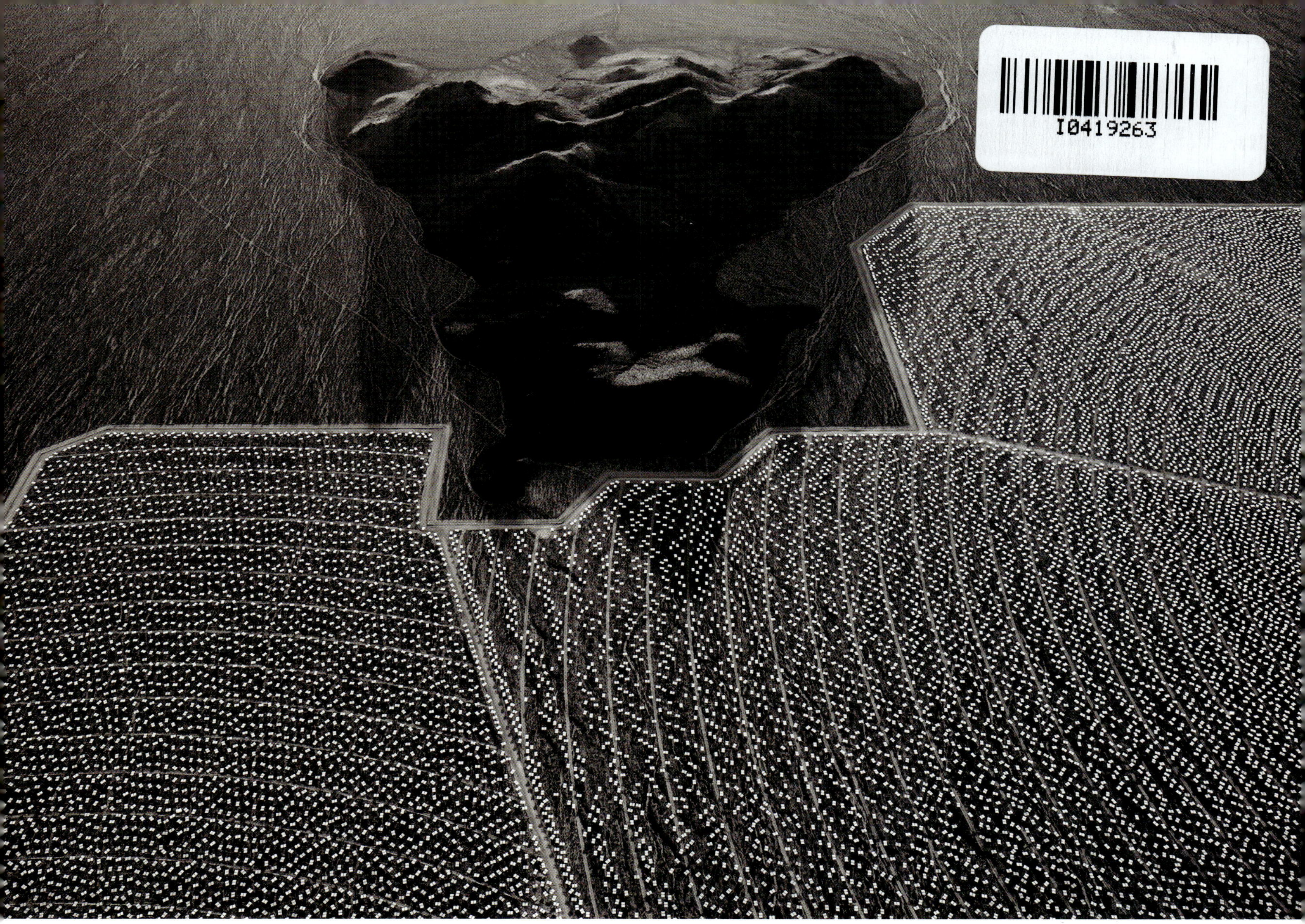

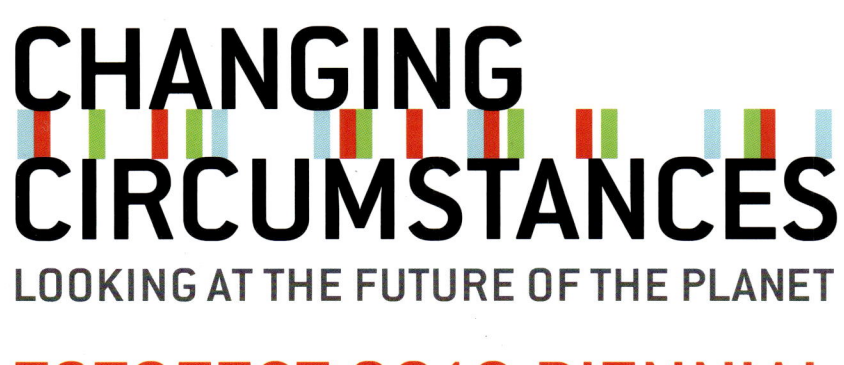

Jamey Stillings, #9499, 21 March 2013, from the series *The Evolution of Ivanpah Solar*. A hill formation rises above the alluvial slope at the eastern boundaries of Units 2 and 3 with heliostat installation complete. Courtesy of the Artist.

CHANGING
CIRCUMSTANCES
LOOKING AT THE FUTURE OF THE PLANET

FOTOFEST 2016 BIENNIAL

Over 30 Leading International Artists

March 12–April 24, 2016 | Houston, Texas USA

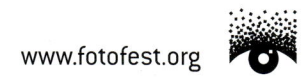

www.fotofest.org

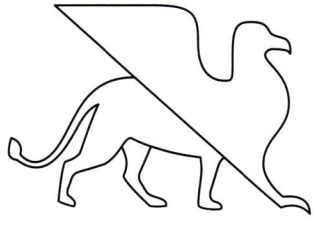
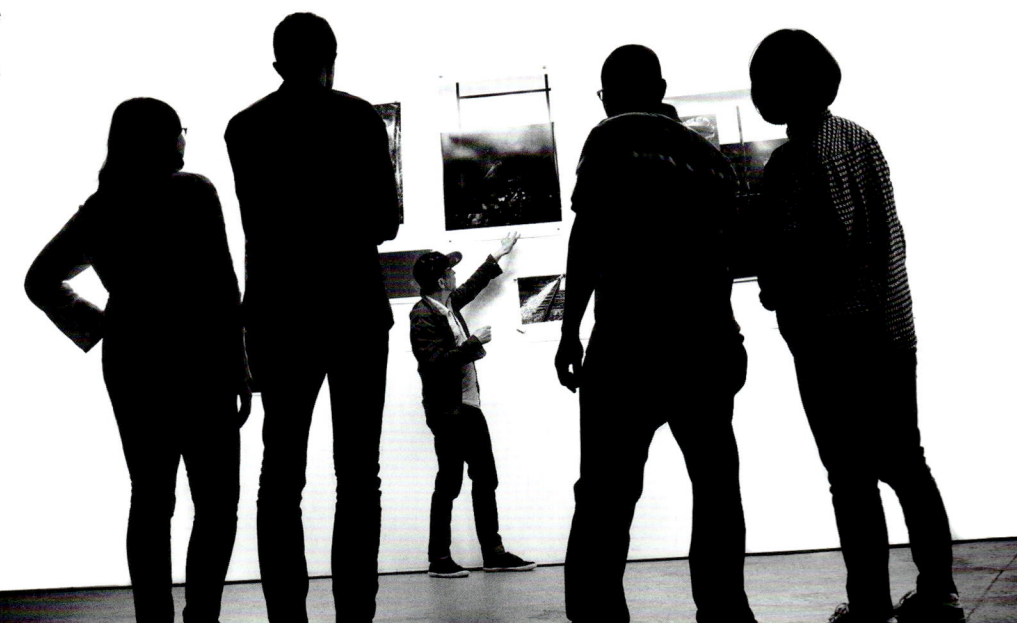

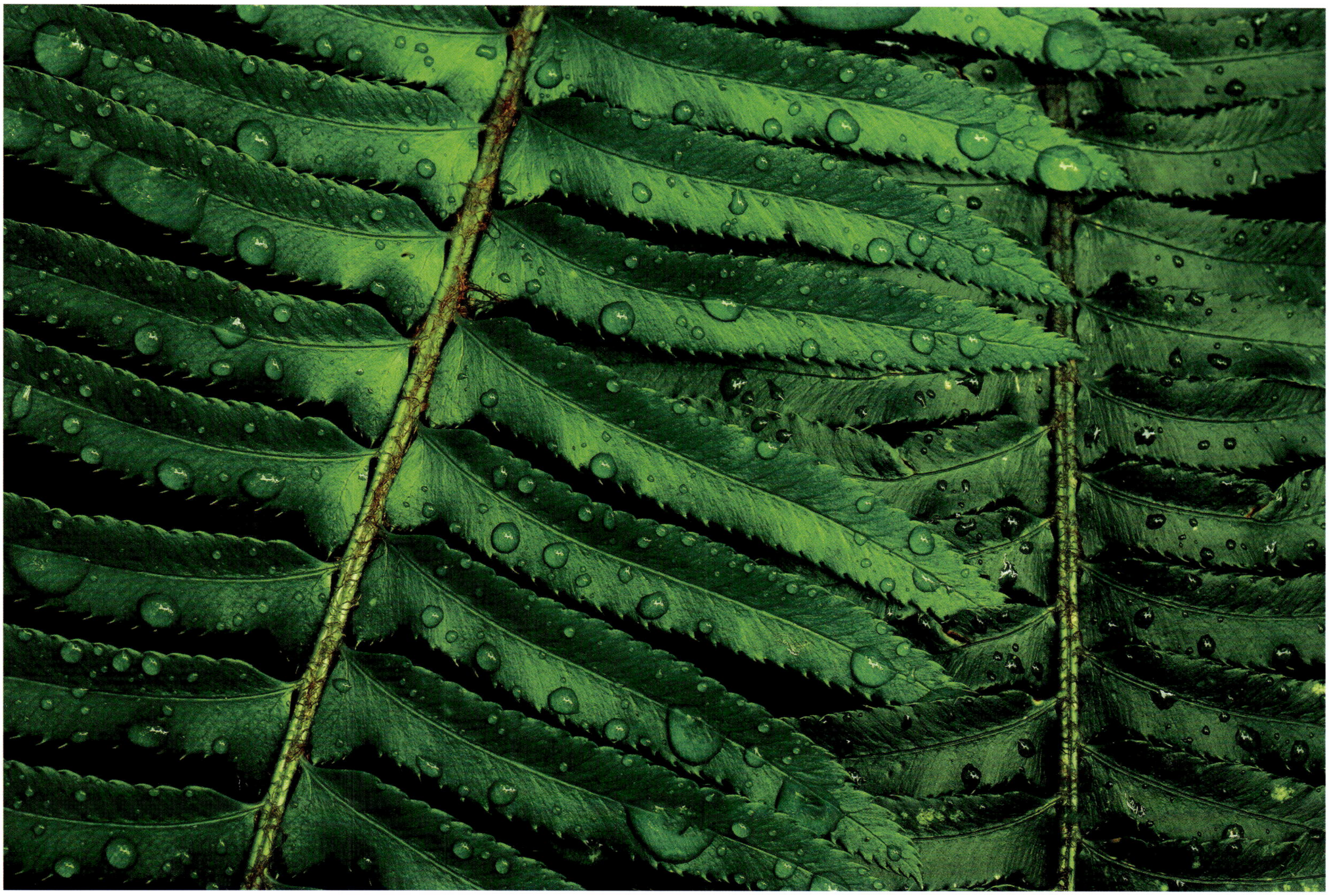

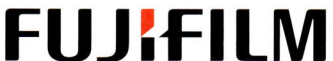
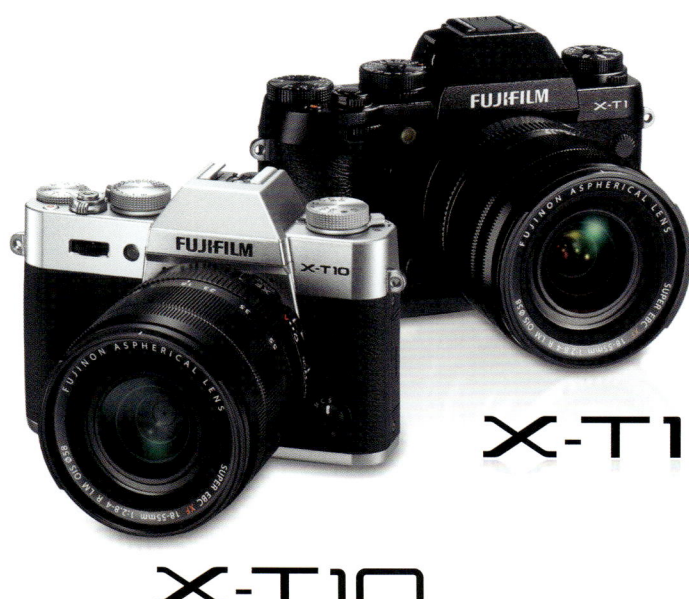
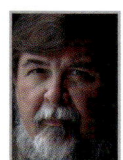

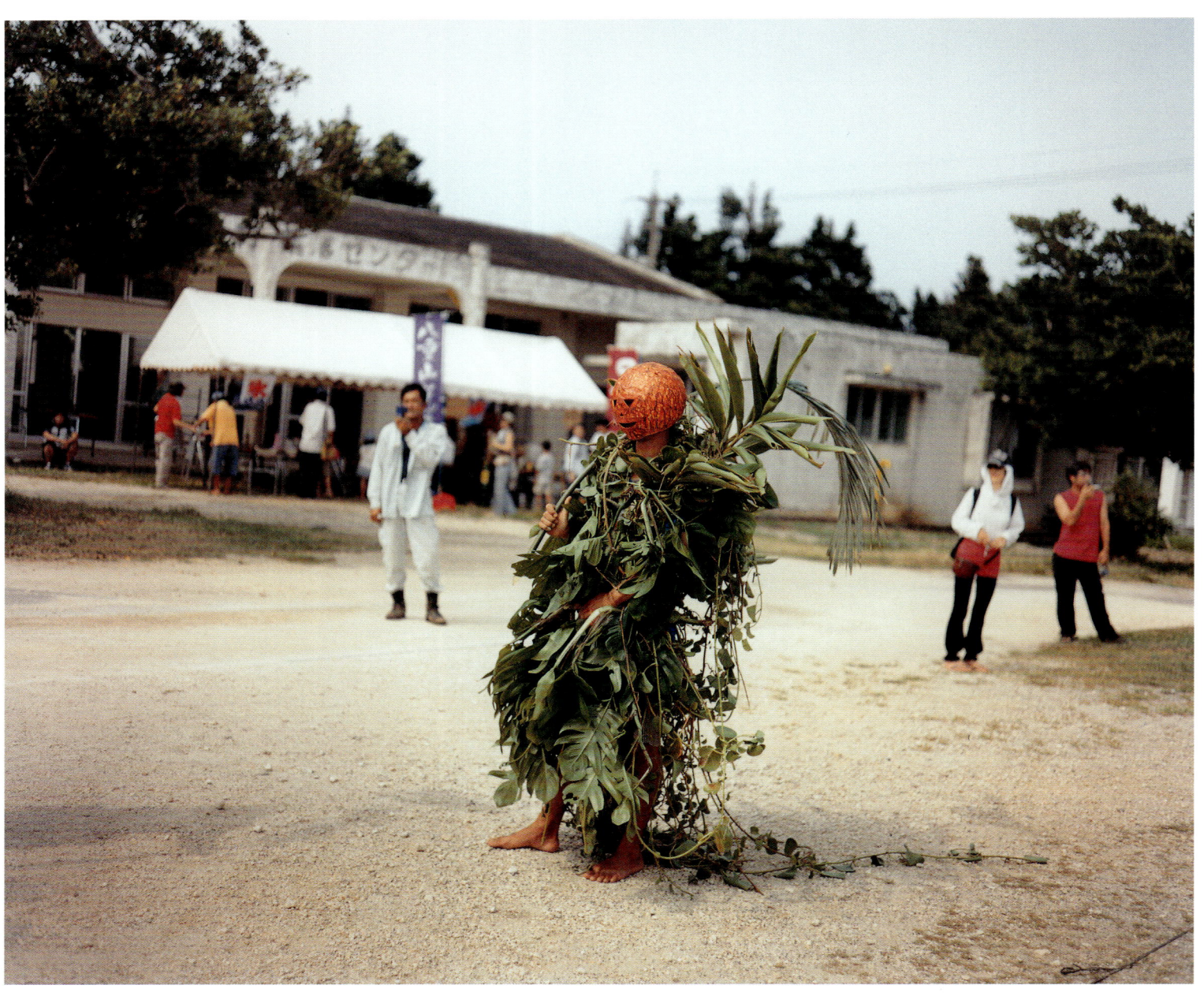

Spring 2016

Words

26 **Unconscious Journey:**
   Tacita Dean in Conversation
   with Travis A. Diehl

32 **Wilfred Thesiger:**
   The Last Nomad
   by Eric Banks

38 **Vittorio Sella: Higher Ground**
   by Alexander Stille

44 **Open Roads & Invisible Borders**
   by Sean O'Toole

50 **Into the Void: Taryn Simon in**
   Conversation with Kate Fowle

Pictures

58 **Samuel Gratacap: Empire**
   Introduction by Bronwyn Law-Viljoen

68 **Taiyo Onorato & Nico Krebs:**
   Eurasia
   Introduction by Aaron Schuman

78 **Trevor Paglen: Landing Site**
   Introduction by Brian Wallis

88 **Jacob Aue Sobol:**
   Arrivals and Departures
   Introduction by Pico Iyer

98 **Carly Steinbrunn:**
   The Voyage of Discovery
   Introduction by Stanley Wolukau-
   Wanambwa

106 **Maha Maamoun: Domestic Tourism**
   Introduction by Natalie Bell

110 **Yto Barrada: Dinosaur Road**
   Introduction by Carmen Winant

118 **Ishikawa Naoki: Archipelago**
   Introduction by Niwa Harumi

126 **Justine Kurland: Highway Kind**
   Introduction by David Campany

Front

9 **Editors' Note**

11 **Collectors: The Philosophers**
   Contributions by Diarmuid
   Costello, Cynthia Freeland,
   Michael Hardt, Dominic McIver
   Lopes, Jerry Miller, Peter Singer

16 **Curriculum**
   by Dayanita Singh

19 **On Portraits**
   by Geoff Dyer

23 **Redux**
   Sara Knelman on *Mieux Vivre*
   (1936–39)

Back

136 **Object Lessons**
   Annie Smith Peck's Postcards,
   1908

Opposite:
Ishikawa Naoki,
from the series
Archipelago, 2009
© and courtesy Ishikawa
Naoki

Front cover:
Samuel Gratacap,
from the series *Empire*,
Choucha Camp, Tunisia,
2012–14
Courtesy the artist and
Galerie Les Filles du
Calvaire, Paris

Aperture, a not-for-profit foundation, connects the photo community and its audiences with the most inspiring work, the sharpest ideas, and with each other— in print, in person, and online.

Aperture (ISSN 0003-6420) is published quarterly, in spring, summer, fall, and winter, at 547 West 27th Street, 4th Floor, New York, N.Y. 10001. In the United States, a one-year subscription (four issues) is $75; a two-year subscription (eight issues) is $124. In Canada, a one-year subscription is $95. All other international subscriptions are $105 per year. Visit aperture.org to subscribe. Single copies may be purchased at $24.95 for most issues. Subscribe to the *Aperture Digital Archive* at aperture.org/archive. Periodicals postage paid at New York and additional offices. Postmaster: Send address changes to *Aperture*, P.O. Box 3000, Denville, N.J. 07834. Address queries regarding subscriptions, renewals, or gifts to: *Aperture* Subscription Service, 866-457-4603 (U.S. and Canada), or email custsvc_aperture@fulcoinc.com.

Newsstand distribution in the U.S. is handled by Curtis Circulation Company, 201-634-7400. For international distribution, contact Central Books, centralbooks.com.

Help maintain Aperture's publishing, education, and community activities by joining our general member program. Membership starts at $75 annually and includes invitations to special events, exclusive discounts on Aperture publications, and opportunities to meet artists and engage with leaders in the photography community. Aperture Foundation welcomes support at all levels of giving, and all gifts are tax-deductible to the fullest extent of the law. For more information about supporting Aperture, please visit aperture.org/join or contact the Development Department at membership@aperture.org.

Library of Congress Catalog Card No: 58-30845.

ISBN 978-1-59711-364-9

Printed in Turkey by Ofset Yapimevi

Aperture magazine is supported in part by the New York City Department of Cultural Affairs in partnership with the City Council.

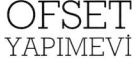
OFSET
YAPIMEVİ

Editor
Michael Famighetti

Managing Editor
Brendan Wattenberg

Copy Editors
Clare Fentress, Donna Ghelerter

Production Director
Nicole Moulaison

Production Managers
Thomas Bollier, Bryan Krueger

Work Scholars
Sophie Klafter, Nicole Maturo, Melissa McCabe, Cassidy Paul

Art Direction, Design & Typefaces
A2/SW/HK, London

Publisher
Dana Triwush
magazine@aperture.org

Partnerships and Advertising
Elizabeth Morina
917–691–2608
emorina@aperture.org

**Executive Director,
Aperture Foundation**
Chris Boot

Minor White, Editor (1952–1974)

Michael E. Hoffman, Publisher and Executive Director (1964–2001)

Statement of Ownership, Management, and Circulation (Required by 39 U.S.C. 3685). 1. Publication Title: Aperture; 2. Publication no.: 0003-6420; 3. Filing Date: October 1, 2015 4. Issue Frequency: Quarterly; 5. No. of Issues Published Annually: 4; 6. Annual Subscription Price: $75.00; 7. Complete Mailing Address of Known Office of Publication: Aperture Foundation, 547 West 27th Street, 4th Floor, New York, NY 10001-5511; Contact Person: Dana Triwush; Telephone: 212-946-7116; 8. Complete Mailing Address of Headquarters or General Business Office of Publisher: Aperture Foundation, 547 West 27th Street, 4th Floor, New York, NY 10001-5511; 9. Full Names and Complete Mailing Addresses of Publisher, Editor, and Managing Editor: Publisher: Dana Triwush, Aperture Foundation, 547 West 27th Street, 4th Floor, New York, NY 10001-5511; Editor: Michael Famighetti, Aperture Foundation, 547 West 27th Street, 4th Floor, New York, NY 10001-5511; Managing Editor: Brendan Wattenberg, Aperture Foundation, 547 West 27th Street, 4th Floor, New York, NY 10001-5511; 10. Owner: Aperture Foundation, Inc., 547 West 27th Street, 4th Fl., New York, NY 10001; 11. Known Bondholders, Mortgagees, and Other Security Holders Owning or Holding 1 Percent or More of Total Amount of Bonds, Mortgages, or Other Securities: None; 12. Tax Status: The purpose, function, and nonprofit status of this organization and the exempt status for federal income tax purposes: Has Not Changed During Preceding 12 Months; 13. Publication Title: Aperture; 14. Issue Date for Circulation Data Below: Summer 2015 #219; 15. Extent and Nature of Circulation (Average No. Copies Each Issue During Preceding 12 Months; No. Copies of Single Issue Published Nearest to Filing Date): a. Total Number of Copies (Net press run): 16,011; 15,160; b. Paid Circulation; (1) Mailed Outside-County Paid Subscriptions Stated on PS Form 3541: 7,519; 7,096; (2) Mailed In-County Paid Subscriptions Stated on PS Form 3541: 38; 38; (3) Paid Distribution Outside the Mails Including Sales Through Dealers and Carriers, Street Vendors, Counter Sales, and Other Paid Distribution Outside USPS: 3,992; 4,318; (4) Paid Distribution by Other Classes of Mail Through the USPS: 35; 35; c. Total Paid Distribution: 11,593; 11,487; d. Free or Nominal Rate Distribution: (1) Free or Nominal Rate Outside-County Copies included on PS Form 3541: 27; 9; (2) Free or Nominal Rate In-County Copies Included on PS From 3541: 0; 0; (3) Free or Nominal Rate Copies Mailed at Other Classes Through the USPS: 132; 117; (4) Free or Nominal Rate Distribution Outside the Mail: 650; 600; e. Total Free or Nominal Rate Distribution: 809; 726; f. Total Distribution: 12,392; 12,213; g. Copies not Distributed: 3,619; 2,947; h. Total: 16,011; 15,160; i. Percent Paid 93.5%; 94.1%; 16. Electronic Copy Circulation. a. Paid Electronic Copies: 409; 307; b. Total Paid Print Copies + Paid Electronic Copies: 11,992; 11,794; c. Total Print Distribution + Paid Electronic Copies: 12,801; 12,520; d. Percent Paid (Both Print & Electronic Copies): 93.7%; 94.2%; I certify that 50% of all my distributed copies (Electronic & Print) are paid above a nominal price. 17. Publication of Statement of Ownership: Will be printed in the Spring 2016 issue of this publication.; 18. I certify that all information furnished on this form is true and complete. I understand that anyone who furnishes false or misleading information on this form or who omits material or information requested on the form may be subject to criminal sanctions (including fines and imprisonment) and/or civil sanctions (including civil penalties). Signature and Title of Editor, Publisher, Business Manager, or Owner: Dana Triwush, Publisher, October 1, 2015

aperture.org

AVEDON WARHOL

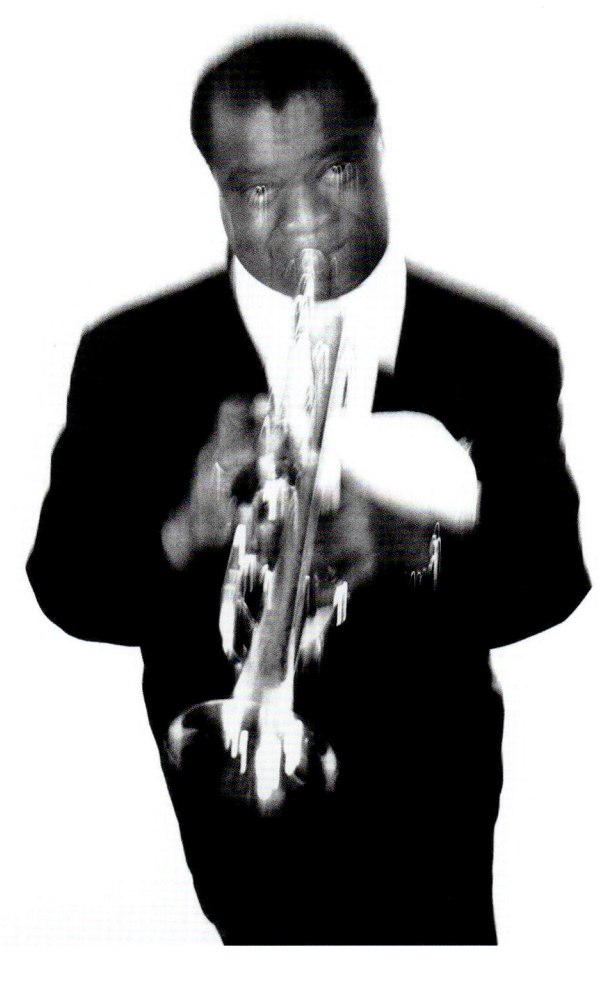

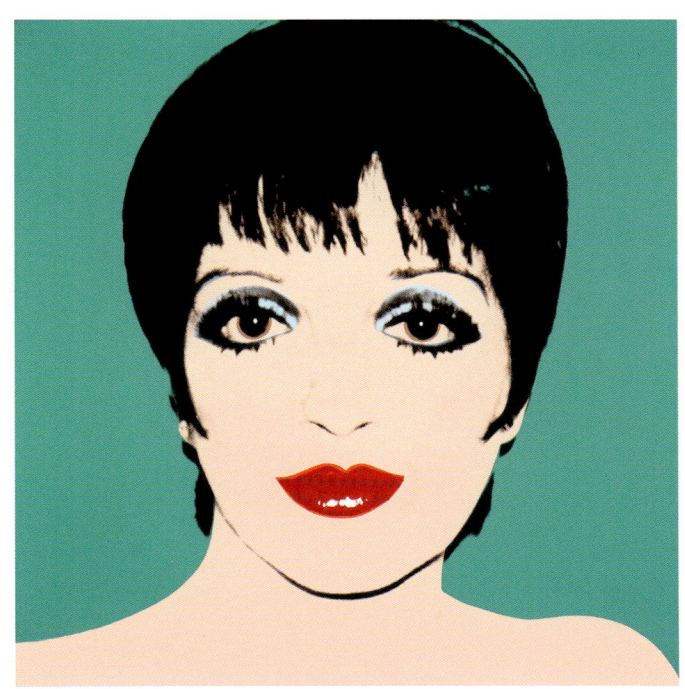

Gagosian Gallery February 9–April 23, 2016

6–24 Britannia Street London WC1X 9JD +44.207.841.9960 www.gagosian.com

**Taiyo Onorato & Nico
Krebs,** *Traffic,* **2013,
from the series** *Eurasia,*
2013–15
Courtesy the artists,
RaebervonStenglin,
Sies+Höke, and Peter
Lav Gallery

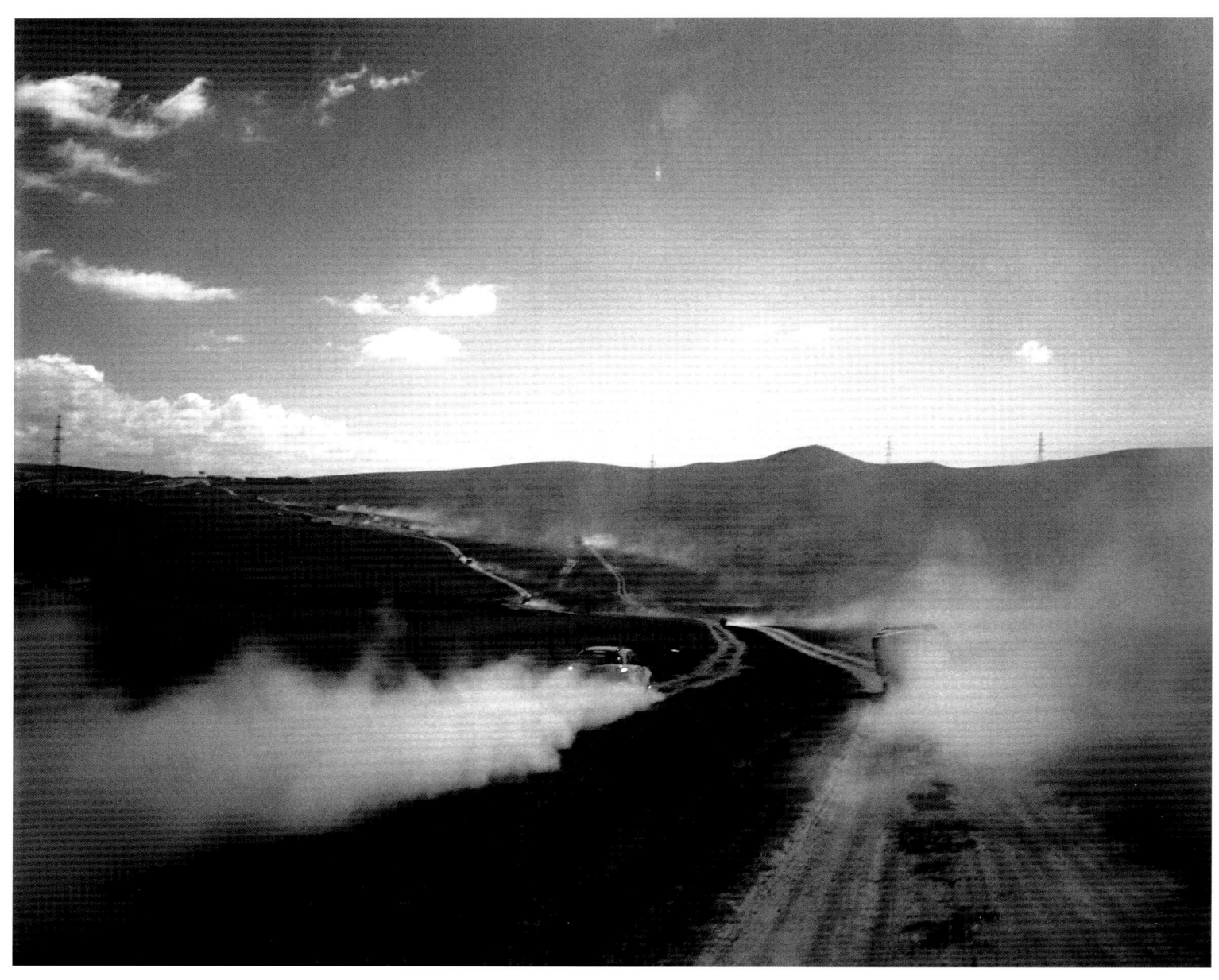

Odyssey

"The tourist hopes to catch something through his lens, while the traveler seeks to surrender, even to be claimed by a surprise in very real life," celebrated travel writer Pico Iyer notes in his introduction to a portfolio of Jacob Aue Sobol's photographs made while riding on the Trans-Siberian Railway. The unexpected route, the captivating spell of wanderlust, and the lure of the unpredictable bind the images in this issue. From early twentieth-century expeditions like those of Vittorio Sella, who created sublime views of the world's most treacherous mountains, to the recent documentary projects of Invisible Borders, a West African photography collective, the camera is central to the journey—not just a means to prove the trip was made. Even so, for Emeka Okereke, the artistic director of Invisible Borders, "The purest form of the project is while we are on the road."

Among the peripatetic wanderers brought together in these pages are Taiyo Onorato and Nico Krebs, who drove a four-wheeler from Switzerland to Mongolia, photographing unfamiliar landscapes and futuristic architecture, and Justine Kurland, who has crossed the United States in a weathered van, adding thousands of miles to her odometer while pursuing a chronicle of American drifters. Precedence can be found in the travelogues of Wilfred Thesiger, who opted for camel over automobile in his arduous midcentury expeditions throughout the Arabian Peninsula, slowly pushing forward into the desert. "I had no desire to travel faster," he wrote. "In this way there was time to notice things."

Likening her artistic process to an "unconscious journey," Tacita Dean, known for her prodigious output in film, still photography, and other forms, is attracted by the hunt for found images. Her oeuvre is marked by references to personal quests: one in search of Robert Smithson's then-submerged land work *Spiral Jetty*, another for a boat, languishing on a remote island, that once belonged to a doomed amateur sailor. Yto Barrada also traces the path of submerged relics. Following the "dinosaur road"—the lucrative trade of purloined fossils between Morocco and Arizona—Barrada constructs her own map of archaeological exploits, constructing a sequence of landscape collages and found paintings, published here for the first time.

Some journeys are undertaken at moments of upheaval; some maps extend past the realm of public knowledge, or into an uncharted future. In his latest project, Trevor Paglen has plunged beneath the ocean to document the Trans-Atlantic cables that carry the bulk of Internet traffic now heavily monitored by government surveillance. Taryn Simon's *Black Square* contains a letter to the future, a project expected to achieve its full realization in one thousand years. But the odyssey emblematic of our time, perhaps the most pressing issue of contemporary international consequence, is the flow of mass migration across North Africa and the Middle East toward Europe. Powerfully represented by Samuel Gratacap in his series *Empire*, refugees from many nations have reached a standstill at Choucha Camp in Tunisia and await passage to an elusive haven. To their north, the islands of Lesbos, Kos, and Lampedusa, among many others that figured in the geography of Homer's epic poem, form an archipelago of uncertainty. At the edge of the Mediterranean, the longest journey is still to come, the territory just beyond the horizon.

— The Editors

WE HAVE A DIFFERENT WAY OF LOOKING AT **AUCTIONS**

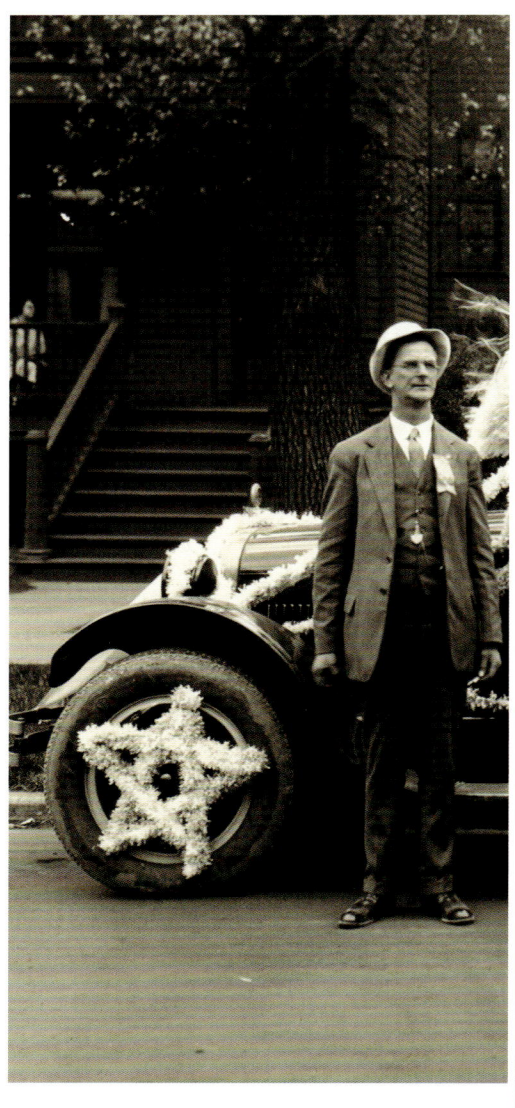
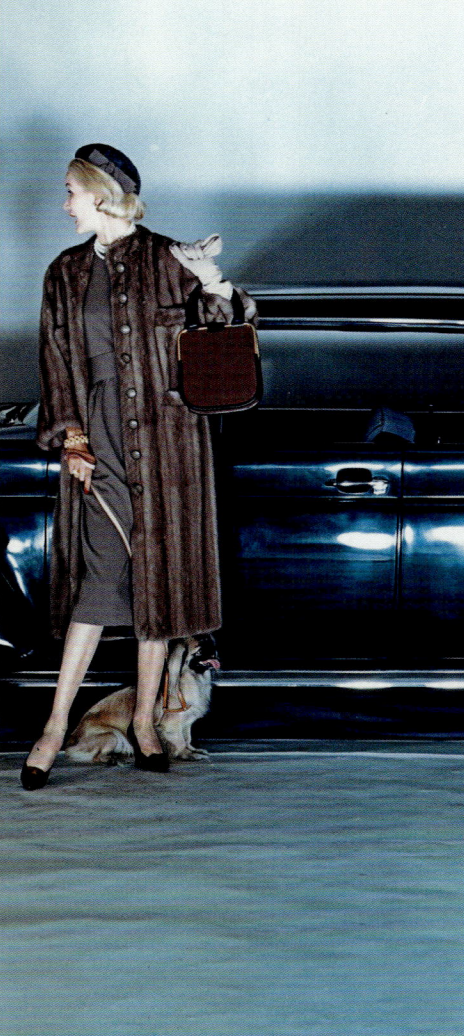
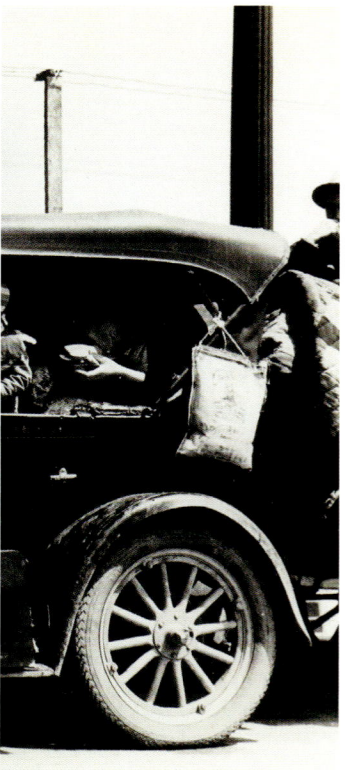

Find something new at Swann Auction Galleries. Our departments assemble sales that are unusually rich. In fact, we were the first American house to offer auctions of photographs, and our Photographs & Photobooks specialists remain innovators in their field. Swann understands more than art and books, we understand you, whether you're a lifelong collector, a first-time buyer, or looking to sell. We approach auctions with a blend of high-brow knowledge and low-brow fun. For a different perspective on auctions, come to Swann. We create our own culture.

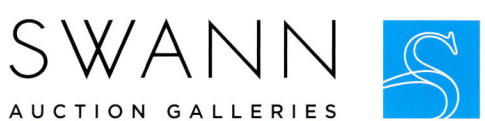

SWANN
AUCTION GALLERIES

104 East 25th St, New York, NY 10010 • 212 254 4710 • SWANNGALLERIES.COM/PHOTOGRAPHS

Collectors
The Philosophers
On Recent Acquisitions

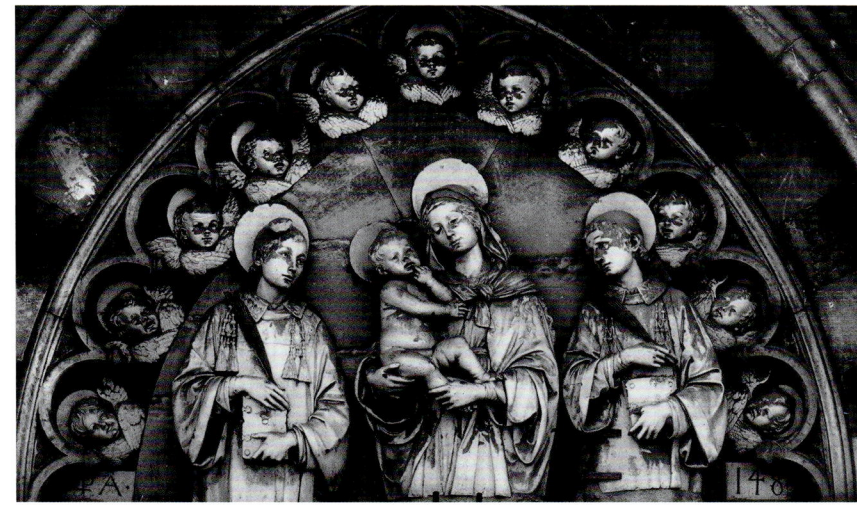

Fratelli Alinari, Madonna and Child with St. Lawrence and St. Stephen, Prato Cathedral Courtesy Archivi Alinari, Firenze

Cynthia Freeland

I don't own many historical or old photographs. Much of the appeal of this Alinari Brothers print was in the beauty of the Andrea della Robbia sculpture grouping, *Madonna and Child*, from Prato Cathedral (1489). The figures in the lunette have a typical della Robbia blue majolica backdrop, but I prefer the restrained tones of this image. I love antiquarian photographic prints: platinum-palladium, hand tinted, or selenium toned. I was told this is an albumen print. Its clarity and detail are amazing. You can see the central figures' delicate, expressive hands, the folds of the Christ child's chubby legs, the stone at St. Stephen's head, and bits of the grid on which St. Lawrence was roasted. I am not religious, nor did I grow up knowing all about saints, but my current writing project is about the power and danger of sacred images—those that inspire devotion or fear and frenzy enough to motivate destruction.

Cynthia Freeland is Chair, Department of Philosophy, at the University of Houston. She is the author, most recently, of *Portraits and Persons: A Philosophical Inquiry* (2010).

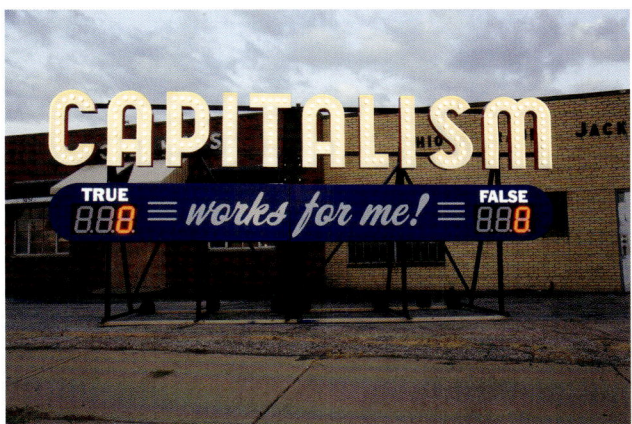

Steve Lambert, *Capitalism Works For Me! True/False*, 2011 Courtesy the artist

Michael Hardt

We have entered an era—let's call it the post-Occupy era—in which questioning the benefits of capitalist society has become commonplace. Steve Lambert's installation, which a friend told me about last year, grasps this new political condition by deploying the spectacle of commodity culture, with Times Square billboard lights and a salesman's enthusiastic exclamation point. This is not, of course, the aesthetic of contemporary capital but that of some bygone era, one in which the answer to Lambert's question was a foregone conclusion—or, really, one in which the question couldn't even be asked. The temporal disjunction created by recalling the past confidence and hegemony of Cold War capitalist ideology emphasizes all the more clearly its fragile basis today. And the political effect of Lambert's project doesn't even depend on the results of the survey. The simple fact that capital works for some and not others already opens a broad avenue for critique, and even suggests the need to construct alternatives.

Michael Hardt, a political philosopher, teaches in the Program in Literature at Duke University. He is the author, with Antonio Negri, of *Empire* (2000), *Multitude* (2004), *Commonwealth* (2009), and *Declaration* (2012).

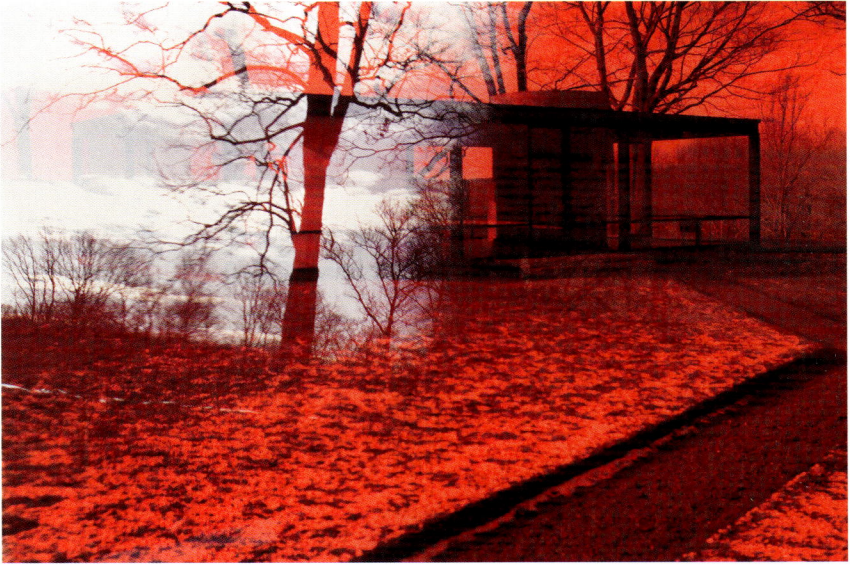

James Welling, *8067*, 2008 Courtesy the artist and David Zwirner, New York/London; Philip Johnson Glass House is a site of the National Trust for Historic Preservation.

Diarmuid Costello

I first saw James Welling's *8067* in 2011 at Maureen Paley in London. Unlike standard architectural photography, its notional subject, Philip Johnson's Glass House in Connecticut, can only just be made out behind the reflection of a silhouetted tree against a pale winter sky. The latter almost overwhelms an oblique view of the house, itself seen through a crimson filter, set in a frost-covered landscape. Three years later, Jim gave me this print as a gift.

Because the images in Jim's series *Glass House* are made by holding diverse filters before the lens during exposure, the results are harder to predict, and often harder to resolve, than they would have been in postproduction. As a whole, the series conveys Jim's interest in circumventing his own intentions, and the lure of the tried and tested. The print hangs in our bedroom, where the crimson fairly leaps off the gray-green walls. Consonant with the work's jarring juxtapositions, strong shadows cast by the frame of a sash window in direct sunlight regularly bisect the print. I like to think it fully in the spirit of the work to welcome this intrusion.

Diarmuid Costello teaches philosophy at the University of Warwick. He is currently completing the monograph *On Photography* for the Routledge series *Thinking in Action*.

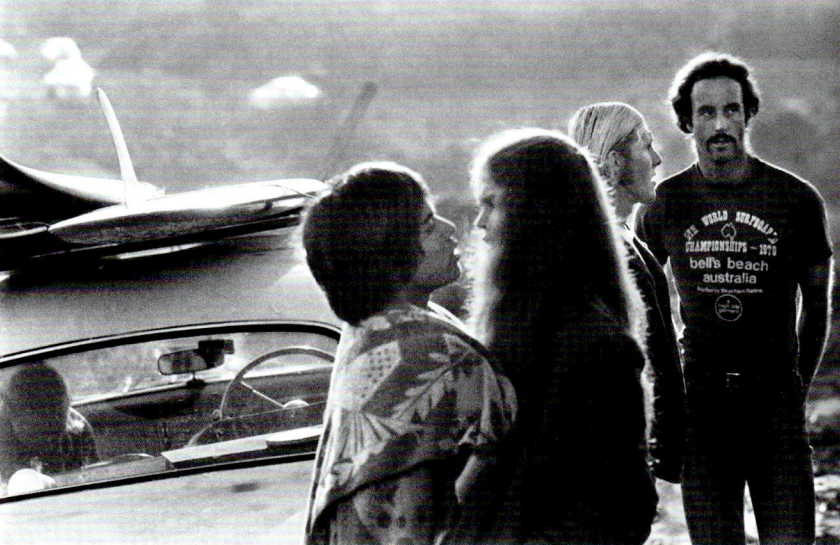

Rusty Miller, *Reno Kissing Joanne*, World Surfing Championship, Bells Beach, Victoria, Australia, 1970
Courtesy the artist

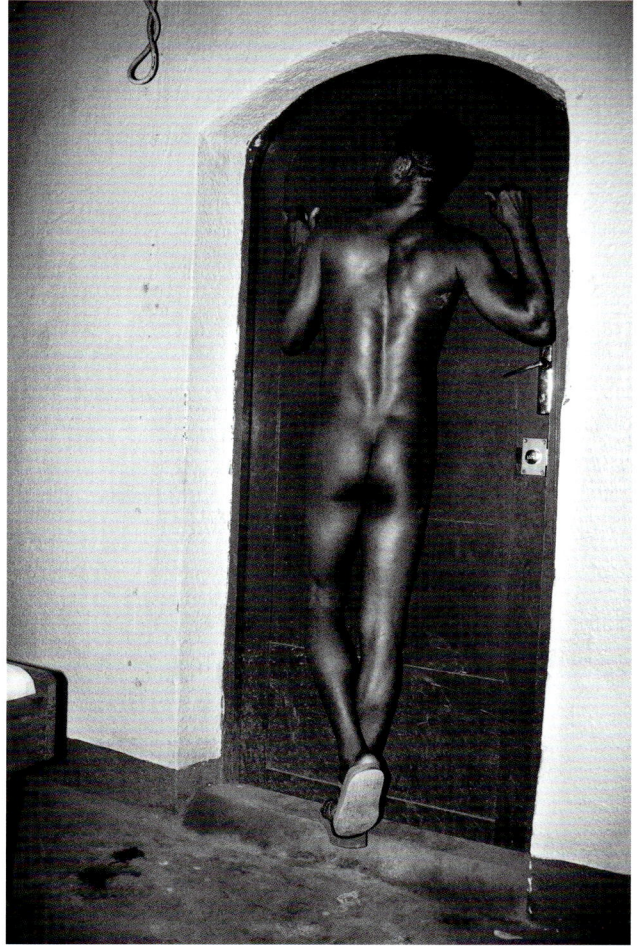

Samuel Fosso, *Self-Portrait*, from the series *Mémoire d'un ami*, 2000
© Samuel Fosso and courtesy Jean Marc Patras Galerie, Paris

Jerry Miller

For a period in my midtwenties I slipped into a kind of social coma, doing little and speaking less. Like the figure in Samuel Fosso's photograph, I felt pitched against a door, awaiting a message or sign that I knew would not come. Seeing Fosso's body visually melt into the threshold, trepidatious of moving forward or turning back, revived this hazy recollection of my past immobility.

My reasons for leaving the bookstore with Fosso's 2008 monograph in hand, however, derived from more than a sympathetic connection to my previous self. Lately I have been contemplating the historical possibility of what I call "postcaricature" racial imagery: representations dimly beholden to colonialist Western imaginaries or reinstatements of the precolonial. While Fosso's more ebullient work plays with stock images of both traditions, his pieces that, as above, gesture to a new, almost aloof expression of racialized being were what convinced me to bring the book into my library.

Jerry Miller is Associate Professor of Philosophy and Chair, Philosophy Department, at Haverford College. His book, *Stain Removal: Ethics and Race*, is forthcoming in 2016.

Peter Singer

Rusty Miller's photograph *Reno Kissing Joanne* is an evocative mix of elements that change and elements that remain constant. Hairstyles, clothing, cars, and surfboards all show the period when the photograph was taken in 1970, but Bells Beach, on Victoria's coast, not far from Melbourne, is still the venue for Australia's most famous surfing competition, and we instantly recognize the mutual attraction between Reno and Joanne. Rusty captured a poignant moment in the lives of two people, and leaves the viewer wondering what happened to their romance, and to them.

I learned surfing from Rusty, who was America's top-ranked surfer in 1965, before moving to Byron Bay, Australia's most easterly point. But I didn't know about his photography until 2011, when he brought some of his pictures down to Bells Beach for an exhibition marking the fiftieth anniversary of the competition. The photo appears in *Turning Point: Surf Portraits and Stories from Bells to Byron 1970–1971*, a book that was put together by Rusty and his wife, Tricia Shantz, in 2013. I'm happy to have the print hanging on a wall where I can look at it and be reminded of my own summers spent on Australian beaches, and of my aspirations to be more of a hippie than my cautious nature and purpose-driven lifestyle would ever permit me to be.

Peter Singer is Ira W. DeCamp Professor of Bioethics at Princeton University. The author, most recently, of *The Most Good You Can Do* (2015), he has published numerous books including *Animal Liberation* (1975) and *Practical Ethics* (1979).

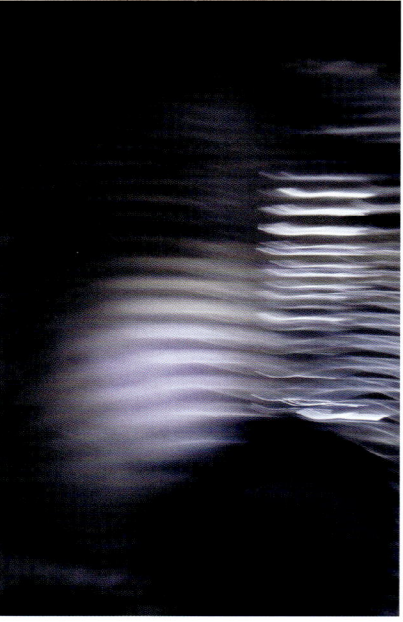

Shirine Gill, Untitled, 2008 Courtesy the artist

Dominic McIver Lopes

Shirine Gill's use of intentional camera movement foregrounds two overlooked building blocks of photography: the motion of the camera and of the photographer's body. Except in special circumstances, we set these variables to zero. Yet the retina registers nothing without motion, so the eye continuously, involuntarily, and subconsciously saccades. This photograph is as much biological and retinal as optical. It calmly accepts motion, with no thirst to bring a scene into focus or to fix a world that lies behind the light. Critics describe Gill's abstract work as impressionistic, impalpable, evanescent, and playful. I would like to pair this photograph on a wall with a mezzotint by Hamanishi Katsunori, whose palette matches Gill's, and whose depiction of manila knotted around a steel pole suggests bound limbs. Together, these artists playfully reverse philosophers' ideas about the boundary between photographs and other images.

Dominic McIver Lopes is Distinguished University Scholar and Professor of Philosophy at the University of British Columbia. His most recent book is *Four Arts of Photography* (2016).

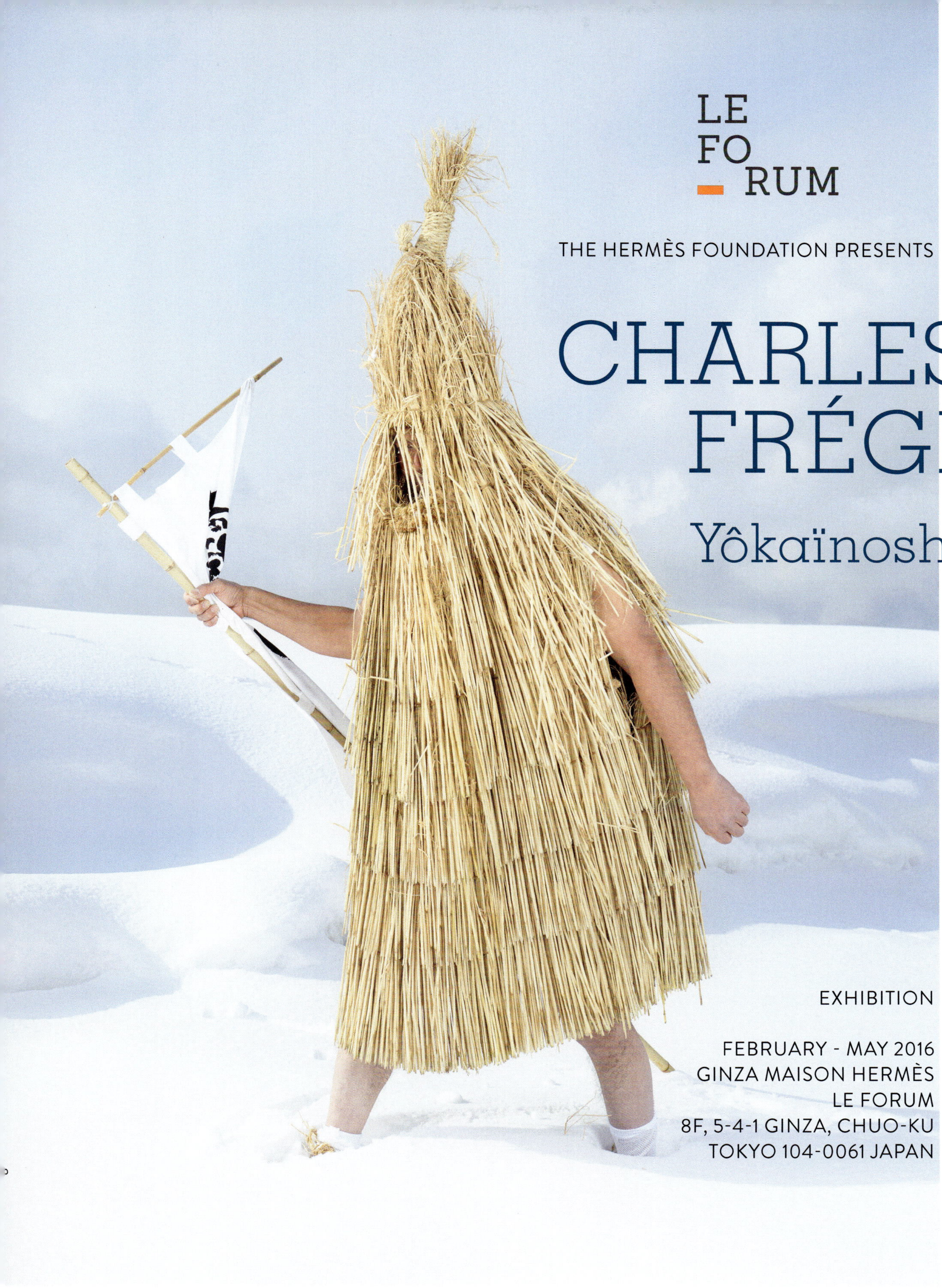

LE
FO
_
RUM

THE HERMÈS FOUNDATION PRESENTS

CHARLES FRÉGER

Yôkaïnoshima

EXHIBITION

FEBRUARY - MAY 2016
GINZA MAISON HERMÈS
LE FORUM
8F, 5-4-1 GINZA, CHUO-KU
TOKYO 104-0061 JAPAN

www.fondationdentreprisehermes.org

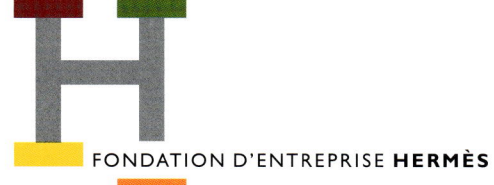

FONDATION D'ENTREPRISE **HERMÈS**

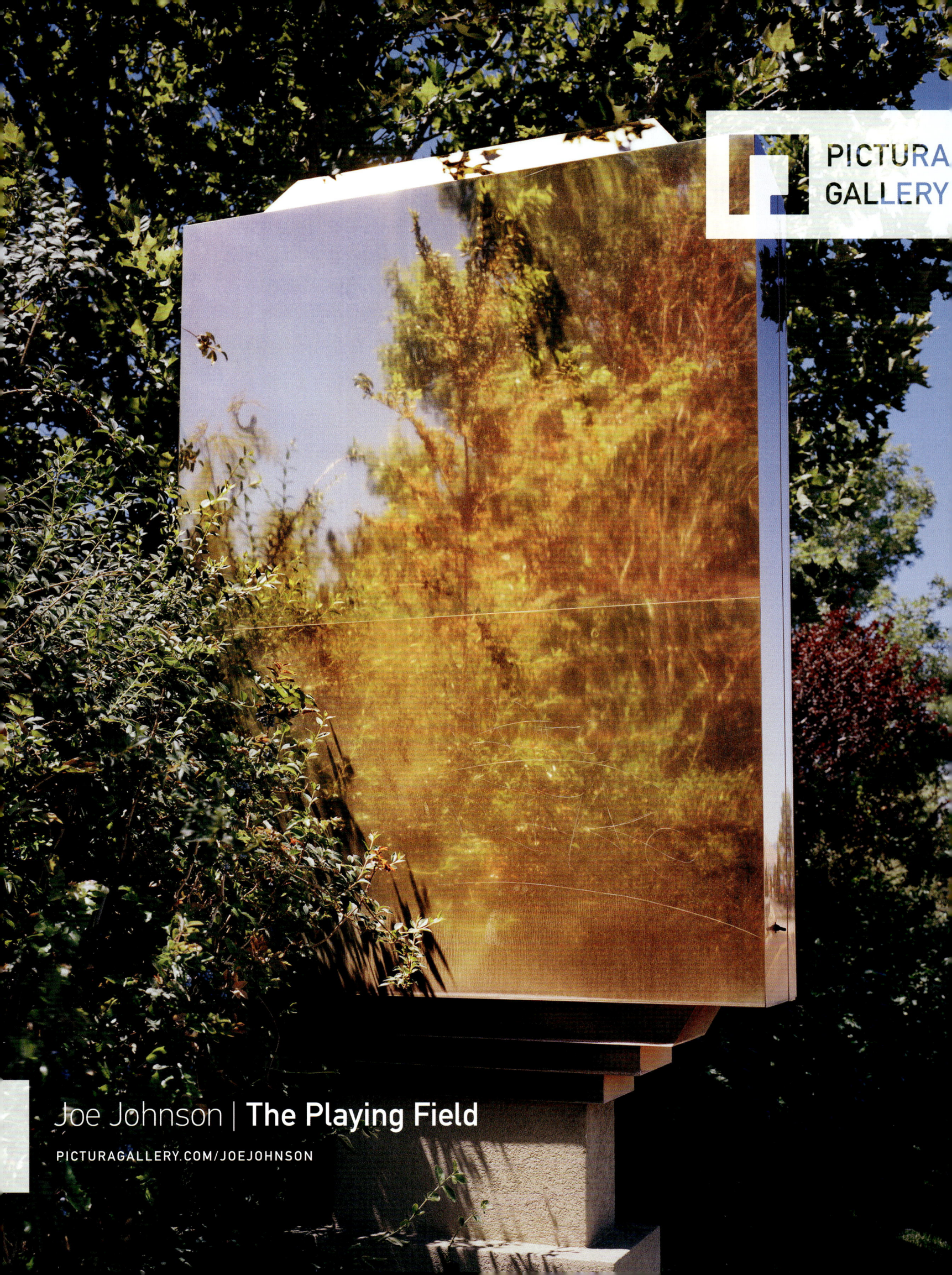

20

SCOTIABANK
CONTACT
PHOTOGRAPHY
FESTIVAL

MAY 2016

TORONTO

CELEBRATING PHOTOGRAPHY FOR 20 YEARS

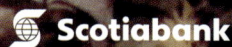 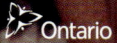 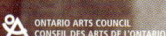 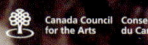

Curriculum
A List of Favorite Anythings
by Dayanita Singh

From her intimate portraits of India's elite to her forensic study of bureaucratic file rooms, Dayanita Singh (b. 1961) has approached photography with the detailed eye of a novelist. Beyond the frame of her austere, atmospheric interiors, landscapes, and character studies, collected since 1986 in twelve monographs, a portal opens onto a narrative at once mysterious and vivid. Singh, who trained in New York as a photojournalist, considers herself a bookmaker, and her reading of experimental fiction and poetry informs her own labyrinthine visual storytelling in highly crafted photobooks and inventive exhibition structures—"portable museums" built to display interconnected visions.

Rainer Maria Rilke, *Letters to a Young Poet*, 1929

I have held on to this book since I was eighteen, the same copy, and it's my first gift to anyone wishing to pursue the creative life. Most importantly Letter Eight, which poses and answers all the difficult questions ("How should it not be difficult for us?"), or suggests how you live the questions, or why one does what one does, how to sustain it, where the sources lie. All of this written in the most poetic language, as only Rilke could.

Virginia Woolf, *A Room of One's Own*, 1929

I like to use a phrase—stream of consciousness editing in photography. I built my *Museum of Chance* (2015) sequence from this, moving freely between cities, dreams, and spaces. Woolf is an extremely important writer for any artist. But I am suggesting, more specifically, *A Room of One's Own*, especially for women, possibly for all creative people, because it addresses the importance of that designated space where one sits and waits for the muse to arrive. Space and circumstances nurture the muse; everyone needs a room for inquiry.

Italo Calvino, *Difficult Loves*, 1970

"Adventures of a Photographer" is one of the short stories in this gem of Calvino. It would certainly be the first chapter in my new reader, not only for alluding to the madness of photography and the obsession of the artist, but also because Calvino is my role model in that he finds a form for each work of his. There is no Calvino-esque formula, but if there were, it would be to have no formula, ever. I could have made this entire list from Calvino books; *Six Memos for the Next Millennium* (1988) would be next after this. It's not about what he writes, but how he writes. It's the same in photography.

Vikram Seth, *All You Who Sleep Tonight*, 1990

When I made *Go Away Closer* (2007), a single sequence of black-and-white images connected by a single emotion and no text other than the title, I thought the concise book held within it images that had no words, feelings that had no vocabulary, until I read *All You Who Sleep Tonight*, and I actually cut out the poems from the book and pasted them into a copy of my book and gave it to the author. Poetry is essential to get to the "something else" in photography. I would have included Ramanujan and Kabir in the list, if I had more space.

Jun'ichiro Tanizaki, *In Praise of Shadows*, 1933

I think this book shaped my black-and-white aesthetic. His description of light, shadows, and architecture, it's almost a meditation on space … the beauty of withholding, of concealment, the same attributes that I ascribe to Michael Ondaatje. All the keys for black-and-white photography are held in this pithy book.

Geoff Dyer, *The Ongoing Moment*, 2005

Like Calvino, Geoff Dyer is genre defying. Each time he has a new obsession, he finds a new form for it. His interest in photography led him to write a history of photography through the themes in photography. His interest in the film *Stalker* led to his book called *Zona* (2012), where he describes *Stalker* shot by shot, with a parallel story in the footnotes; *But Beautiful* (1991) from his interest in jazz; *Out of Sheer Rage* (1997) from his frustration on not being able to write a book about D. H. Lawrence. It seems so effortless, as though he wandered into a situation, got obsessed, researched around it, left all that behind, and saw what remained. Geoff Dyer is beyond brilliant.

W. G. Sebald, *Austerlitz*, 2001

My favorite photobook. Alongside it I would like to mention a catalogue, *Searching for Sebald: Photography after W. G. Sebald* (2007). I am no writer, and no writer could come close to Sebald, but *Austerlitz* to me is the zenith of a photobook. I often give it to young students to read and then invite them to come back to talk about it, but no one has ever returned, perhaps because I had set such a different bar from what they expected from photography conversations. And now as we become, once again, a more image-based society, writers may need to consider photography as a tool in their writing. I am surprised *Austerlitz* did not start a trend of using images in fiction, though trends are dangerous.

Michael Ondaatje, *The Conversation: Walter Murch and the Art of Editing Film*, 2002

From Ondaatje I have learned editing. He is the master of withholding, of knowing just when to stop. I would have recommended *Running in the Family* (1982), but then this book, a long interview with the master editor Walter Murch, seemed more appropriate in a photo-centric mix. It is a book where I have underlined almost every page, as editing is key to photography, now more so than before. Making photographs is relatively simple, but the magic of photography lies in editing, sequencing pacing, and finding the right form. This book leads one through some of those stages.

Opposite, clockwise from top left: Emilio Ronchini, *Italo Calvino*, Turin, Italy, July 1959; pages from W. G. Sebald, *Austerlitz*, 2001; Virginia Woolf, 1932; cover of Rainer Maria Rilke, *Letters to a Young Poet*, 1954; Greg Williams, *Walter Murch*, 2002; cover of Vikram Seth, *All You Who Sleep Tonight*, 1990; Marser, *Tamamo Park, Kagawa City, Japan*, n.d.

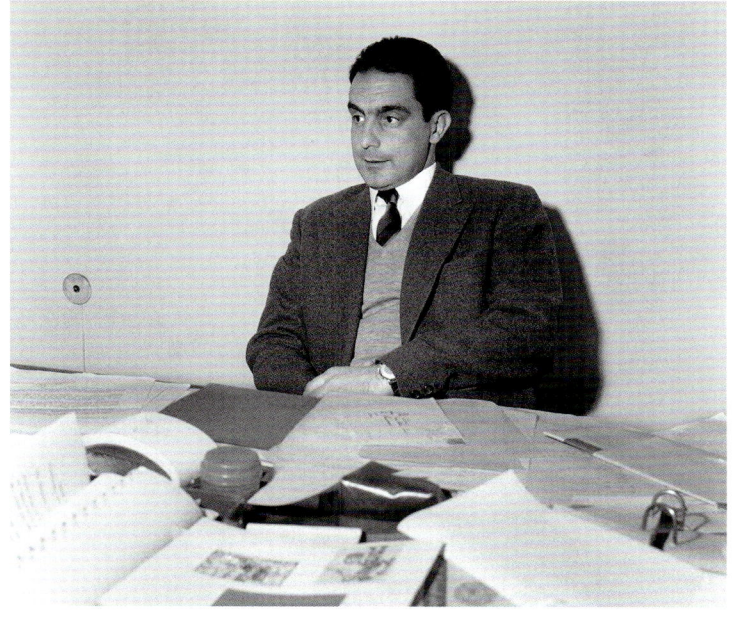
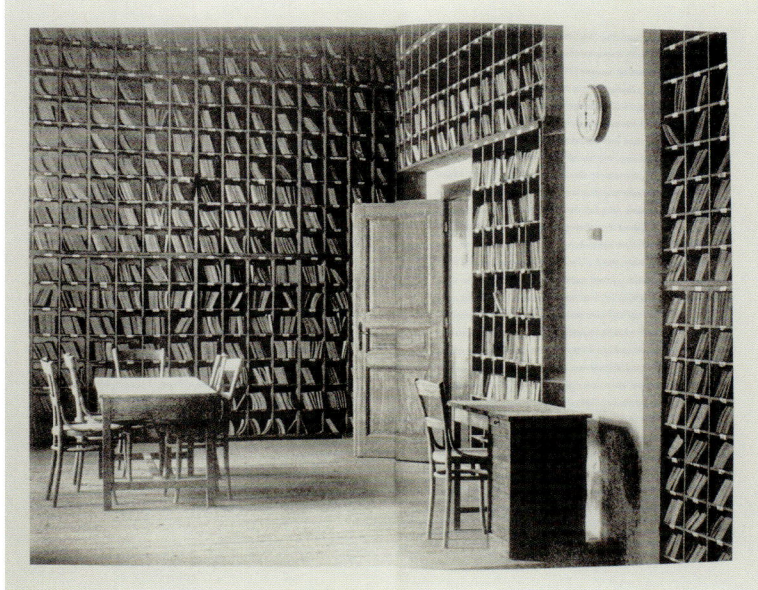
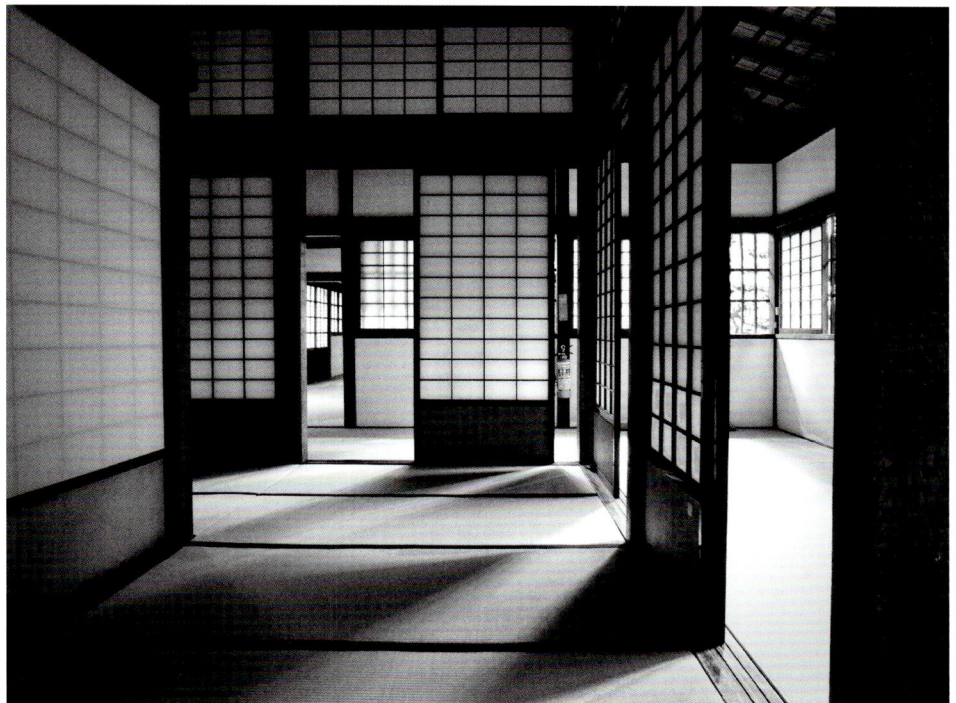
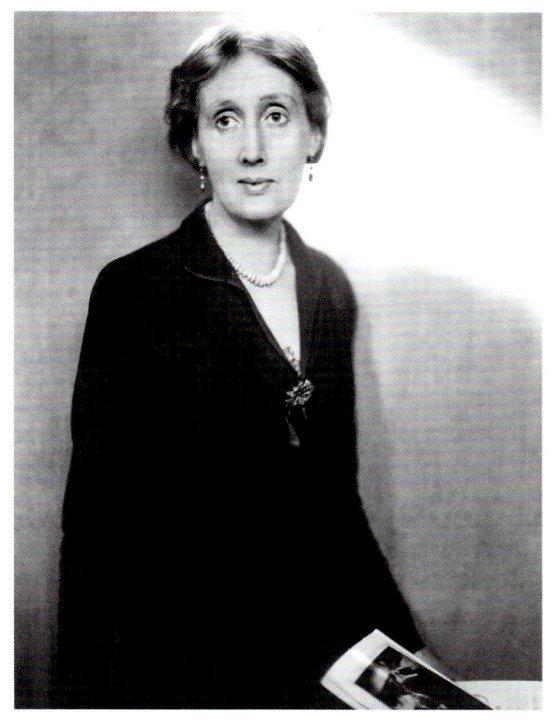
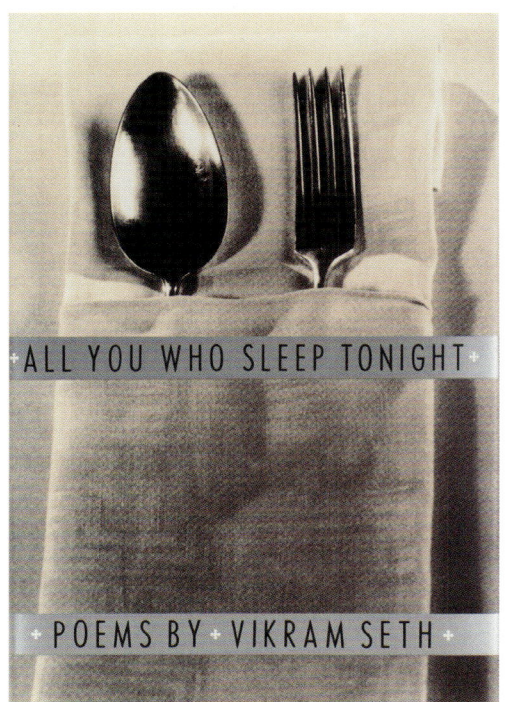

ALL YOU WHO SLEEP TONIGHT

POEMS BY VIKRAM SETH

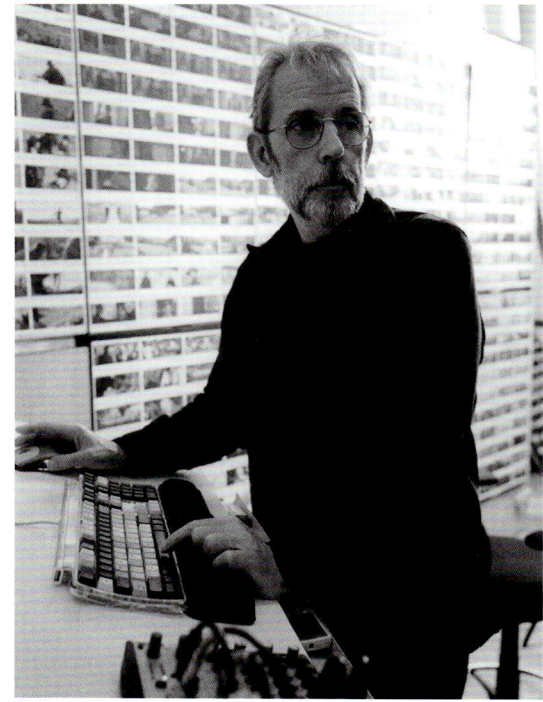

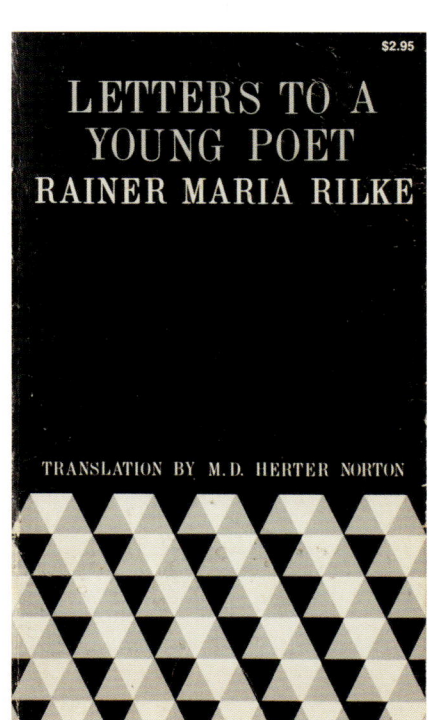

$2.95

LETTERS TO A YOUNG POET
RAINER MARIA RILKE

TRANSLATION BY M.D. HERTER NORTON

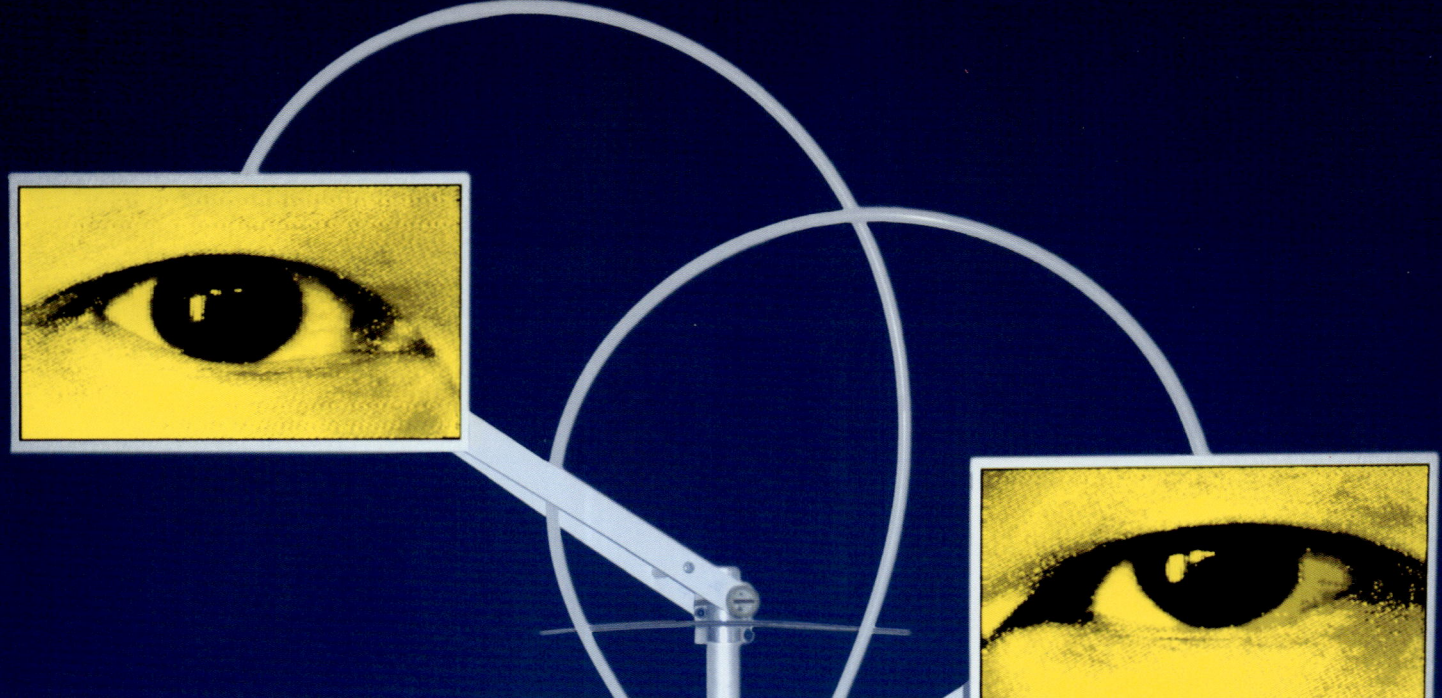

April 14–17, 2016

April 13
Opening Night Preview

Park Avenue Armory
New York

The
Photography
Show

presented by
AIPAD

**The world's leading
photography art galleries**

The Association of International
Photography Art Dealers

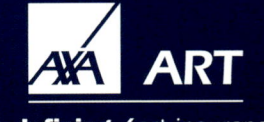
AXA ART

redefining / art insurance
Premier Corporate Partner of AIPAD

On Portraits
Geoff Dyer

In this regular column, Dyer considers how a range of figures have been photographed. Here, he remembers the life and work of French photographer Christophe Agou.

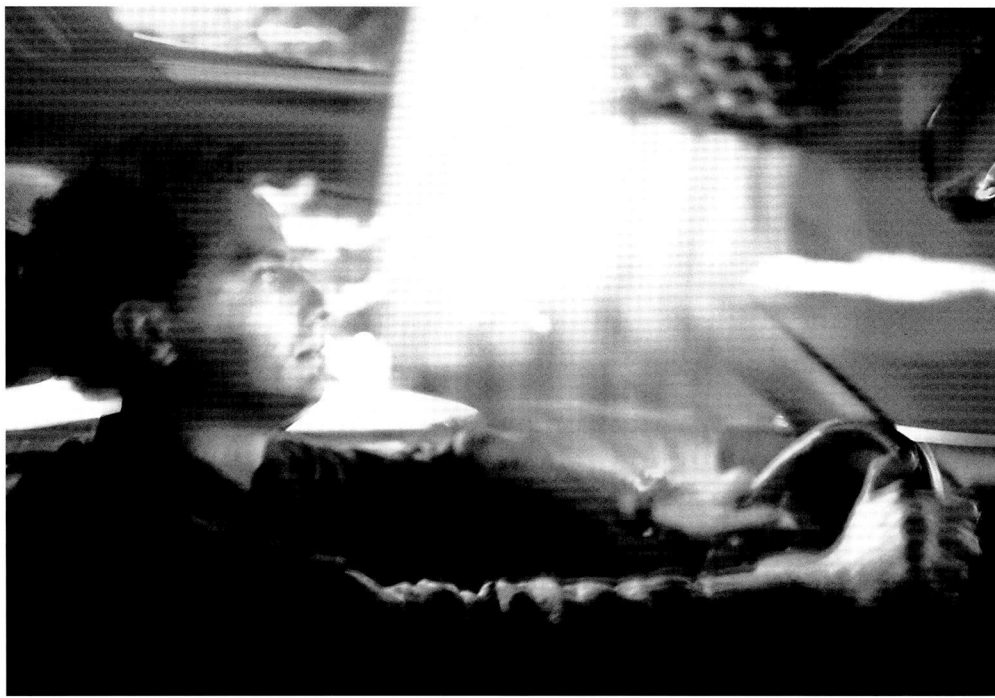

Untitled (Portrait),
from the series *Les faits
secondaires*, 2013

I'm guessing that some readers of this magazine attended an event held at the Aperture Gallery in New York in the fall of 2013 to celebrate the publication of *Understanding a Photograph*, a collection of essays on photography by John Berger. I'd edited the book and on the panel with me were fellow writers and admirers, including Lawrence Weschler and Wendy Lesser, who spoke wittily and cleverly about what Berger meant to them. But by far the most memorable contribution came, appropriately, from the only photographer on the panel, Christophe Agou.

I'd met him years earlier at the Frieze London Art Fair through Matt Stuart, a street photographer who, unlike Garry Winogrand—famously contemptuous of the term—considers

it the best job description in the world. We had dinner, drank a lot. Christophe gave me a copy of his book of photographs taken on the New York subway, *Life Below* (2004). The work was obviously in the tradition of Walker Evans's series of subway portraits from the 1930s and '40s—that same sense of the guard being down—but with a quality that was anathema to Evans, partly because of technical restraints, partly by temperament. For Evans it was precisely the impersonal nature of the encounters that compelled his attention. For Christophe it was the accepted and abided-by intimacy of life in the crowded, swaying cars that proved alluring and subtly revealing.

We became friends, saw each other whenever Christophe was in London or I was in New York. We played Ping-Pong at Fat Cat in the West Village. He was very serious about his work, but in person was always light-footed, funny. When he heard that Pico Iyer and I were contributing essays to a little book of Alec Soth's found photographs of Ping-Pong matches he sent an old snap of his own. No one would claim it's a great photograph but I love its strange air of extreme listlessness. In the accompanying message he signed off with the words, "As always ... *Ouvre-l'oeil!*"

The big project Christophe was engaged in post–*Life Below* was of farm workers in the Forez region of France, where he had been born and raised. This work was as heavily lined and deeply felt as the Ping-Pong pic was lighthearted. You know the expression "as tough as old boots"? There's a famous passage in a lecture by Heidegger about van Gogh's painting of a farm woman's boots. The faces of these people were like those boots: all the more expressive for being so locked into the rhythm of their silence. These are people fully at home in effort. Generously, crazily, Christophe asked if I would write an introduction to the planned book but it was obvious that the only person who could do this was John Berger (from whom I stole that phrase about peasants being fully at home in effort). I put them in touch and they collaborated on what would become *In the Face of Silence* (2011). So many of the themes of Berger's *Into Their Labours* trilogy—especially the first two volumes, *Pig Earth* (1979) and *Once in Europa* (1987)—are manifest in these pictures. The fit between author and photographer is perhaps closer than that between James Agee and Evans in *Let Us Now Praise Famous Men* (1941).

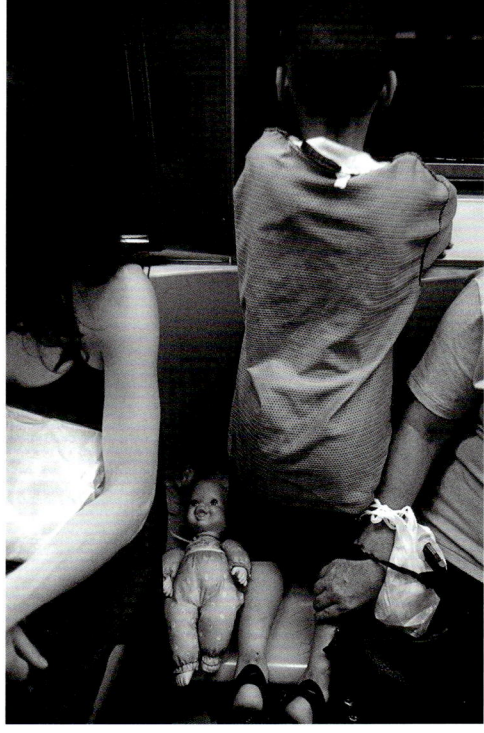

Claudette at her home, with her dog: not waiting for death but with a constant, daily reminder of the increasing pain and *weight* of being alive. When he spoke of John's incredible compassion and generosity it became almost too painful for him. It's not unusual for young writers when they read from their work in public to be overcome with emotion and cry. It's always embarrassing because there's a touch of vanity about it. In Christophe's case the passion was *appropriate*. And you didn't need to know his full story—as only a few of us at the event did—to sense this.

He rallied, recovered, fell ill again and then, on September 18, I received an email from Matt saying that he had died. He was forty-five.

A few days later Matt sent a short video of Christophe on his motorbike in New York—a passion he shared with John—shot, I'm guessing, with an iPhone. The headlight stares straight into the camera. He pulls away from the sidewalk, laughs, roars along the street, leans into the bend and is gone, around the corner. Watching this tiny clip I experienced the nonrider's habitual reaction to such footage: how *dangerous* it is to ride a motorbike in a city. But what difference did that make to him? What danger was there left? I would like to say that after he turns the corner the street seems emptier than it had before, but the truth is that as soon as he disappears a postal truck comes hulking into view: another subject, more happenings, further errands. More life. Other lives.

How quickly the water closes over our heads.

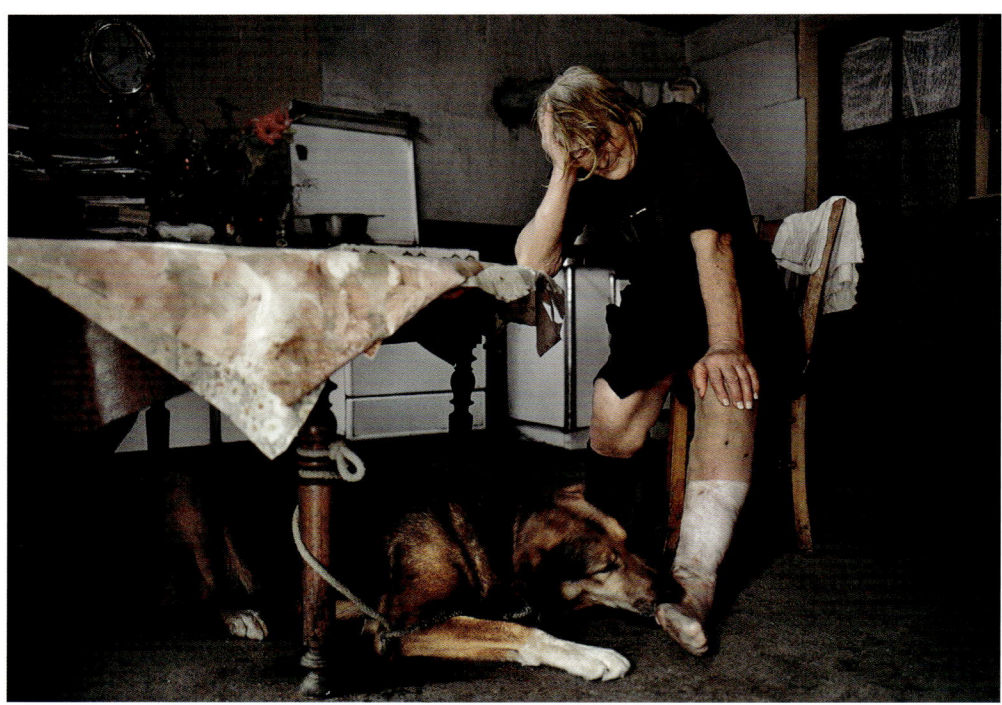

The faces of these people were like those boots: all the more expressive for being so locked into the rhythm of their silence.

About four years ago I heard through Matt that Christophe was ill. He survived an operation and much painful therapy, but by the time of the Aperture event he looked far older and frailer. All of the surface vitality—the silliness that I enjoyed—had gone. The vitality was still there but it had retreated deeper into his being in order to keep him alive, as the body will allow extremities to grow cold in order to maintain its core temperature.

That was why, when Christophe talked about the farmers he had photographed, many of them old, ill, or dying—some of them dead by the time of our event—he was so filled with emotion. Look at the picture of

Geoff Dyer's new book,
White Sands, will be
published by Pantheon
in May 2016.

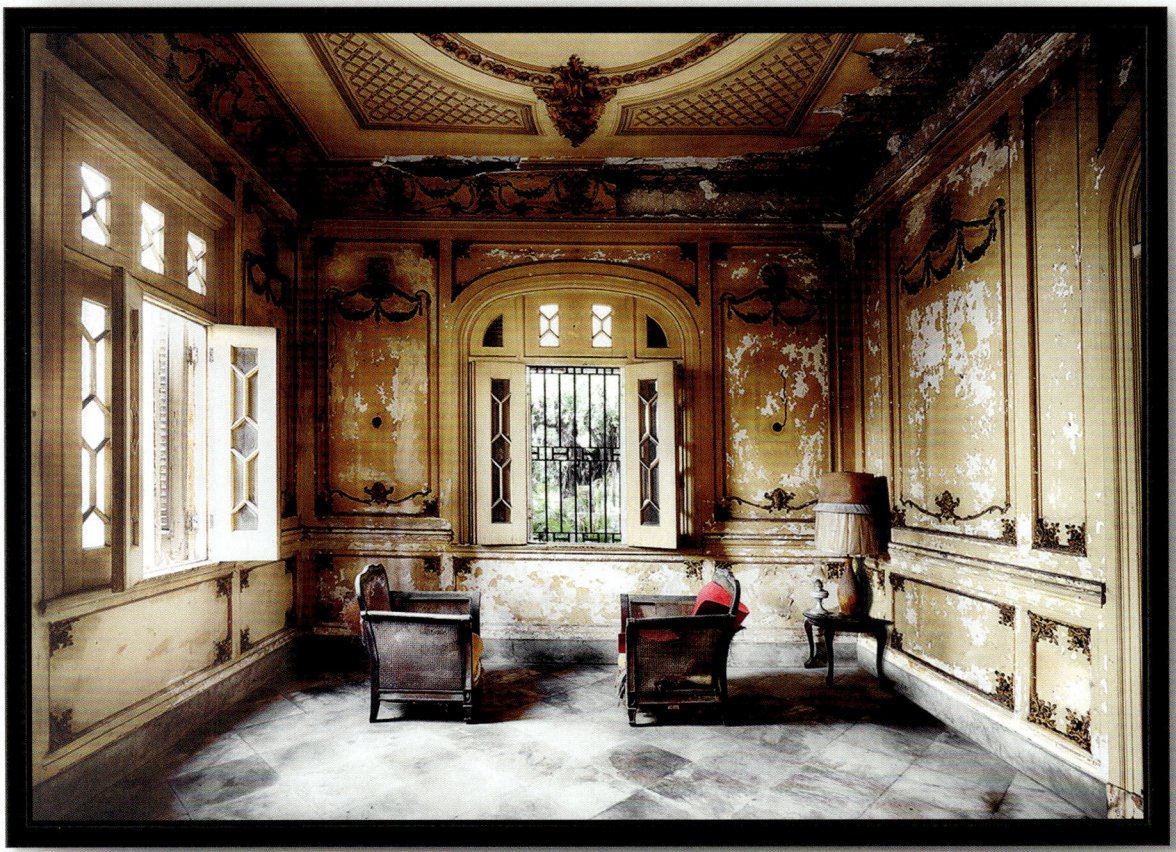
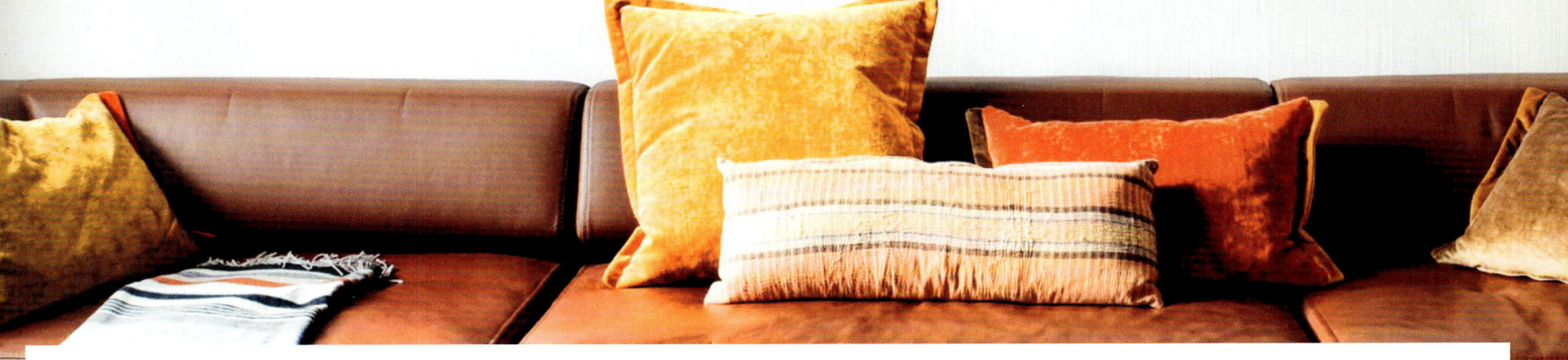

Art | Basel
Hong Kong | March | 24–26 | 2016

Galleries | 10 Chancery Lane | 303 Gallery | **A** | Acquavella | Aike-Dellarco | Air de Paris | Alisan | Andréhn-Schiptjenko | Applicat-Prazan | Arario | Arndt | Athr | Atlas | Aye | **B** | Balice Hertling | Beijing Commune | Bernier/Eliades | Blindspot | Blum & Poe | Boers-Li | Marianne Boesky | Ben Brown | Buchmann | **C** | Gisela Capitain | Cardi | carlier gebauer | Carlos/Ishikawa | Casa Triângulo | Chambers | Chemould Prescott Road | Chi-Wen | Yumiko Chiba | Mehdi Chouakri | James Cohan | Sadie Coles HQ | Contemporary Fine Arts | Continua | Pilar Corrias | Alan Cristea | Chantal Crousel | **D** | Thomas Dane | Massimo De Carlo | de Sarthe | Dirimart | The Drawing Room | **E** | Eigen + Art | Eslite | Gallery Exit | **G** | Gagosian | Gajah | Galerie 1900-2000 | Gandhara-Art | gb agency | Gerhardsen Gerner | Gladstone | Gmurzynska | Goodman Gallery | Marian Goodman | Richard Gray | Greene Naftali | Karsten Greve | Grotto | Kavi Gupta | **H** | Hakgojae | Hanart TZ | Hauser & Wirth | Herald St | Xavier Hufkens | **I** | Ibid. | In Situ - fabienne leclerc | Ingleby | Taka Ishii | **J** | Bernard Jacobson | Jensen | Johnen | Annely Juda | **K** | Kaikai Kiki | Kalfayan | Paul Kasmin | Sean Kelly | Tina Keng | Kerlin | Kewenig | David Kordansky | Tomio Koyama | Krinzinger | Kukje/Tina Kim | **L** | Pearl Lam | Simon Lee | Lehmann Maupin | Lelong | Dominique Lévy | Lin & Lin | Lisson | Long March | **M** | Maggiore | Magician Space | Mai 36 | Edouard Malingue | Marlborough | Hans Mayer | Mazzoleni | Fergus McCaffrey | Meessen De Clercq | Urs Meile | Mendes Wood DM | kamel mennour | Metro Pictures | Meyer Riegger | Francesca Minini | Victoria Miro | Mitchell-Innes & Nash | Mizuma | Stuart Shave/Modern Art | mother's tankstation | **N** | nächst St. Stephan Rosemarie Schwarzwälder | Nadi | Nagel Draxler | Edward Tyler Nahem | Nanzuka | Taro Nasu | Nature Morte | neugerriemschneider | nichido | Anna Ning | Franco Noero | **O** | Lorcan O'Neill | Nathalie Obadia | One and J. | Ora-Ora | Ota | Roslyn Oxley9 | **P** | P.P.O.W | Pace | Pace Prints | Paragon | Peres Projects | Perrotin | PKM | Plan B | Platform China | Polígrafa | Project Fulfill | **R** | Almine Rech | Nara Roesler | Tyler Rollins | Thaddaeus Ropac | Andrea Rosen | Rossi & Rossi | Lia Rumma | **S** | SCAI | Esther Schipper | Rüdiger Schöttle | ShanghART | ShugoArts | Sies + Höke | Silverlens | Skarstedt | Soka | Sprüth Magers | Starkwhite | STPI | Sullivan+Strumpf | **T** | Take Ninagawa | Tang | team | Thomas | TKG+ | Tokyo Gallery + BTAP | Tolarno | Tornabuoni | **V** | Vadehra | Van de Weghe | Isabelle van den Eynde | Susanne Vielmetter | Vitamin | **W** | Wentrup | Michael Werner | White Cube | White Space | Wilkinson | Hubert Winter | Jocelyn Wolff | **X** | Leo Xu | **Y** | Yamamoto Gendai | Yavuz | **Z** | Zeno X | David Zwirner | **Discoveries** | 11R Eleven Rivington | 313 Art Project | a.m. space | Sabrina Amrani | Artinformal | Isabella Bortolozzi | Thomas Erben | Experimenter | Selma Feriani | François Ghebaly | Hopkinson Mossman | Pippy Houldsworth | Darren Knight | Michael Lett | Mujin-to | Night | Raster | ROH Projects | Rokeby | Side 2 | Société | Weingrüll | Workplace | Yeo | **Insights** | 1335Mabini | A Thousand Plateaus | Antenna Space | Arataniurano | Hadrien de Montferrand | du Monde | EM | Exhibit320 | Fost | Gallery 100 | Ink Studio | Yoshiaki Inoue | iPreciation | L-Art | Lawrie Shabibi | Leeahn | Liang | Longmen | MEM | Osage | Park Ryu Sook | Pékin | Pi Artworks | Star | This Is No Fantasy + dianne tanzer | Vanguard | Yamaki | Yang

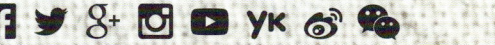

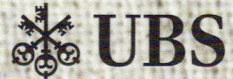

Redux
Rediscovered Books and Writings

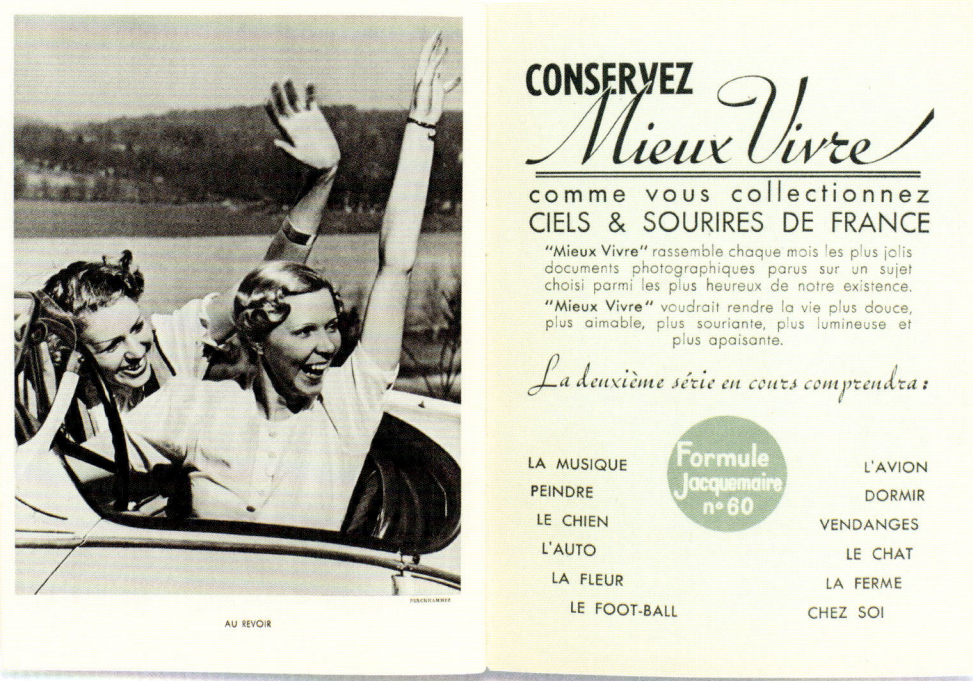

A French pharmacist's magazine reflected the avant-garde of its day.

Mieux Vivre
Sara Knelman

Spread from *Mieux Vivre* No. 2: *L'Auto*, 1937, including photograph by Peckhammer

In January 1936, Jean Bonthoux, a French pharmacist, began publishing *Mieux Vivre* (Live better), his second monthly arts revue. It joined Bonthoux's already successful *Ciels & Sourires de France* (Skies and smiles of France), which also provided the blueprint: hire a well-respected artist as creative director, insist on high production values, invite the best writers and contemporary photographers to contribute content around everyday themes with a wide appeal, and—you might have guessed— incorporate smart, exclusive advertising for new pharmaceutical products. Issues were freely distributed to doctors and other medical professionals for patients to browse, precursors, in their way, to the lifestyle magazines we're now accustomed to finding in medical offices and waiting rooms. While *Ciels* traded on picturesque landscapes from around the country, *Mieux Vivre*'s themes were immersive experiences and active verbs: skiing, sailing, cycling, painting, sculpture, cinema, and, of course, photography.

Directed by photographer and critic George Besson, every issue opens with a short essay on the chosen theme— Colette on flowers, Maurice de Vlaminck on farming, Kees van Dongen on painting—followed by images by some of the most talented photographers of the day, including Brassaï, Nora Dumas, André Kertész, Ergy Landau, André Steiner, Paul Wolff, and Ylla. Every slim, 5-by-7-inch installment conforms to exactly the same format: twenty-four illustrated pages, all richly toned, attentively printed heliogravures, stapled together inside sturdier cover stock. The title text offers the only flash of color, a thin, modern font inscribed in deep, bright orange. Above it, a single image (sometimes a photograph, more often a well-known painting) is invariably presented within a frame, each one with distinct wood grains and beveled edges, as though ready to hang on a museum wall. It's an odd design feature, and may look kitschy to us now. On the other hand, it expresses the kind of meticulous consideration and attention to detail that infused the whole enterprise, and signals the publication's self-regard as an object of worth— emphasized again at the close of the issue, where text on the inside back cover encouraged readers to save and collect each volume.

Collectible but free, the booklets were far from exclusive or elitist. Besson was acutely aware of his broad readership, and the interpretations of themes are purposefully varied and playful. In *Peindre* (Painting), for example, the issue opens with an image of an aged Pierre-Auguste Renoir, regal yet frail at his easel. A few pages on we get an image of youthful house painters hard at work, followed on the next page by another pair, smiling in the sunshine, enjoying a break from their labors. We see more "masters" (Le Corbusier, André Derain) interspersed amid Sunday painters busily rendering landscapes and metropolitan views, all equally absorbed in their canvases. These shifts between art and craft, extracurricular

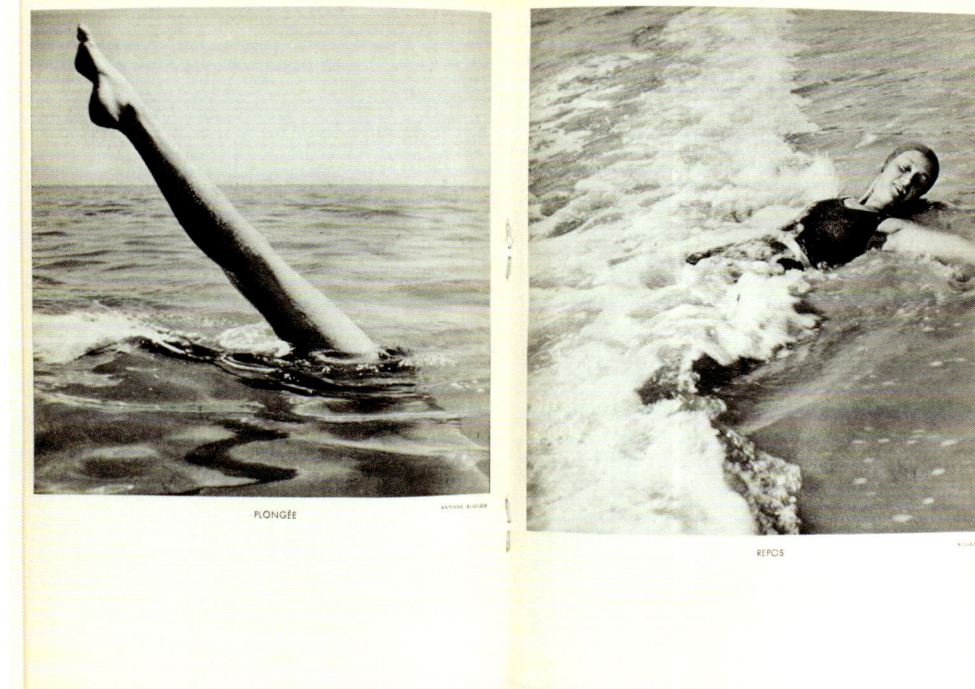

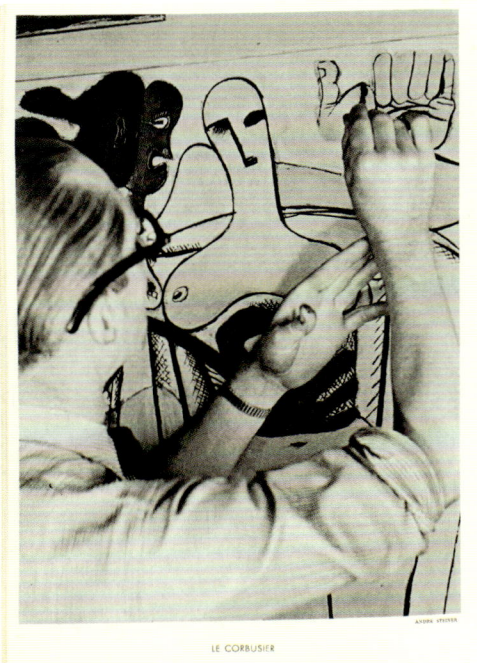

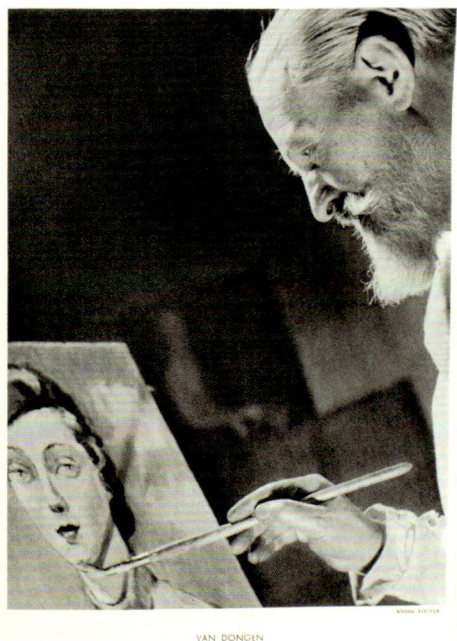

n° 60 ... également Quiétude!" (... also tranquility!), aligning the calm moments of reading with the general peace of mind the drug might furnish. There are also ironic discords, most obviously the many images of habitual smokers writing, painting, playing cards, and taking photos—activities that go especially well with cigarettes, it would seem—that share space with a drug marketed for use *"aux terrains précancéreux"* (in precancerous territory). Indeed, November 1937 was dedicated to *Fumer* (Smoking), portraying smoking as a lifestyle choice that might go hand-in-hand with these everyday lozenges.

The forty-five published issues of *Mieux Vivre* were of their time, produced at the close of a creatively potent decade when Surrealism, jazz, and experimental literature flourished, and, like a lot of mass-cultural products, also slipped away with it. Bonthoux died in 1937 in the midst of the magazine's short life; it would abruptly fold two years later. September 1939 ushered in the German invasion of Poland and the publication of the series's final published issue: *Les Fruits.* (The subsequent three issues, on wine, trees, and singing, were advertised but never completed.) By the time the war ended many of the contributors had fled Europe, and the lighthearted energy of the period was scattered or dissolved. Surviving copies also scattered, though they are easy enough to find for cheap in French used bookstores. The sudden end and perpetual incompleteness of *Mieux Vivre* are heavyhearted reminders of the immense creative potential of the time, which would never be fully realized. But the revue's spirit is remarkably intact, a testament to the inventive collaborations between art and commerce, the expanding and conflicting possibilities for photography, and the vivid imaginations and experimental spark of this moment in and around Paris of the 1930s. *Mieux Vivre*? Maybe. Then again, living better so often looks best in retrospect.

hobby and paid labor are apt reflections of the lives of the jobbing photographers who made them, and of a wider cultural sensibility, one that preferred not to distinguish high from low, placing value instead on pleasure and pride. In a similar way, *Mieux Vivre*'s heterogeneity also makes its present-day appeal hard to pin down—we may be interested in the photographs, but historians of pharmacology or collectors of vintage advertising might find it equally fascinating for different reasons.

The images were, let's not forget, in the service of selling pharmaceuticals, and astutely set against ads for a new drug called Formule Jacquemaire n° 60. Readers were led to believe that taking

this pill twice daily could support the energy levels and general health needed to pursue all of the wonderful fun illustrated by the pictures. The ads were often conceived and executed with each issue's subject in mind: A Formule Jacquemaire ad in *L'Auto* (The car) gives readers a jagged motorway route, with junctures along the line listing the evolving benefits of the product, from preventing warts to combating depression to, ultimately, deterring precancerous cell development. In *Lire* (Reading), an ad showing a young girl contentedly absorbed in a book carries the captions *"Lire un bon livre ... Quiétude!"* (Read a good book ... tranquility!) and *"Formule Jacquemaire*

Top:
Spread from *Mieux Vivre
No. 8: Le Bain*, 1936,
including photographs
by Antoine Rougier
and Emmanuel Sougez
Bottom:
Spread from *Mieux Vivre
No. 3: Peindre*, 1937,
including photographs
by André Steiner

Sara Knelman is a writer,
curator, and lecturer living
in Toronto.

Words

Vittorio Sella, Climbers
Descending the Hoffman
Route, Gross Glockner,
1893
© Fondazione Sella and
courtesy Decaneas Archive
(See page 38)

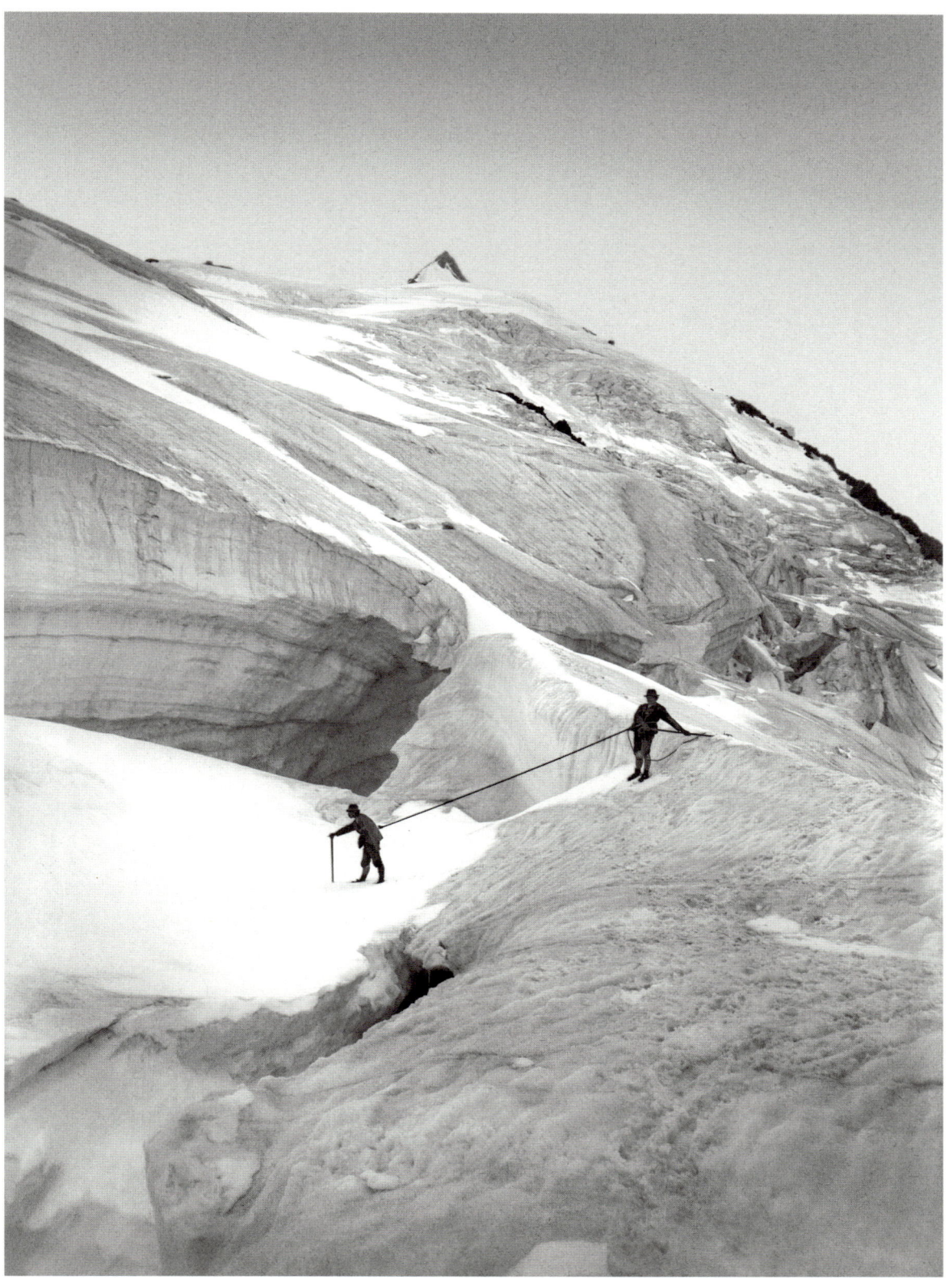

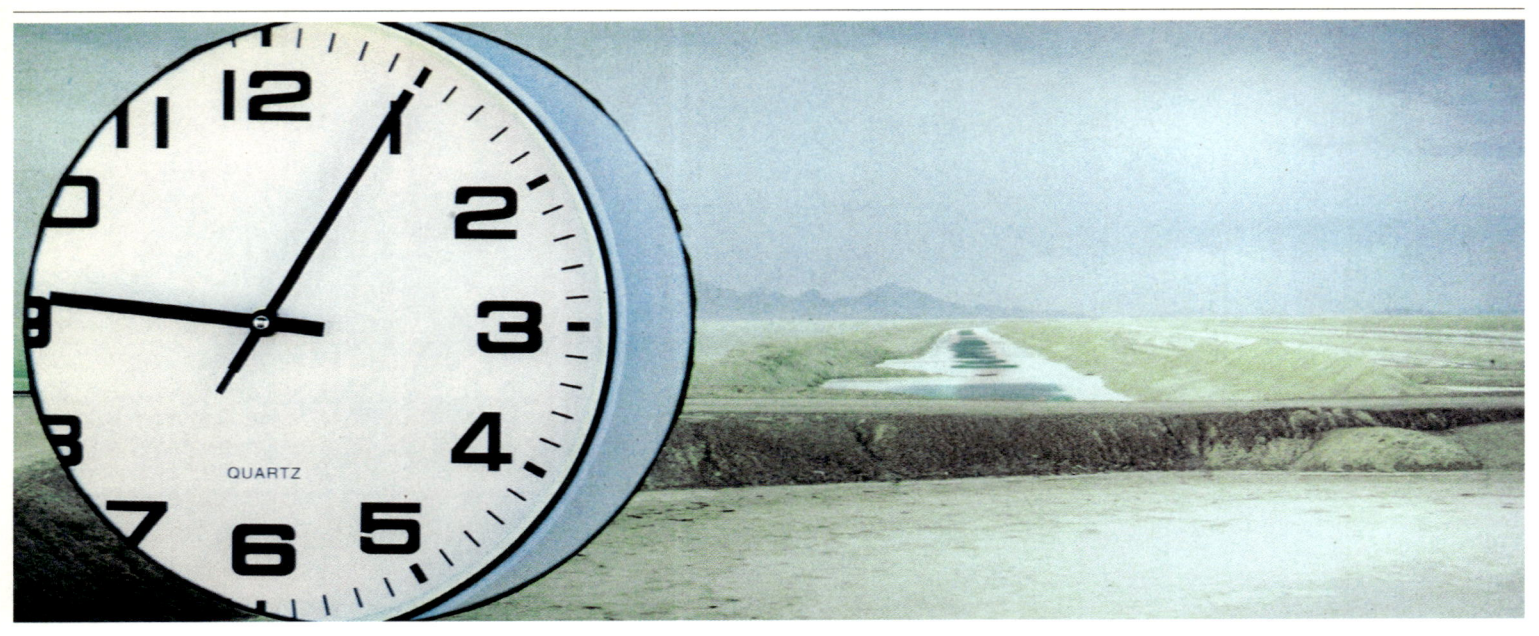

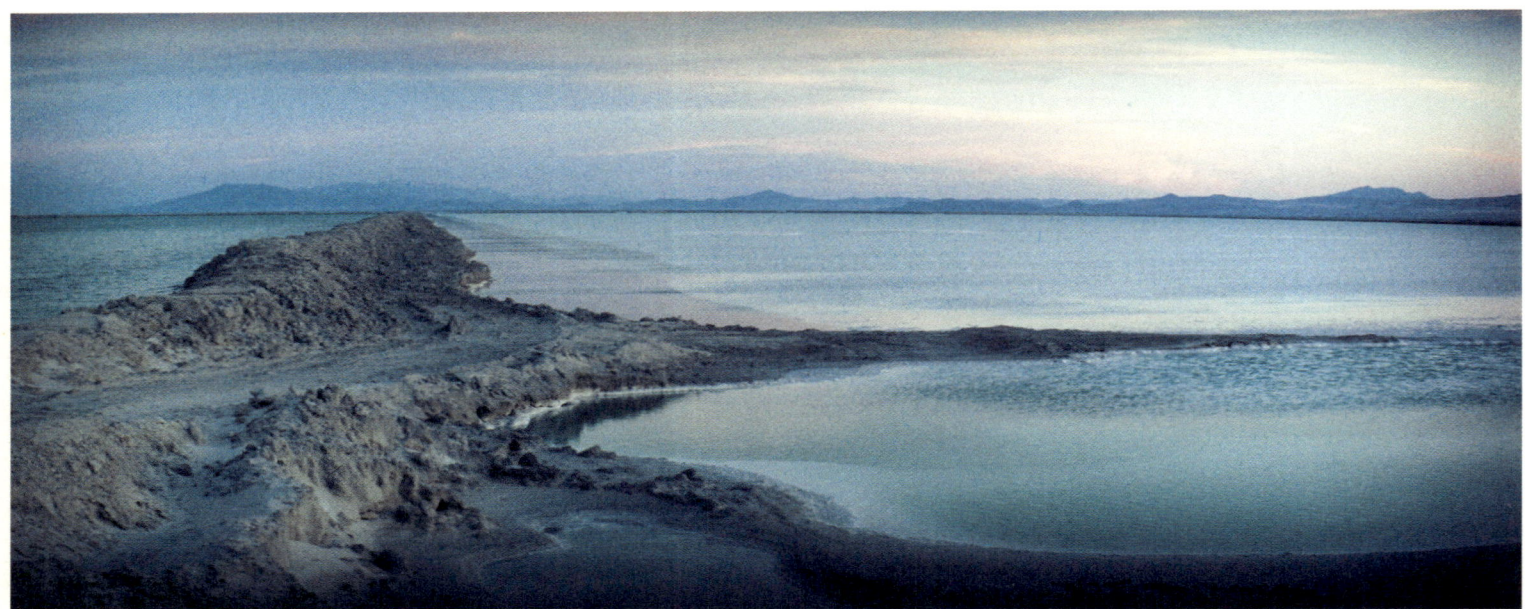

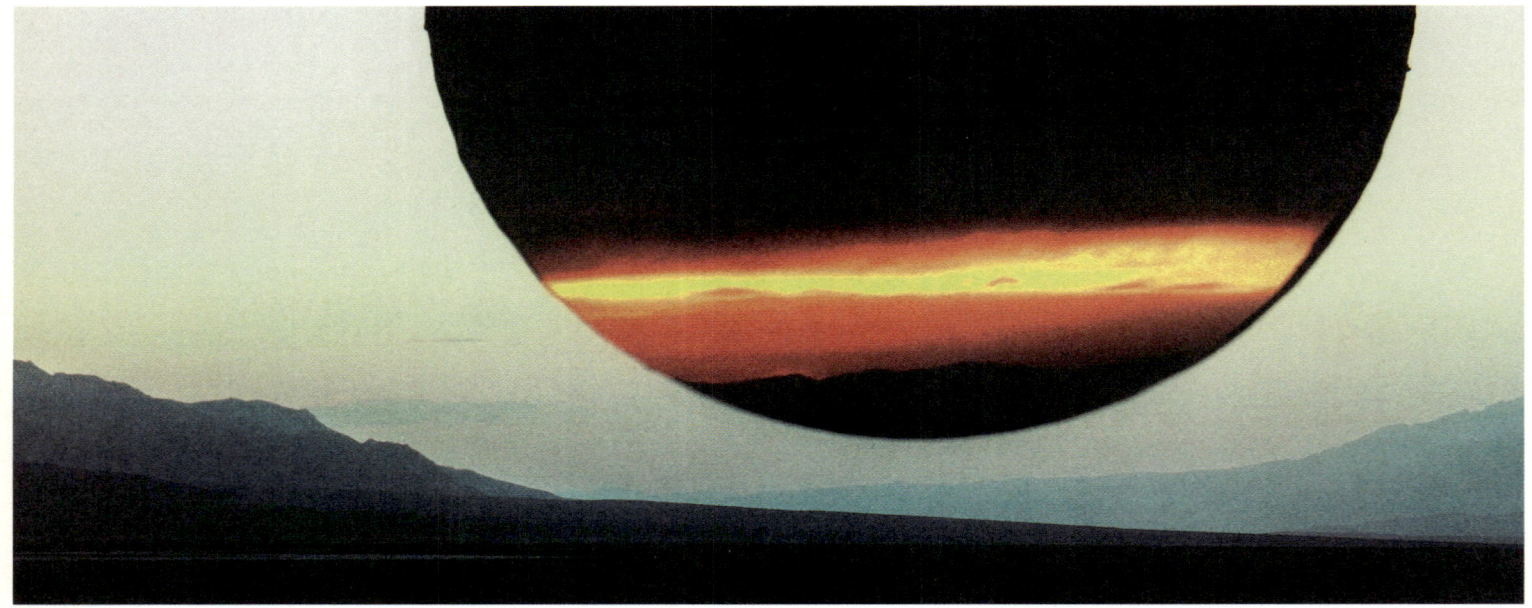

JG, 2013 (film stills). 35mm color and black-and-white anamorphic film with optical sound, 26½ minutes

Unconscious Journey

Tacita Dean in Conversation with Travis A. Diehl

In the shopping district a few blocks from Berlin-based artist Tacita Dean's Los Angeles apartment, concrete compass roses decorate the street corners, and plaques inlaid in the sidewalks read "All Roads Lead to Westwood." LA imagines itself as the end of the earth. It's not—and Dean would know. Since the early 1990s, her artworks—which include 16mm and 35mm films, as well as found photographs, audio recordings, photogravures, pressed clovers, books, gouaches on postcards, and large-scale chalk drawings on blackboards, among other mediums—have led her to ends as far flung as the island of Cayman Brac in search of the wreck of a yacht in *Teignmouth Electron* (2000), Utah's lifeless Great Salt Lake in *Trying to Find the Spiral Jetty* (1997), and the westernmost edge of Madagascar to capture a particular ray of sun in *The Green Ray* (2001). If LA has a short memory, Dean takes the long view; exploring the shape of time with J. G. Ballard and Robert Smithson in the film *JG* (2013), photographing Prague on the brink of westernization in *Czech Photos* (1991/2002), and arcing back to a Germany before the war in *c/o Jolyon* (2012–13). Yet the city and the artist share an obsession. LA is a place fixated on image, filmic and otherwise. Following her residency at the Getty Research Institute, Dean stayed on in LA to complete the monumental task of archiving the negatives of her more than fifty films, and to advocate for the endangered medium she loves in the higher circles of The Industry. Within months, she will return to Europe. Travis A. Diehl reached Dean in her living room on a weekday night, just before supper.

Travis A. Diehl: **In your Kassel project, *c/o Jolyon* (2012–13), you've gone on a journey, back to the origin of the image. You've returned to the scenes shown in old postcards to complete the work by adding an image of the modern city. A car, a new window, a modern apartment building …**

Tacita Dean: When I go to a strange town, I try to buy second-hand postcards of it to get a better understanding. On a site visit to Kassel for dOCUMENTA, the first shop I went into, I found over one hundred postcards from prewar Kassel. So I bought them all. Kassel was so disfigured by World War II because it was a Nazi stronghold and was blitzed. I asked a historian to track down each location in the postcard and photograph it as close to the original as was possible. It was quite a job. Then it became this ongoing process for me of pulling out a postcard, comparing it to the contemporary image, and then overpainting it. Fifty of them were shown in Kabul in 2013. The resonance for that city, then (and now) in the process of being destroyed, was poignant, like some sort of painted future for them.

TAD: **There's a connection between the Kassel postcards and your *Czech Photos* (1991/2002), in terms of returning to the site of an image through the image, or the time of that image's making, if not actually to Prague.**

TD: Well, I didn't return to Prague, but I returned in the sense that I refound the photographs. I took those images when I was a student, a postgraduate student at the Slade School of Fine Art, and I had just bought my first SLR camera and a lot of cheap Russian film—and it was really cheap. Normally when you're a student, one film has to last you a long time. It was exhilarating. I just started to take photographs, unselfconsciously. This was 1991. The Velvet Revolution had only just happened, and there were still posters and handwritten notes from Václav Havel all over the city. There was a raw energy there. Prague is very touristified now.

The point about all of those photographs I took was that I left them to be processed in Prague. When a packet arrived in London many months later, it contained these tiny, beautiful, hand-printed photographs with white borders. Usually you have a strong sense of what you've taken on a roll of film; you can remember. But by the stage they arrived, it already had become another land, so it was like a gift from Prague's past but also from my past.

TAD: **A kind of found photography.**

TD: I work a lot with found images. I like the unconscious journey that happens when you're in a flea market, or when you're in some sort of situation where you can just come across things, and what that does in terms of either triggering something else or renewing a memory. Do you know about "objective chance"? It's an unconscious journey that comes out of Surrealism. You allow yourself to be interrupted on your journey and led elsewhere by whatever you encounter. "*Chance objets*," Breton used to say. I'm not as deliberate as it might look. And I don't want to be either. Sebald talks about his research as being like a dog sniffing a field. Dogs don't go in a straight line but follow their noses and go all over the place. I find that's also a great metaphor for how it is for me.

I've made a lot of projects with found works. With *Die Regimentstochter* (2005), I found these opera programs in a flea market in Berlin. There were thirty-six of them and something had been cut out of every cover quite neatly—making them like found collages. You could see the page underneath through the

gap. They were just immediately arresting. Maybe it's a British thing, but I knew instantly that the swastika had been cut out. I eventually re-presented them and made a facsimile book. Every program cover was scanned by Steidl, the German publisher. The person scanning them had no idea what had been cut out. For me, it was completely clear.

TAD: **You've written an essay entitled "W. G. Sebald" (*October*, Fall 2003), and have referenced Sebald obliquely in a few other projects. He inserted found photos in his texts, and was also interested in the way Germany dealt with having been destroyed. How has Sebald's writing influenced the form of your work?**

TD: I wouldn't say that it has, exactly. Sebald's method is quite like my method, so I was drawn to him for that reason. He is a great writer.

TAD: **When you work on a project, do you know whether it's going to be moving or still film?**

TD: It's usually moving. I make those decisions intuitively.

TAD: **It's sometimes both, no? With *Teignmouth Electron*, which is a series of photographs, a book (1999), and a film (2000), you worked with the story of amateur sailor Donald Crowhurst, who risked everything to enter a solo yacht race around the world. He ended up faking his position, sending misleading reports, and jumping overboard rather than face the repercussions of his deceit. You even went in search of his boat.**

TD: In that case, the photographs came before the film. I had tracked down Crowhurst's trimaran to the island of Cayman Brac, and was commissioned by the National Maritime Museum in Britain to go and photograph it. I took my 16mm camera with me, and ended up filming not only *Teignmouth Electron*, but also *Bubble House* (1999), which features a deserted oval-shaped house farther along the same coast. I often show the two films together, as they are connected. Both were visionary designs that have fallen into disrepair and both of the men who invested in them paid dearly for their fraud.

TAD: **What attracted you to Crowhurst?**

TD: A friend told me about the 1980 book *The Strange Last Voyage of Donald Crowhurst*, by Nicholas Tomalin and Ron Hall, because I was working with the gap between fact and fiction. But the more I got involved in the story, the more I became interested in the madness and the existential dilemma that Crowhurst faced.

TAD: **How do you think of your own working process in relation to the kind of stories you're telling?**

TD: "Stories" is a misleading word, really because I don't actually think I tell stories particularly. What is narrative? It's definitely not a three-act system or whatever it is in cinema. Often my stories are of a day, or passage of time, and so forth, or a depiction of an afternoon, or a person. I see my work much more in relation to a painting discourse than to a cinematic one. Nothing really happens much, other than somebody or something being present in that moment.

TAD: **In *Teignmouth Electron* there's a kind of backstory.**

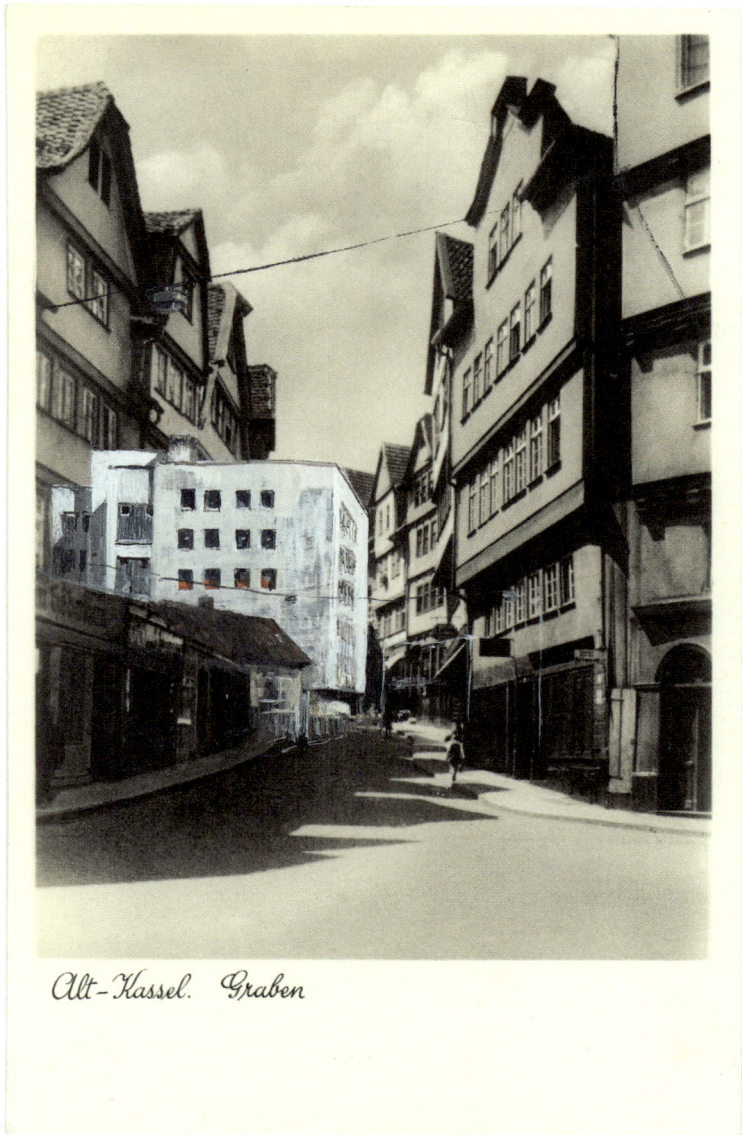

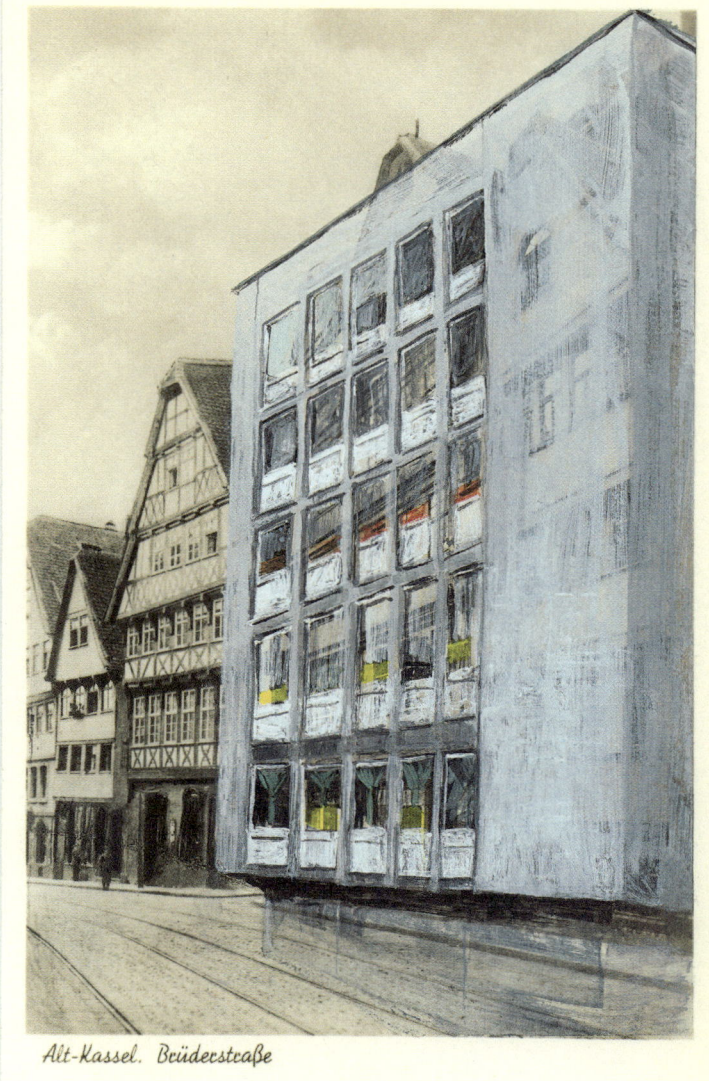

c/o Jolyon, 2012–13 (detail).
Postcards hand painted
with gouache

Dogs don't go in a straight line but follow their noses and go all over the place. I find that's also a great metaphor for how it is for me.

TD: There was a backstory, I guess, a preexisting story. You wouldn't really get to know anything about that from the film. The book is different, of course. The book is a story that is an approach to someone else's story. That's what that book is. I also write, but I write anecdotally more than narratively. I don't put those narratives over the films. Perhaps they're the genesis of the idea but they don't explain it.

TAD: I think of your film *JG* (2013), which composites shots of Mono Lake in California and the Great Salt Lake in Utah, and includes words from the writer J. G. Ballard, as following Robert Smithson and Nancy Holt's *Mono Lake* (1968), and Smithson's *Spiral Jetty* (1970), which are both travel films, in a way.

TD: *JG* is related to Ballard and Smithson. Ballard obviously was a storyteller, and he wrote this particular short story, "The Voices of Time," that for me had a strong connection to Smithson's *Spiral Jetty*. Probably even inspired it, but we won't really ever know. It was this relationship between these two personages in relation to that particular Utah/Southern Californian landscape and deep time, and all the different times that happen within that land, like creatural time, geological time, cosmic time, prehistoric time. Also, it was a film about film itself, and the spiral. *Spiral Jetty*, the film that Smithson made, is very much about prehistory. Ballard told me that he saw the *Spiral Jetty* as a clock. Smithson and Ballard were both interested in each other, even wrote about each other, but, of course, they never met.

I don't know whether we will have the same level of emotional longing for a digital iPhone picture as for a gelatin-silver print.

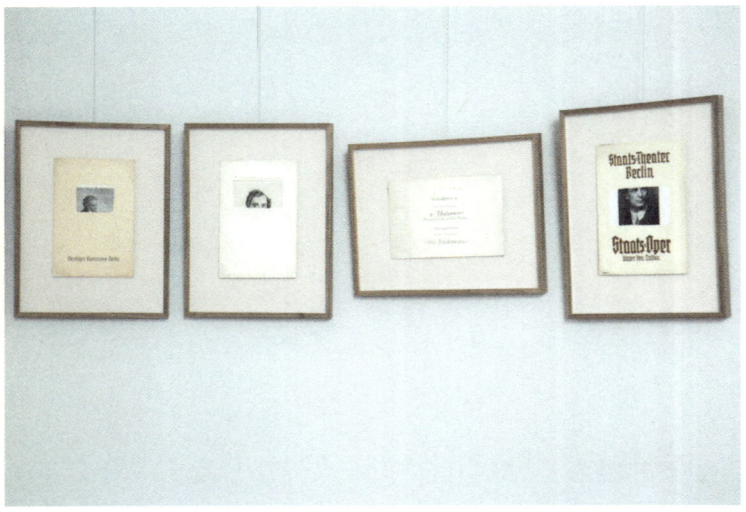

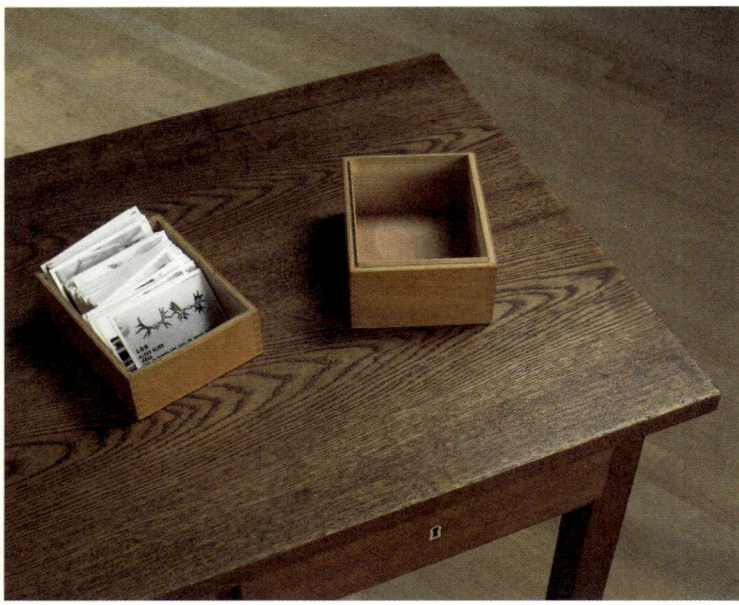

Top:
Installation view of
Die Regimentstochter,
Landestheater, Salzburg
Festival, 2005

Bottom:
Installation view of
Czech Photos, Norton
Museum of Art, Miami,
1991/2002

TAD: **Making that film, you had to travel to the *Spiral Jetty*, and you traveled to Mono Lake. You had your own kind of parallel travel.**

TD: I filmed mostly in a potash plant in Wendover and also in Death Valley. I had developed this aperture gate–masking system for *FILM* in Tate Modern's Turbine Hall (2011–12), and it suddenly seemed the perfect way to bring time and place, which are the two central aspects of that film, into the same pictorial film frame—the physical film frame. I didn't know whether to have a voiceover. That was something that came about quite late. But of course, it doesn't really have a narrative. It just has an atmosphere.

TAD: **Would you say the sound piece, *Trying to Find the Spiral Jetty* (1997), has a narrative?**

TD: Again, I didn't know I was going to make that work. I was in Sundance at the Scriptwriter's Lab, and I had been in this other world with cinema people, and was wondering if I should make a narrative film. I'd heard that the *Spiral Jetty* had risen. I had a few days left at the end of the lab so I phoned up Utah Arts Council and got instructions of how to get there faxed to Sundance. I ended up going on this adventure with another of the lab's participants. This was 1997—no one was looking for the *Spiral Jetty*. There was a lull in interest and it had dropped out of our history to some extent. Now there are signposts. There is a car park that has been been tarmacked. It has lost its pilgrimage aspect, I think. In fact, it's crowded.

TAD: **Do you think of taking photographs or making films as collecting in some way?**

TD: I think it's the same. I've been dysfunctional about making films in LA. I don't know why. I've been a bit dysfunctional here generally. I hear it's common. There's a lot of things about my behavior I'm not quite understanding in LA. It's a strange relationship to history.

I've been mostly concerned with saving the medium of film. A bloody awful time I've had since 2011 trying to find a lab. Now I've just moved it all here, to FotoKem. I was the artist-in-residence at the Getty last year. So that's what's brought me to LA. Why I'm staying for another year is mainly because the Academy Film Archive invited me to store my negatives there in perpetuity.

TAD: **Are you archiving both your still negatives and the films?**

TD: My still negatives are in total disarray, actually; that's for the future. I'm concentrating on my film negatives here in LA. I have fifty-eight original cut negatives. That's a lot of work. I exhibit my films on film. My whole identity is showing films in museums as film. I have no interest in digitizing them; that would be a corruption of the experience of them. So, with the threat to photochemical film, I was looking at extinction. People need to understand it's not just technological extinction. It's medium extinction. Cinema actually is history.

TAD: **Do you mean the history that is recorded on film, or is there something about film that's particularly historical?**

TD: Well, it's not recorded. That's the wrong word. Film is printed. It's a printed medium. What I'm saying is that we have a huge history of film. Like we have a history of painting, we

Teignmouth Electron,
Cayman Brac **(general),**
1999. Color photograph
All works courtesy the artist;
Frith Street Gallery, London;
and Marian Goodman
Gallery, New York/Paris

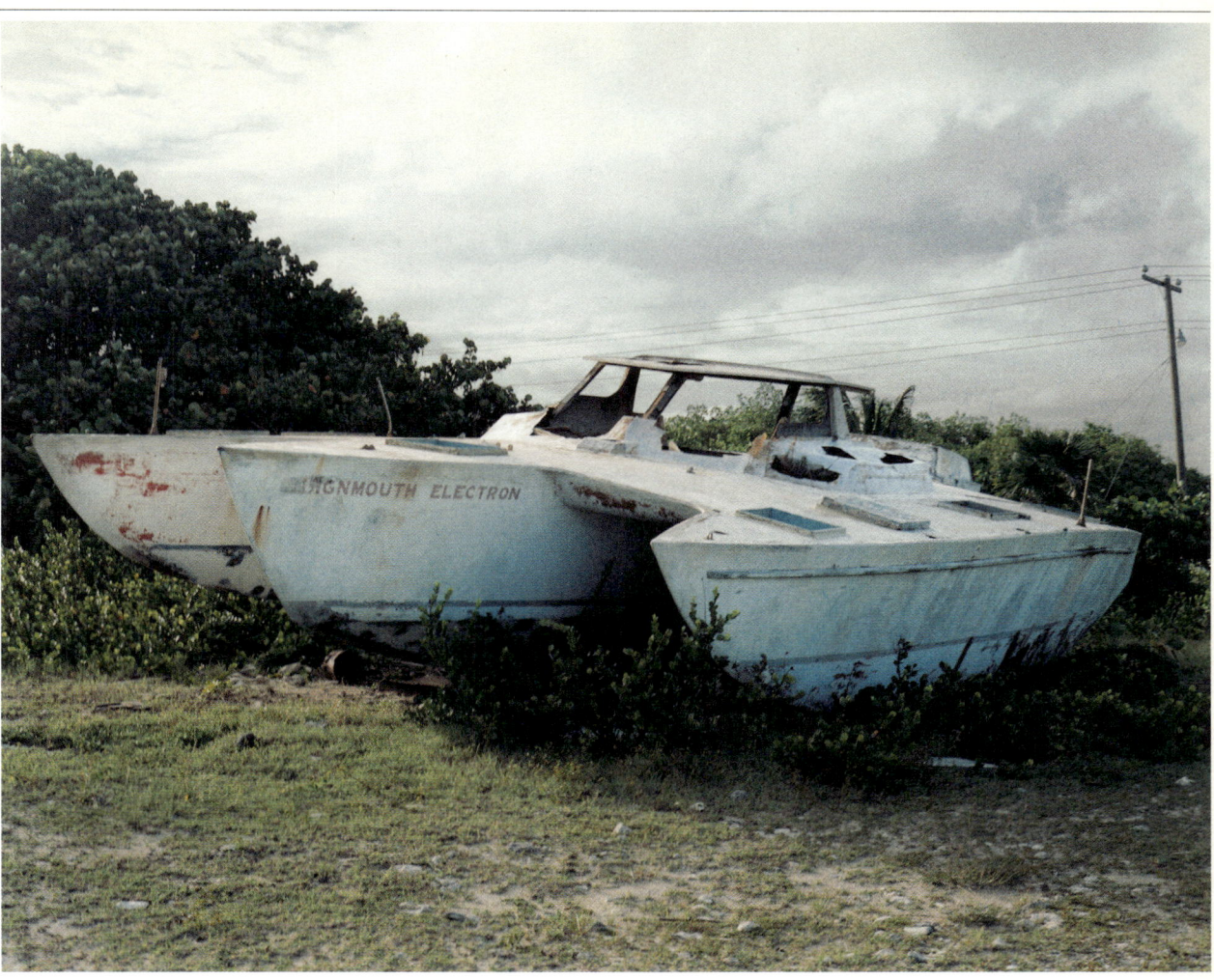

have a history of sculpture, we have a history of photography—
we have a history of film. It is clear they are never going to show
a digitized version of a canvas in a museum without calling
it a facsimile. But even in 1994, when I showed my film *Girl
Stowaway* (1994) at the Institute of Contemporary Arts, London,
they put it on video (I tried to have it on 16mm and it promptly
broke). That was my first real exhibition, or one of them. It was
immensely painful and I made them put up a note: "This is
supposed to be shown on 16mm film."

TAD: **Digital lacks some of the deathly aspect of film,
maybe.**

TD: There's the organic nature of film. Each film frame is
composed differently: it has a different grain structure, like a
snowflake. Getting somebody's likeness who is dead, of course,
has the memento mori aspect. I don't know whether we will
have the same level of emotional longing for a digital iPhone
picture as we will have for a gelatin-silver print. We don't know
what's going to happen about the fetishization of the future.
Do we feel the same emotional attraction to a VHS from the
1980s? Maybe. Some people do.

Digital doesn't deteriorate nicely. That's the difference.
Digital errors are not good. Of course, everyone is losing or has
already lost their personal images. Half the frame just disappears.
There's no gentle fading, it just obliterates. Everybody has had
their computer break, hard drives go down, things are routinely
lost. It's a whole different game. Of course, there's a huge
investment in not telling people that.

TAD: **I'm a little terrified to lose this interview, actually.**

TD: You might have done.

TAD: **Thinking about material forms that do endure, you have
a new book,** *Buon Fresco,* **scheduled for publication this year.
Can you tell us about this project?**

TD: It will be a book without words. The images are the frames
from my film *Buon Fresco* (2014), which I made in Assisi in
the Basilica of St. Francis. I filmed, with a macro lens, details
of the fresco, a view that was once unique to the painter, Giotto.
I was always fascinated by this moment in the history of art
and sainthood when both became more human. St. Francis
was the saint-as-man and Giotto was the first painter to achieve
a naturalism in his depiction of figures that was a true departure
from Byzantine art. What the images show is just how radical
Giotto and his assistants were in their paint strokes and use
of abstraction, which you don't see in the same way when you
stand on the floor of the basilica looking up.

Travis A. Diehl is a writer based in Los
Angeles. He is a recipient of a Creative
Capital/Warhol Foundation Arts Writers
Grant.

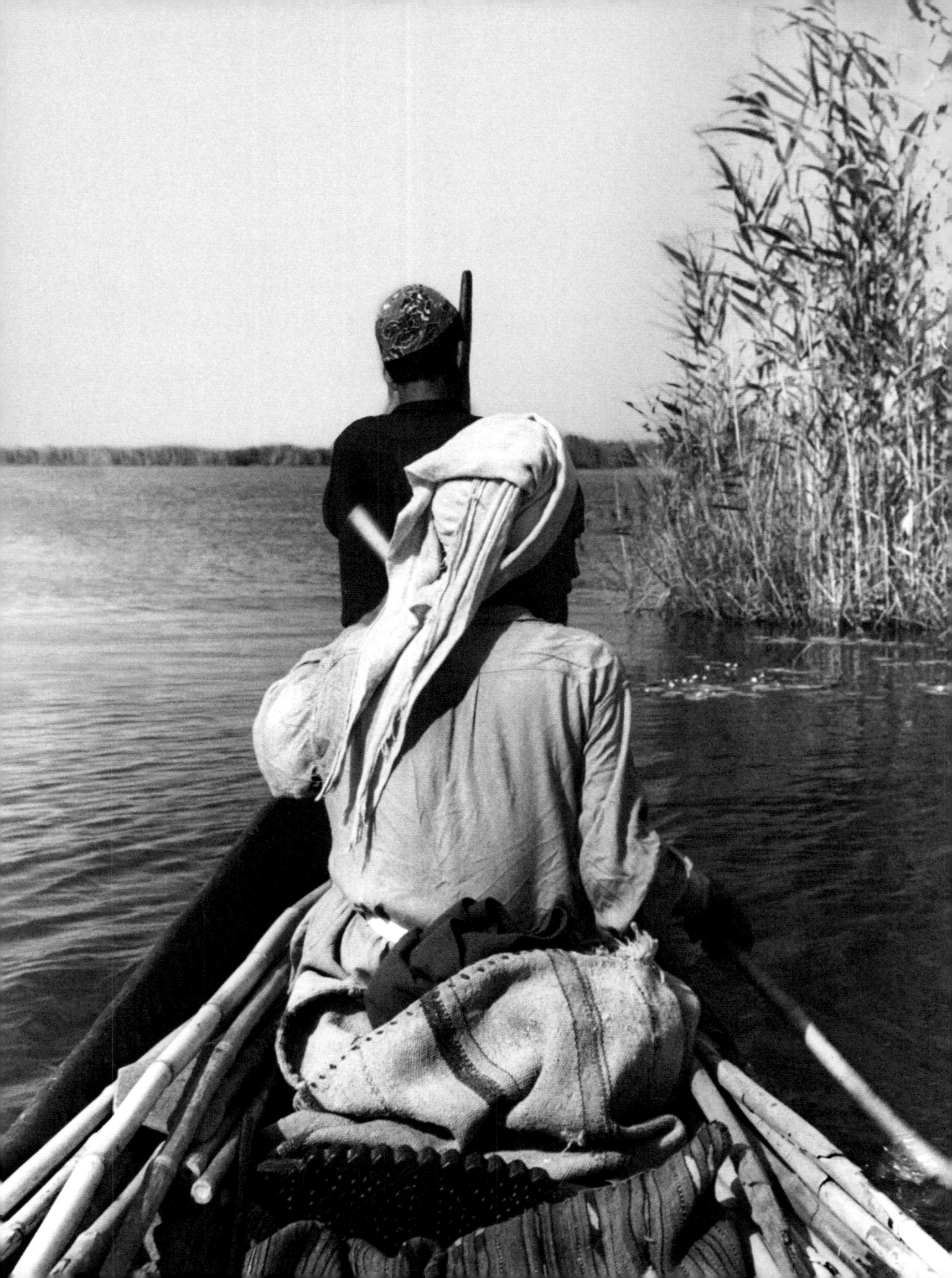

An escapist from modern life, the famed travel writer Wilfred Thesiger journeyed throughout the Arabian Peninsula's remote desert regions and Iraq's salt marshes, recording a region on the brink of change.

The Last Nomad

Eric Banks

"The following pages, then, are written for nieces, or for those who are willing, for the time, to be nieces in wish…. One niece is also more likely than two to carry a kodak and take interest in it, since she has nothing else, except her uncle, to interest her, and instances occur when she takes interest neither in the uncle nor in the journey. One cannot assume, even in a niece, too emotional a nature, but one may assume a kodak."
—Henry Adams, *Mont-Saint-Michel and Chartres*

As early as 1904, when Henry Adams wrote the preface to his hybrid tour manual of the relics of medieval France, it had already become something of an in-joke that no traveler set forth on a journey without a trusty compact camera at the ready. Such was the case with Wilfred Thesiger. Though he may be better known for his prose, his photographs came to mark his renowned midcentury explorations in Africa, Asia, and the Middle East. In 1930, Thesiger journeyed from Oxford, where he was studying, to Addis Ababa, the Ethiopian city where he'd been born twenty years earlier. The occasion was the coronation of Haile Selassie as *Nagusa Nagast*, or King of Kings, and, like the nieces of Adams's telling, the story of the camera Thesiger carried to capture the moment was a family affair—his first machine was a roll-film box camera made by Kodak that his father, a British diplomat, had originally used in the Belgian Congo more than twenty years earlier.

Thesiger, remembered today as a giant of twentieth-century exploration whose name remains synonymous with travel in the Arabian Peninsula and in the marshes of southern Iraq, had already led a remarkable life before he set off into the desert sands in 1945. He had worked for the British government in northern Darfur and among the Nilotic Nuer, and, furious over the horrors of Mussolini's atrocities in Ethiopia, had joined the Sudan Defense Force, at one point capturing a garrison of twenty-five hundred Italian forces in Agibar. Dispatched to Syria, he visited Petra while fighting with a Druze legion, before becoming an adviser to Haile Selassie in 1943. He crowned that wartime work with an odd choice for a dream job—in 1945, he joined the British Middle East Anti-Locust Unit, a group responsible for on-site research on the pest's breeding grounds. But the gig made it possible for Thesiger to pursue his calling: the open-ended project of exploring areas that Europeans had yet to experience, in search of solitude, rigor, escape from the technological present, and the camaraderie of those he saw as yet unsullied by the reach of the West (the last of these desires was paradoxically not at odds with the first). Curiously, Thesiger knew what he wanted to do before he could figure out precisely how to support himself over the longer term, yet the camera and the notebook were his constant companions even before he found the solution. By the time of his death in 2003, at age ninety-three, he had amassed some thirty-eight thousand

In the face of blinding heat, sandstorms, thirst, hunger, and rival tribes, the desert travels made Thesiger the Chris Burden of exploration.

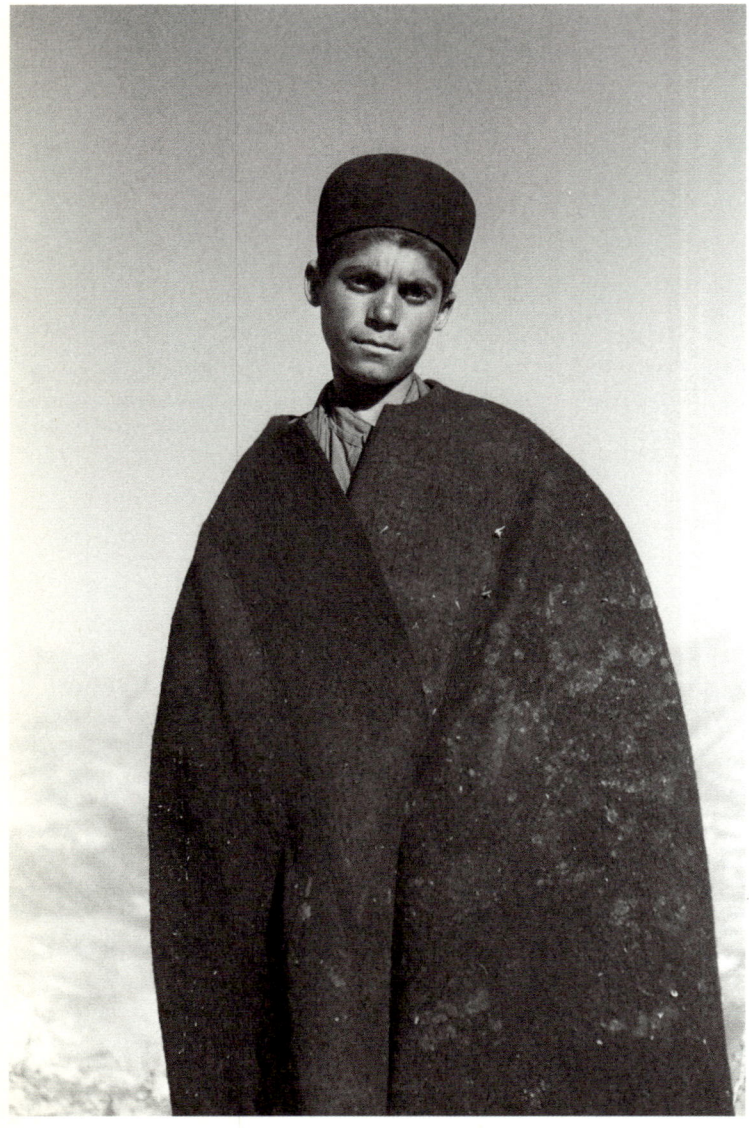

negatives, which he donated to the Pitt Rivers Museum in Oxford, England.

Thesiger's 1930 return to Addis Ababa was a visit that marked, in his later telling, the moment he decided upon the path his life would take. He treasured the memories of his Abyssinian childhood, the "thrill of seeing my father shoot an oryx when I was only three ... of camel herds at water-holes ... the smell of dust and of acacias under a hot sun ... the chorus of hyenas and jackals in the darkness round the camp fire." And he was fixated in particular on an early, bloody memory of the armies of victorious survivors streaming into Addis Ababa in 1916 following the Battle of Segale, where, in hand-to-hand combat, some twenty-six thousand had died. If that sounds horrifically savage, it may be tempered by the fact that millions more were perishing at that moment on the continent to Africa's north.

What Thesiger seemed to discover was that being an explorer could satisfy his desire for a different sort of freedom than he had found at Eton and Oxford, even at a time when, as he put it, there wasn't much left for Europeans to explore. He learned in Addis Ababa that one of the few quests they'd yet to tackle successfully was to find the mouth of the Awash River, so he set off there in exploration in 1933. It was a piffling concern compared to his predecessors' search for the source of the Nile, but it was a challenge nonetheless, which required tremendous cunning in the face of official disapproval, the hostility of warring tribes, and the knowledge that prior parties had been massacred on the lava deserts of the Abyssinian and Somali interior. It gave him a taste of future dangers and forthcoming rewards, none greater than his encounter with what he described as the "ultimate challenge of Arabian exploration," the desert within a desert known as the Empty Quarter.

Thesiger's 1959 book, *Arabian Sands*, recounts the still mind-boggling feat of his 1945–50 journeys in and around the 250,000-square-mile Empty Quarter of the Arabian Peninsula, during which he became the first European to cross the forbidding desert from east to west, then back in the reverse direction. Accomplished in the company of a close band of Bedouin and a retinue of worn-out camels, in the face of blinding heat, sandstorms, thirst, hunger, and rival tribes, the desert travels made Thesiger the Chris Burden of exploration. At one point of his crossing, as the author and diplomat Rory Stewart has recounted, he traveled two thousand miles over seven months while restricting himself to two pints of water a day. No wonder Thesiger lavished such affection on the Bedouin who agreed to cross this desolate land with him. *Arabian Sands* would turn Thesiger into an unlikely literary celebrity—its author was, after all, a fifty-year-old writer making his debut in book form, even as his reports on his travels had cast him as a monumental figure among the cognoscenti of geographers, governmental officials, and enthusiasts. When, in 1964, he followed *Arabian Sands* with *The Marsh Arabs*, his account of seven years living among the comparatively less menacing, but no less exotic, marshlands of southeastern Iraq, he established himself as a singular chronicler of what were soon to be vanished ways of life. Thesiger's observations of his travels in Iraq proved to be no mere literary conceit—by 1994, after Saddam Hussein retaliated against a Shiite uprising by massacring those in the south and building a diversion canal to drain the swamps dry, some 90 percent of the marshlands had disappeared. (Recent restoration efforts have been hopeful, but face ongoing threats from drought and a complicated multinational irrigation and damming system.)

In his writings and in person, Thesiger solidified his image as an anachronism: the greatest nineteenth-century explorer of

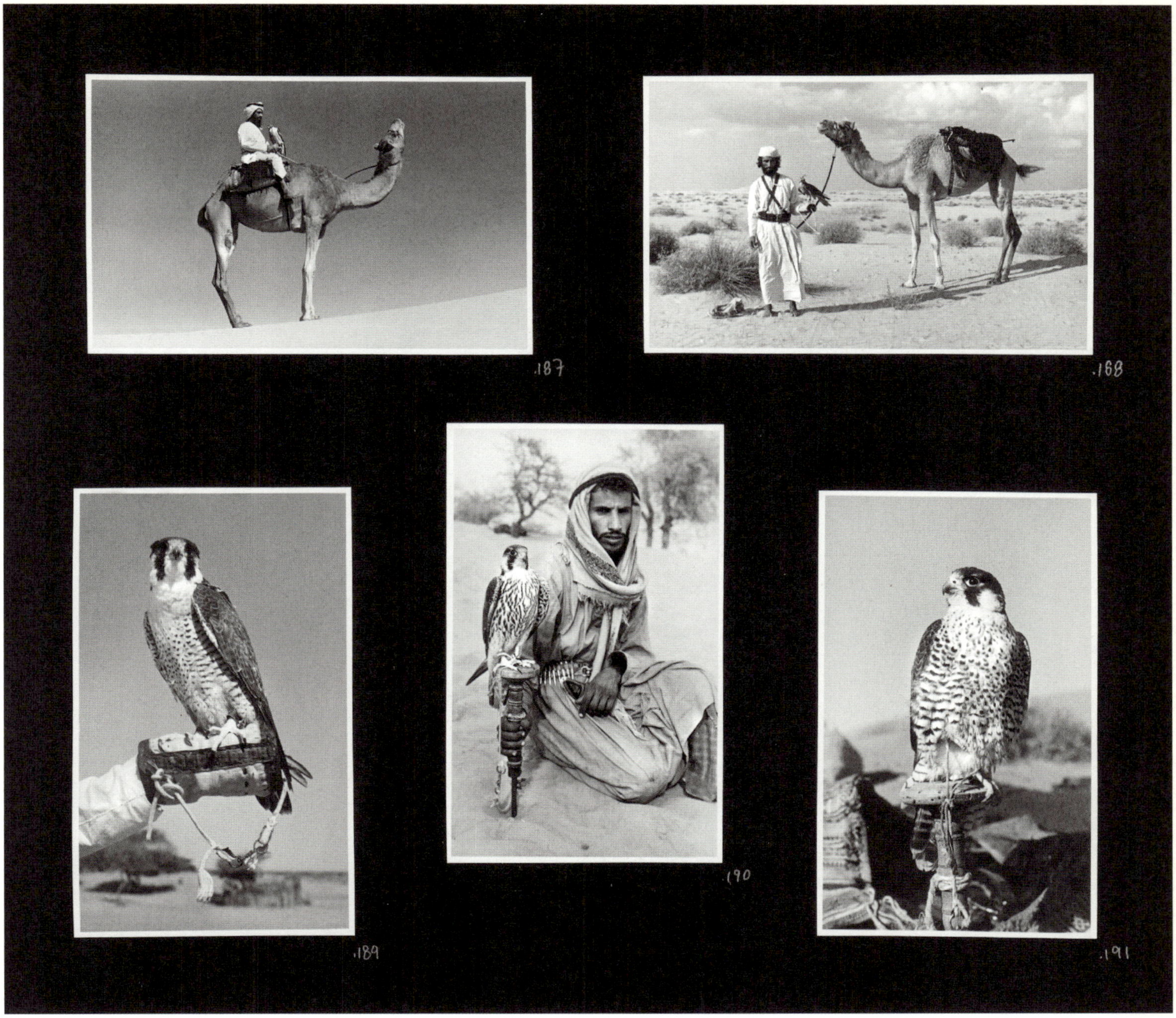

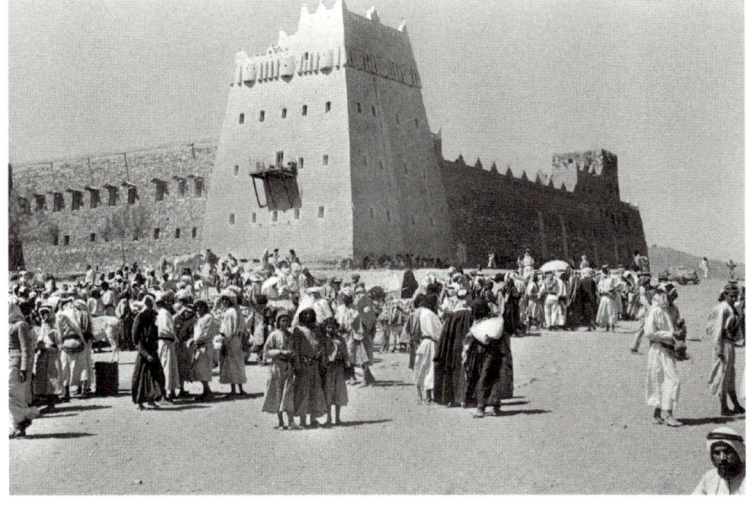

Top:
Album page from
Wilfred Patrick Thesiger's
Dubai, Bahrain, Oman,
1948–49

Bottom:
Al Shada Palace at Abha,
Saudi Arabia, 1947

the twentieth century. He was a scourge of every convenience the 1900s seemed to offer—finding the automobile and the airplane particularly loathsome inventions—and an accidental romantic who knew his peregrinations were undertaken at a moment when the lives he wrote about (the lives of his subjects, and even, for the most part, the life of the explorer) would, like the marshes, soon be curtailed. What would also be lost was a different and salutary sense of time, where slowness delivered its own benefits. In *Arabian Sands*, he recalls the dilatory pace of camel travel, accounting that his tiny caravan averaged only three miles an hour and a mere mile an hour across the steep and difficult dunes:

It often seemed incredible to me, especially when I was on foot and conscious of the steps I was taking, that we could cover such enormous distances going at this pace. Sometimes I counted my footsteps to a bush or to some other mark, and this number seemed but a trifle deducted from the sum that lay ahead of us. Yet I had no desire to travel faster. In this way there was time to notice things— a grasshopper under a bush, a dead swallow on the ground, the tracks of a hare, a bird's nest, the shape and colour of ripples on the sand, the bloom of tiny seedlings pushing

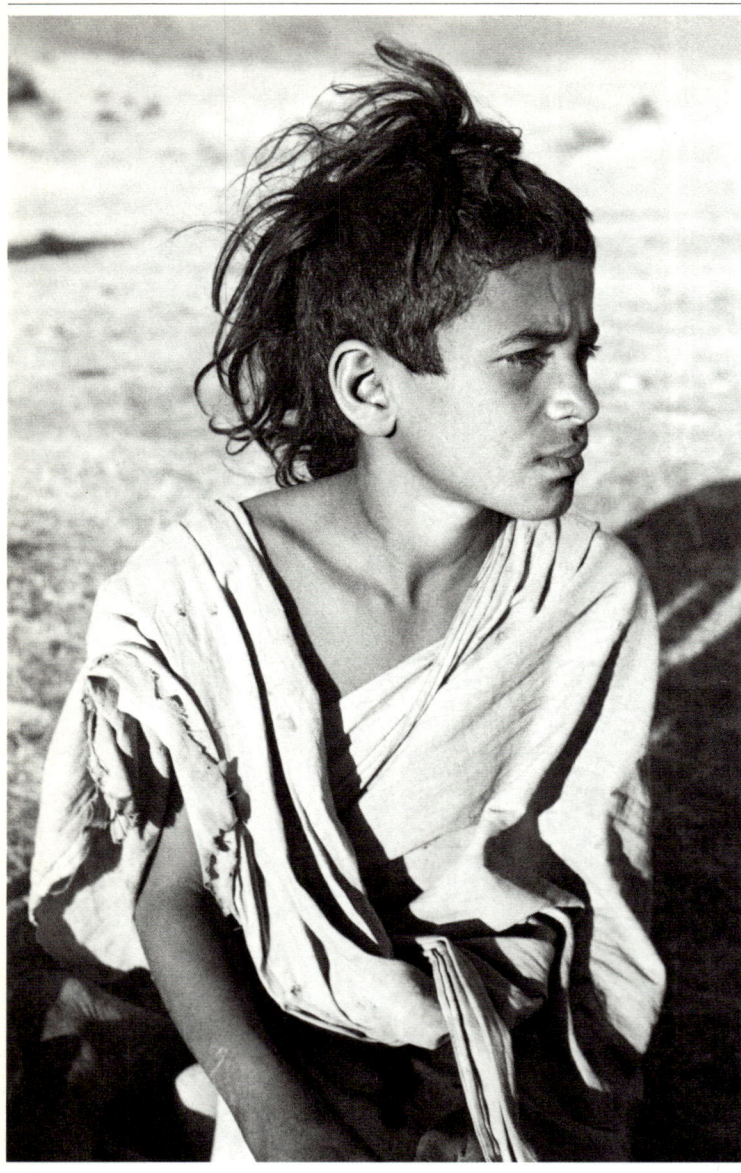

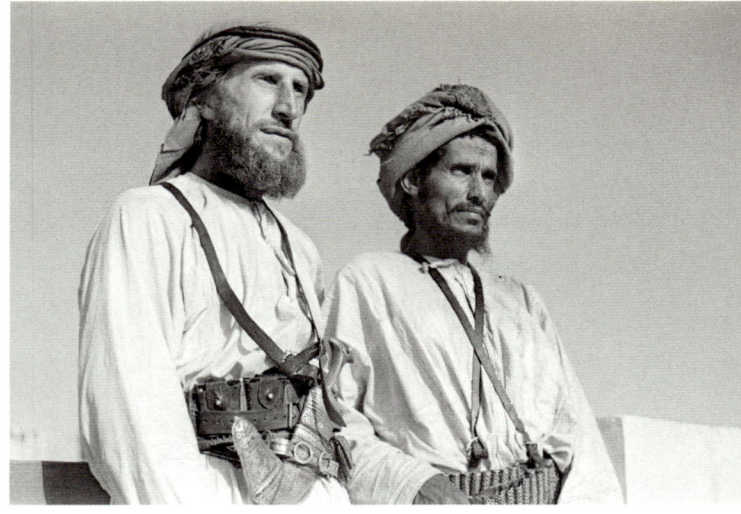

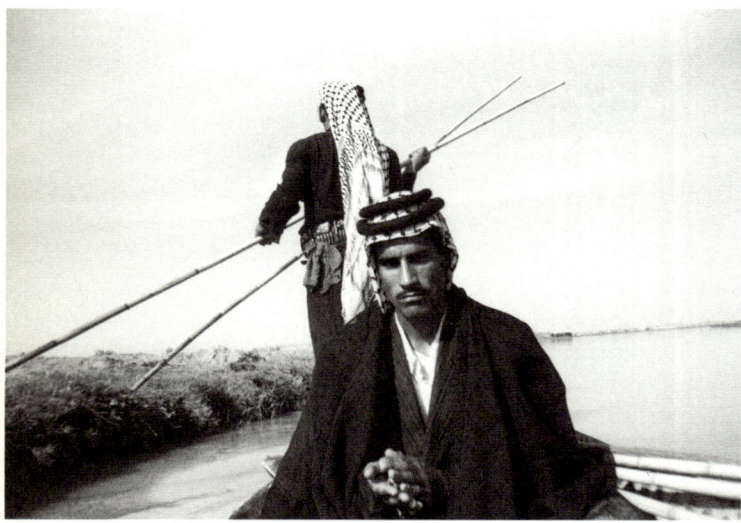

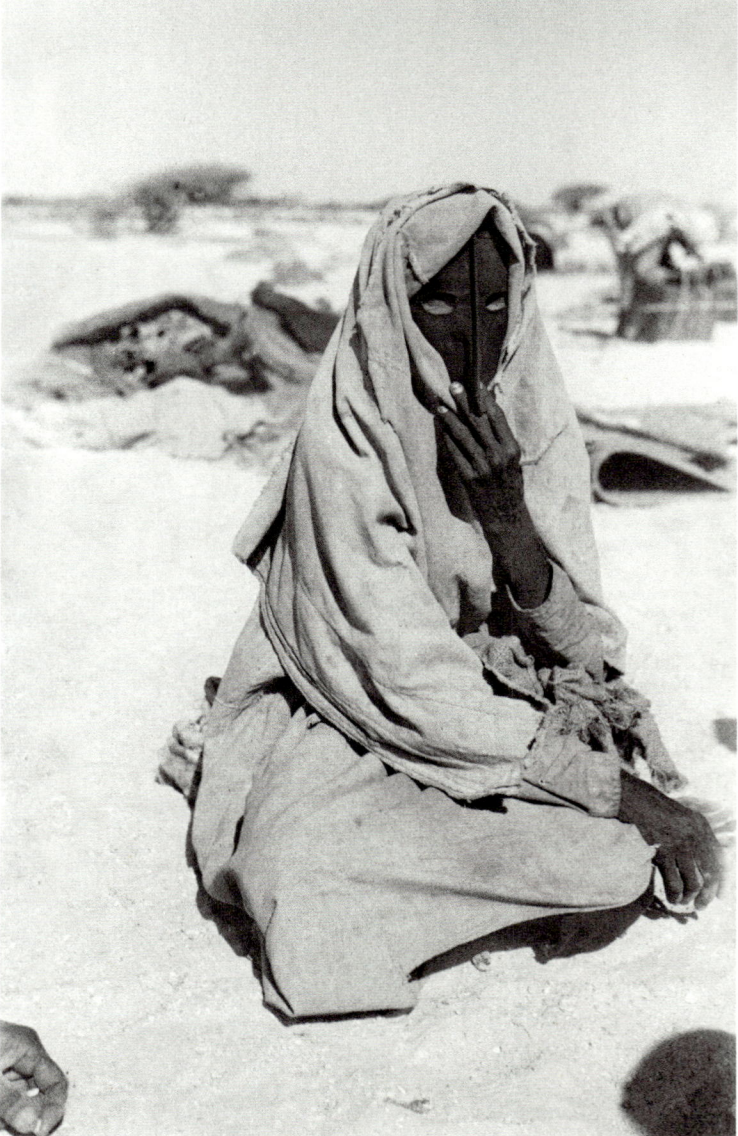

Clockwise from top left: Musallim bin Anauf, Oman, 1946; Photographer unknown, Thesiger and bin Al Kamam on a Dubai rooftop, 1949; Harasis woman with a mask, Oman, 1947; Portrait of a young man (named Amara bin Thuqub), formerly one of Wilfred Thesiger's canoe-boys, sitting in Thesiger's *tarada* (sheikh's canoe), Iraq, 1958

Unless otherwise noted, all photographs by Wilfred Patrick Thesiger © Pitt Rivers Museum, University of Oxford

through the soil. There was time to collect a plant or to look at a rock. The very slowness of our march diminished its monotony. I thought how terribly boring it would be to rush about this country in a car.

That same yearning for the slowness of arduous travel—the proposal that what makes arduous travel worth undertaking is precisely that it requires a deliberate clip proper to observation and alertness if one is to survive—pervades many of Thesiger's photographs as well. His early portraits seem at once relaxed and as if the "sitter" has been holding a pose for eons. His images of the desert itself form a visual essay about the aching slowness of the Arabian landscape: the wavy crests and rippled surfaces of the great dunes formed year after year by the labor of crosswinds; the trails left by his camels' languid march; the untouched quality of the isolated cities on the oases of the interior.

In *Arabian Sands* the photographs take on a shadowy, secondary life, more an appendage to the text than the impetus for its writing. Yet without them the book would perhaps never have found the imaginative juice that made it such an infectious read at the very moment that a different kind of exploration was redrawing the map. The discovery of oil soon transformed the Arabian Peninsula into the economic motor of the wider world and turned the likes of Sheikh Zayed bin Sultan Al Nahyan, the future president of the United Arab Emirates with whom Thesiger practiced falconry and handsomely photographed, into one of the wealthiest men on the planet.

Many of the portraits best known among Thesiger's photographs are of people who traveled alongside him across the desert, opened their homes to him in the marshes, or shared his passion for hunting—a pastime that rivaled only his desire for a nomadic existence throughout his life, yet one from which he eventually turned away as the mass destruction of wildlife became clear. Although Thesiger wrote infrequently about his photographic practice, and typically many years after his pictures had been shot, he averred his preference for intimacy with his subjects and claimed rarely to take photographs of those he didn't know. The closeness of his connection to Salim bin Kabina and Salim bin Ghabaisha, his 1940s Bedouin guides who knew the desert routes that were only sparsely mapped when Thesiger began his crossings, emerges in his numerous portraits of them. These images, like much of his work in the desert, capture both his guides' bitterly handsome features and an intransigent sense of pride and freedom, which he so eagerly attempted to describe in his prose. They have an almost cinematic quality, as if Thesiger's subjects had escaped from bit parts in an early Pasolini film to inhabit life in the desert.

Thesiger was at times criticized for the eroticism of his portraits, for the heavy emphasis on young male figures, and for the lack of women in both his writing and his photographs. (A haunting image of an Omani woman from the Harasis tribe, her face hidden behind a traditional black cloth mask, is an exception not just to the fraternal rule he followed but also for being one of the more nakedly ethnographic images in his early repertoire.) But those he came to know best in the desert were young and male and adventurous enough to accompany him, and their presence let Thesiger focus on the same details that powered his prose—precise accounts of how his fellow travelers dressed and comported themselves, a crisply matter-of-fact description of how they looked to the world, so that their strangeness to him and their growing familiarity remain intact. Like Thesiger's photograph of Musallim bin Anauf, a young boy with a cockscomb arrangement of hair, the images do double-duty with his texts, illustrating a mode of rugged Bedouin vigor while putting faces to named companions.

Thesiger preferred black-and-white photography to color and throughout his life stuck to a kind of vernacular starkness in his use of lighting, which provides a signature style even to the most precise of his later shots, in Iraq, Kurdistan, Afghanistan, Yemen, and Kenya, his last home before his final return to England in 1994. (That stark quality is just as pronounced in the records of architectural relics and desolate cities in the Arabian hinterland.) In the body of images that accompanied *The Marsh Arabs*, he could no longer rely on the enormity of the desert landscape and its harsh emptiness to frame his narrative of the everyday struggle of those he encountered. Perhaps as a response, his photographs took an ethnographic turn, with a more focused eye on the reed-built *mudhif* dwellings of the Iraqis, the construction of their canoes, the herds of water buffalo they maintained, and the vast sheets of water that organized their way of life. He gravitated toward people in groups—sitting in a grand *mudhif* on the Euphrates, tending boats, spearing fish, their weapons angularly filling the upper half of the frames like the army of lances in a Uccello painting of battle. Those spears often seem at one with the tips of wild reeds that poke up out of the marshes.

Thesiger ended both books by writing of doors closing, of experiences no longer possible. By the time of his death, the desert and the marsh had become even more remote both in fact and in imagination. Abu Dhabi and Dubai, when Thesiger first visited them, were small port cities; the Iraqi marshes were flush with wild duck and boar. Thesiger was, at least in one sense, able to stop time—his massive archive of photographs, along with his books and essays, provide a fleeting picture of how people once lived in these irrevocably changed worlds.

Eric Banks, the former editor in chief of *Bookforum*, is the director of the New York Institute for the Humanities at New York University.

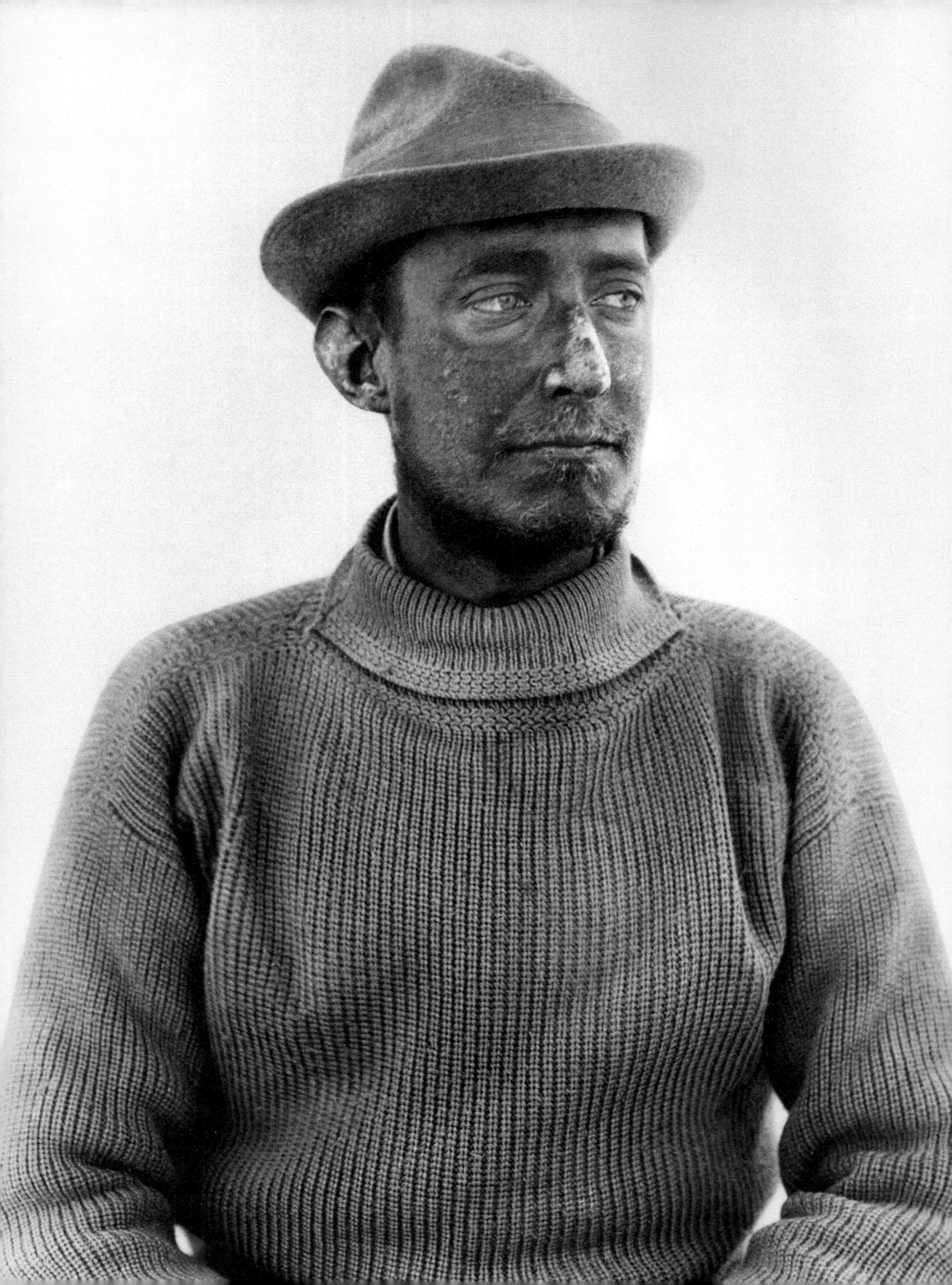

Vittorio Sella, born in the foothills of the Italian Alps, combined his passions of photography and mountaineering to capture the elevated beauty of the world's most inhospitable places.

Higher Ground

Alexander Stille

Mountains are powerful symbols of eternity, of the immensity and grandeur of nature, towering above and indifferent to human civilization and history. Yet our interest in and preoccupation with mountains—climbing, studying, painting, and photographing them—are the products of a very recent history.

High and remote mountains, which earlier European generations avoided, viewing them as dangerous wastelands inhabited by the poorest and most backward people, suddenly took on new appeal in a rapidly industrializing nineteenth-century Europe. Romantic poets longed to escape from the "dark Satanic mills" (William Blake)—the factories beginning to dot the landscape—and from the "getting and spending" (William Wordsworth) of growing urban life. Wordsworth, Coleridge, Byron, and Shelley all wrote about the powerful, formative experiences of their visits to Mont Blanc and their encounters with the mighty Alps. "High mountains are a feeling, but the hum / Of human cities torture," Byron wrote. While the eighteenth-century traveler concentrated on the ancient sites of Italy and Greece, the Alps became an obligatory Grand Tour destination for cultivated young English gentlemen of the nineteenth century. John Ruskin, Victorian England's most influential tastemaker, proclaimed, in 1856, that "mountains are the beginning and the end of all natural scenery."

This sudden awareness of the mountains, together with improved transportation and technical capacity for systematic mountain climbing, tempted Europeans not just to admire the mountains from below but to see the world from their heights. In the mid-nineteenth century there was an active scramble—a kind of friendly, international competition among a new class of gentleman mountaineers and explorers—to reach the remaining unexplored peaks of the Alps, the last frontier of nature in Europe untouched by man. The ascent in 1854 of

Sella managed to get the camera and plates back up the Matterhorn, where he began to make some of the pictures that established him as the premier mountain photographer of his time.

the Wetterhorn—one of the highest peaks in Switzerland— by British climber Alfred Wills was an international event, ushering in the "golden age" of mountaineering and the formation of the Alpine Club in 1857.

Vittorio Sella, mountain-photography pioneer, was born in 1859 into a family of explorers and photographers in the town of Biella, in the foothills of the Italian Alps, where his family ran a successful wool factory. A few years before Sella's birth, his father published the first major treatise in Italian on the new science of photography. When Sella was four years old, his uncle, Quintino Sella, led the first expedition to the top of Monte Viso (or Monviso), the highest mountain in the French-Italian Alps, and in 1863 founded the Club Alpino Italiano, which remains Italy's principal mountaineering club.

Sella's father died when Sella was just sixteen, leaving him in the care of his uncle, an important and emblematic figure in nineteenth-century Italy. After getting an undergraduate degree in engineering, Quintino Sella studied mineralogy at the École des Mines in Paris, then returned to Italy, where he taught mathematics and mineralogy. During his frequent ascents, he gathered samples of unusual rocks, assembling one of Italy's most important collections of minerals. He was placed in charge of a new royal museum of mineralogy in Turin, which was the capital of the Duchy of Savoy, home to what would become the Italian monarchy. Quintino Sella entered politics in 1860 and became Italy's minister of finance in 1862, after Italy was unified. The conquest of the alpine peaks was not entirely divorced from the politics of the newly unified Italian nation: Quintino Sella shrewdly included a member of parliament from Calabria in his ascent of Monte Viso, making the climb a public moment of patriotic unity.

Vittorio Sella synthesized his father's expertise in photography with his uncle's passion for mountaineering. When he was nineteen he made his first serious effort at alpine photography, dragging heavy, borrowed photography equipment up to

Crevasses, Glacier du
Chardon, August 3, 1888

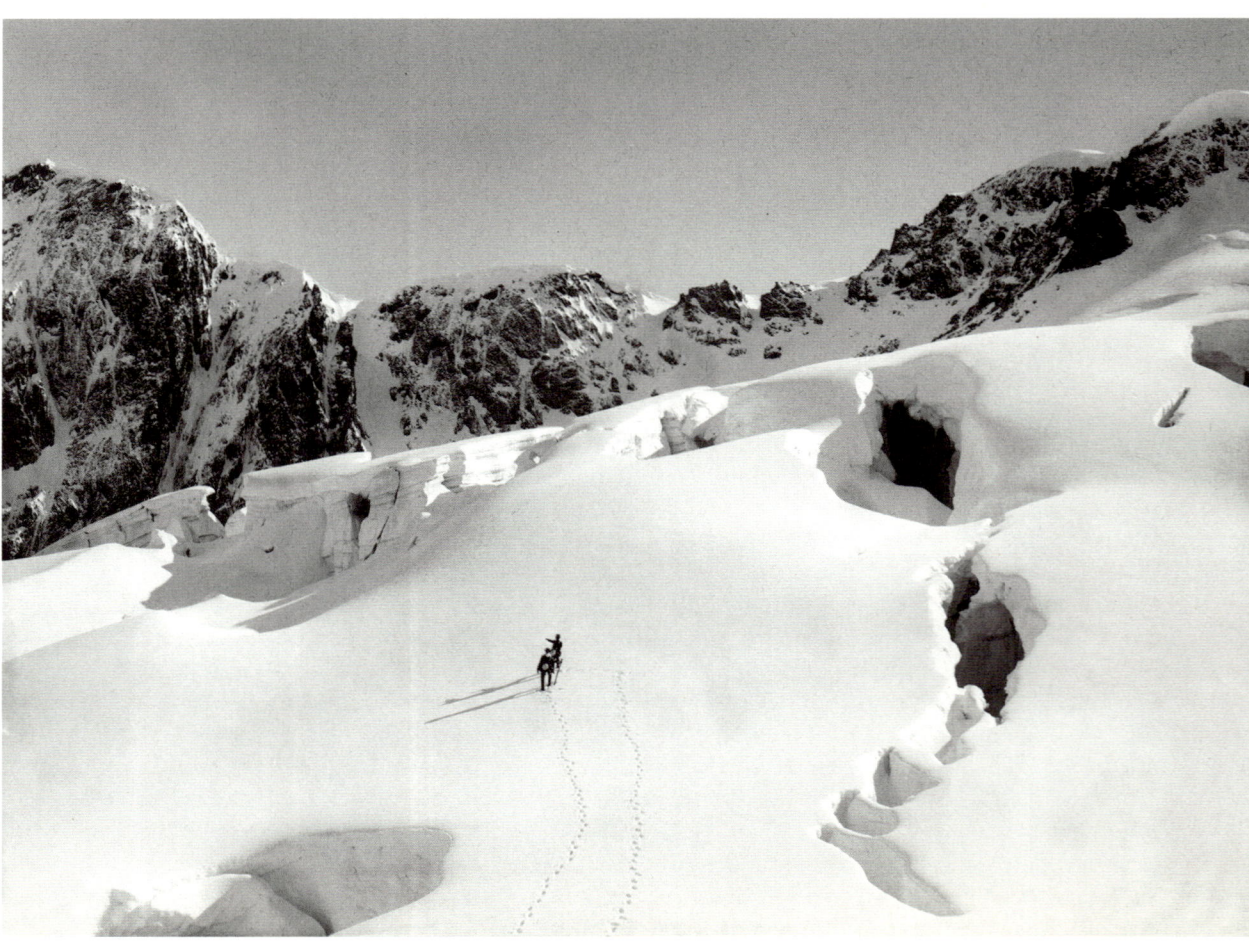

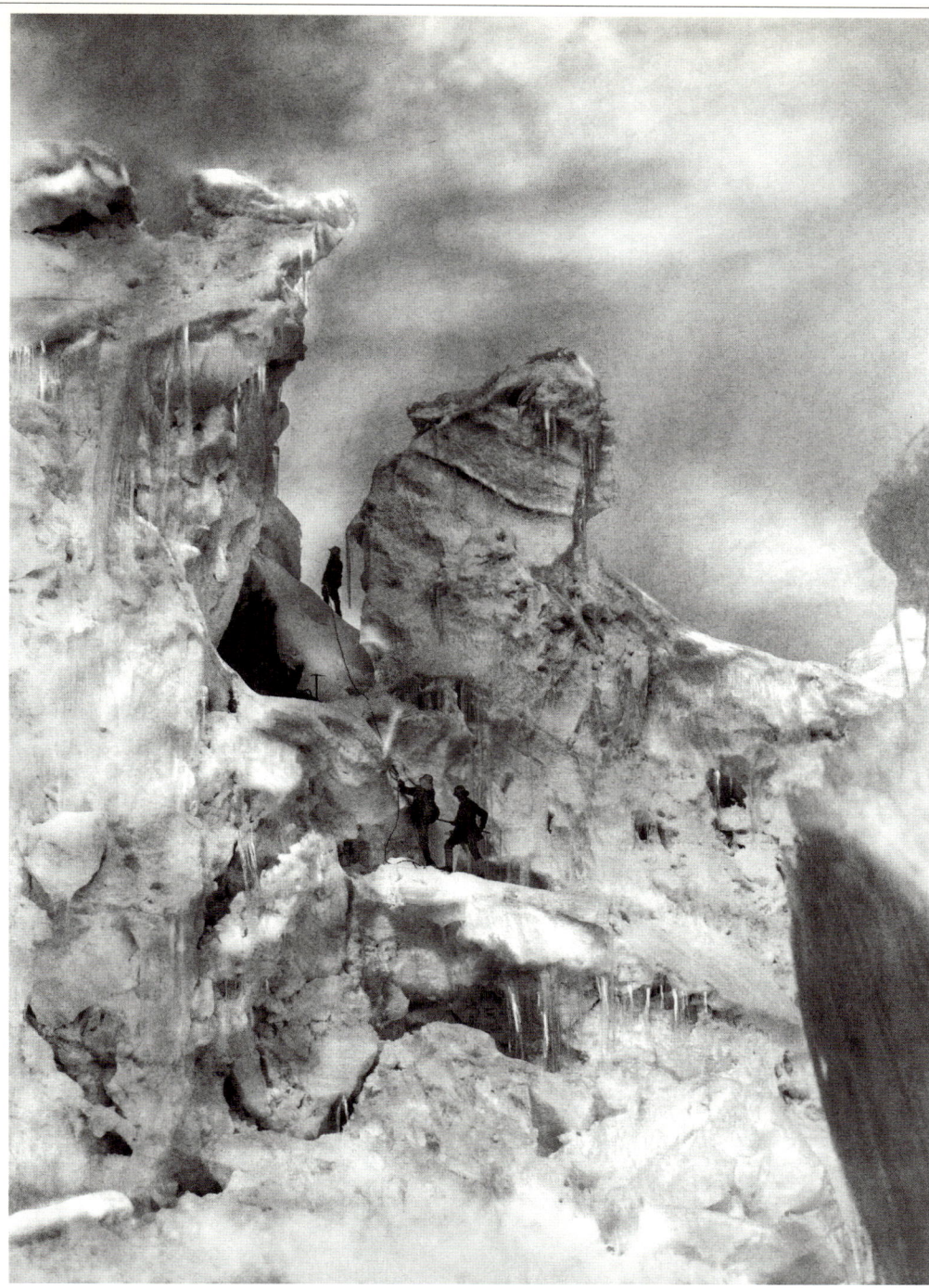

Monte Mars and making his first panoramic views of the Alps. At the time, he was working with extremely cumbersome and volatile wet-collodion glass-plate negatives. With this method a photographer needed to coat each plate with a silver-nitrate solution and develop each shot within ten or fifteen minutes of exposure, while the negative was still wet. This meant that Sella had to carry and improvise a portable darkroom up in the Alps. Despite the technical difficulties and uneven photographic results of these initial efforts, Sella persisted, learning a great deal through the trial and error of an art that was still in rapid evolution. "From 1880," he wrote, "I made up my mind to combine photography with Alpinism, and I took almost no interest at all in the lower parts of the mountains, and confined myself to photographic work on the summits, and to those higher regions of the Alps, which were little known and had not been photographed."

Fortunately for Sella, photographic technology was evolving; particularly revolutionary was the development of the gelatin process—glass plates with a dry photographic emulsion— which meant that negatives could be prepared in advance and developed later. The new dry negatives were both more convenient and exceptionally sensitive, allowing for shorter exposure times and remarkable photographic detail.

Sella was a pioneer in mountaineering as well as photography. In 1882, he led the first group to successfully climb the Matterhorn (known as Cervino in Italian), the largest mountain on the Italian–Swiss border, during the winter—an achievement hailed by the Alpine Club as "beyond doubt the most remarkable that has ever been made during the winter season." Later that same year, in a fever of excitement, he wrote to the camera company J. H. Dallmeyer in London: "I beg you to undertake immediately the camera for plates 30 × 40 cm described in my letter. I beg you to make it in the best mahogany, with every care possible, as I will serve myself of it for taking photographs in the high Alps … Here, we have splendid weather and I burn with impatience to start photographic excursions."

The camera that Sella acquired from J. H. Dallmeyer weighed nearly forty pounds; each glass plate, almost two. Despite this exceptional challenge, Sella managed to get the camera and plates back up the Matterhorn, where he began to make some of the pictures that established him as the premier mountain photographer of his time.

The duke and his inner circle slept in iron bedsteads that porters carried up to 10,000 feet above altitude.

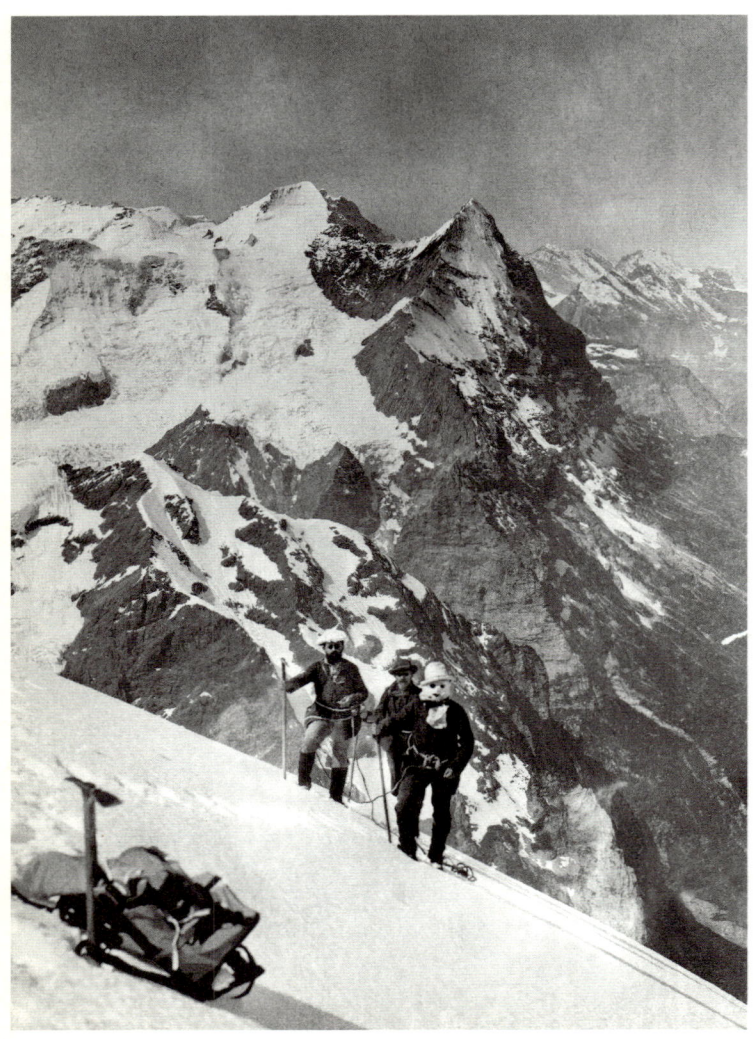

Photography was, of course, both art and science, and documenting the world's most remote spots partook of the scientific spirit of the age. It was the age of positivism, in which scientists believed that, with enough time and the right tools, nature would yield all of its secrets. On the other hand, part of the mountains' appeal was that they could never really be mastered. Experienced climbers like Sella understood that the mountains needed to be approached with great caution and respect, and that human beings were temporary guests at the world's highest peaks. Thus mountain climbing pushed human and technical achievement to new heights, but was also a sober reminder of human limitations. These expeditions always carried a strong element of danger: many of Sella's own climbs were cut short when changing weather or injury made it too risky to proceed. Some expeditions were marked by tragedy. The first ascent of the Matterhorn in 1865—by the British explorer Edward Whymper—was clouded by the deaths of four climbers during the descent.

Sella's interest in towering mountains inevitably led him away from Italy. He traveled to the Caucasus in 1889, 1890, and 1896, making one of the first ascents of Mount Elbrus, the highest mountain in Europe. Here, for the first time, Sella seems to have become captivated by the human population that lived in uneasy coexistence with the mountains. Although Sella's first passion remained the mountain landscape, he was fascinated with the weather-beaten people of the Caucasus, who had adapted to this austere environment.

Sella's desire to explore and document the world's highest summits received a significant boost under the patronage of Prince Luigi Amedeo, Duke of the Abruzzi and cousin of Italian king Victor Emmanuel III, a mountaineer who thirsted to "conquer" the last unexplored mountains in the world. The duke recruited Sella as his official photographer. Royal expeditions were part of the great scramble in which the major European powers competed to divide the world into expanding empires and plant their national flags on the remaining corners of the earth yet untouched by man. The new technologies of the steamship, railroad, and telegraph led Westerners to travel widely, mastering and often conquering every inch of the globe. The North and South Poles as well as the world's few unmapped mountains became the targets of organized international expeditions. Thus, the Duke of the Abruzzi set his sights on being the first to climb Mount Saint Elias in Alaska. The duke and his inner circle slept in iron bedsteads that porters carried up to 10,000 feet above altitude, but this did not diminish the rigors of the final ascent to 18,000 feet.

In 1906, Sella accompanied the Duke of the Abruzzi in the first full exploration of the Rwenzori mountain range, in a remote area along the border of present-day Uganda and the Democratic Republic of the Congo. In 1876, the indefatigable Henry Morton Stanley, the swashbuckling Welsh journalist who helped Belgian King Leopold II colonize the Congo, was supposedly the first European to set his eyes on the mountains, which were often shrouded in mist and cloud cover. The duke and his team scaled sixteen summits on their trip, and the duke named several of the highest peaks. One of them he named after himself, Mount Luigi di Savoia, and the highest peak in the range, Margherita, still bears the name of the Italian queen.

Yet if the mountaineering of the late nineteenth and early twentieth centuries that Sella participated in represented the colonial enterprise of Europeans claiming the "unconquered" parts of the earth, Sella's photography is remarkably free of any rhetorical excess or triumphant self-aggrandizement. There is a clear appreciation of the exceptional beauty of his surroundings. He often preferred climbing in winter because of the freshness

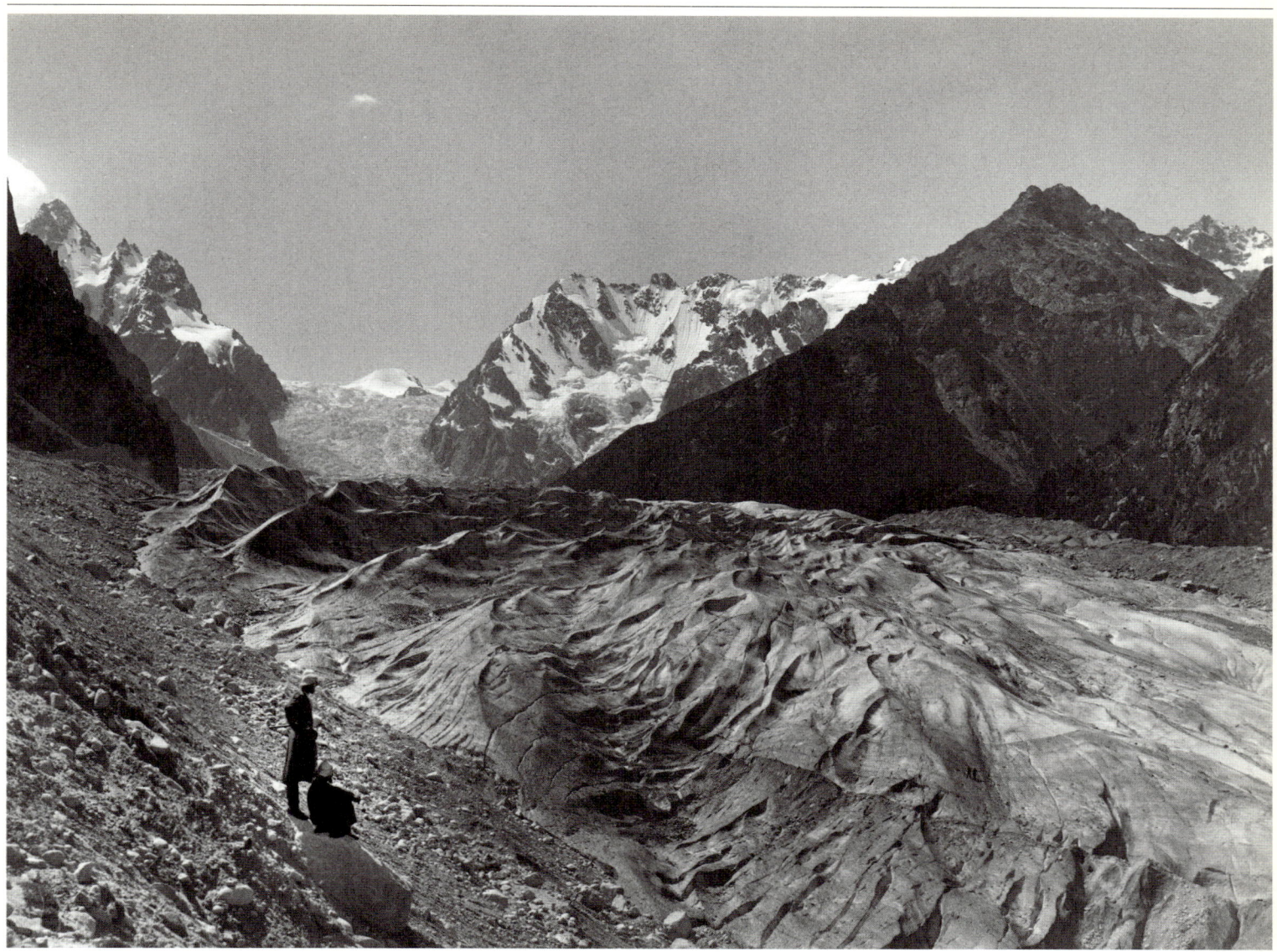

The Karagom Glacier
as seen from its right
moraine, Caucasus, 1890
All photographs ©
Fondazione Sella and
courtesy Decaneas Archive

and clarity of the winter air. He would spend entire days waiting for the right light in which to express through his images the particular moods and nuances of the mountain landscapes. Ansel Adams, perhaps Sella's principal artistic heir, wrote: "We are amazed by the mood of calmness and perfection pervading all of Sella's photographs…. there is no faked grandeur; rather there is understatement, caution, and truthful purpose."

Sella was apparently a relatively taciturn and modest man who downplayed his own achievements and artistic gifts by saying that his principal merit had been lugging cumbersome photography equipment up the sides of mountains. But his letters and journals indicate that the aesthetic side of his work was fundamental to him. In a letter to his wife, Sella expresses disappointment that the beauty of the mountain landscape was entirely lost on many of his fellow mountaineers: "In spite of the alpinistic, geographic, and photographic success, it does not give me any satisfaction because of the daily disappointment about the sentiments and the moral quality of almost all of my companions, in whom you would not find a speck of poetry or of interest for the really beautiful things, should you look for it with a microscope."

In Sella's work, the quiet poetry of an aesthetic sensibility is balanced by a sense of moral and scientific rigor. Sella strove to render "the truth of the sites which fascinated our senses," as well as document for posterity sites that, in many cases, had never before been seen or studied. Thanks to him, we have images that capture a particular moment in our history and our evolving relationship to the natural world.

Alexander Stille is San Paolo Professor of International Journalism at Columbia University and a regular contributor to *The New Yorker*, *The New York Review of Books*, and *La Repubblica*.

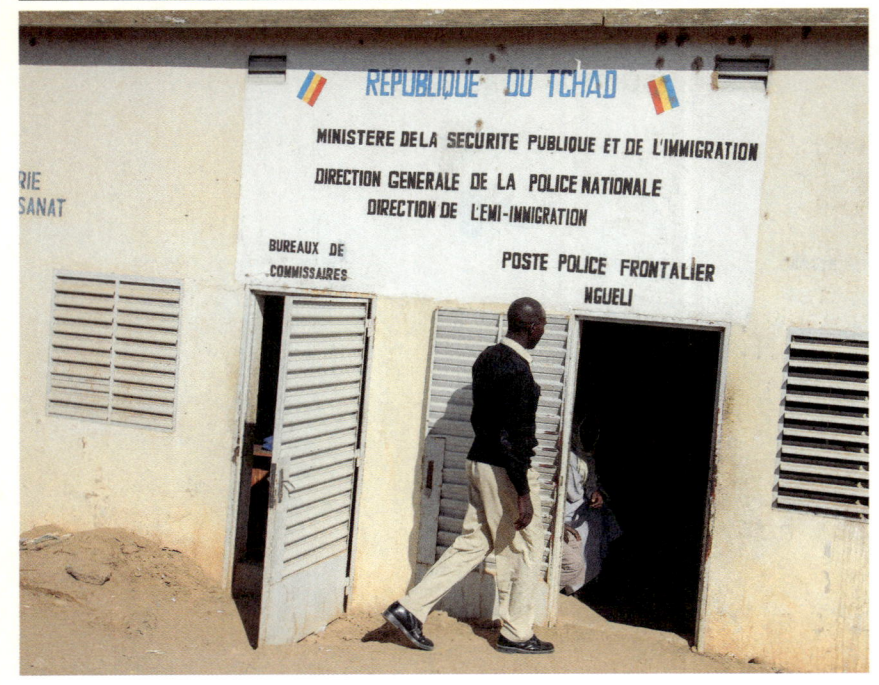

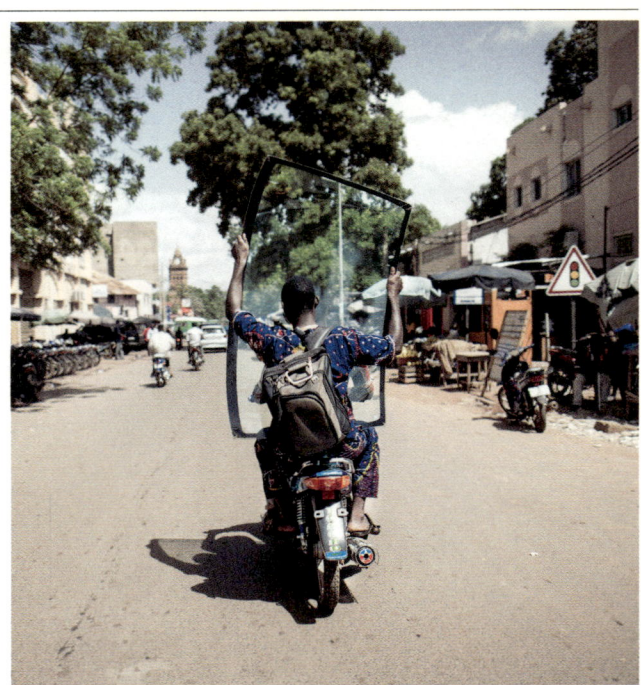

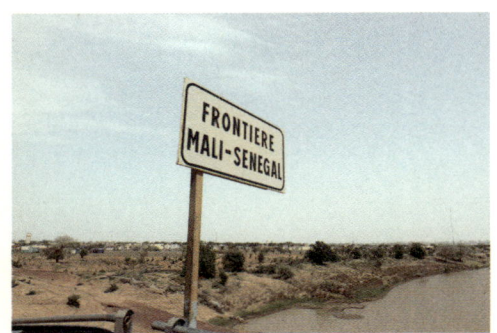

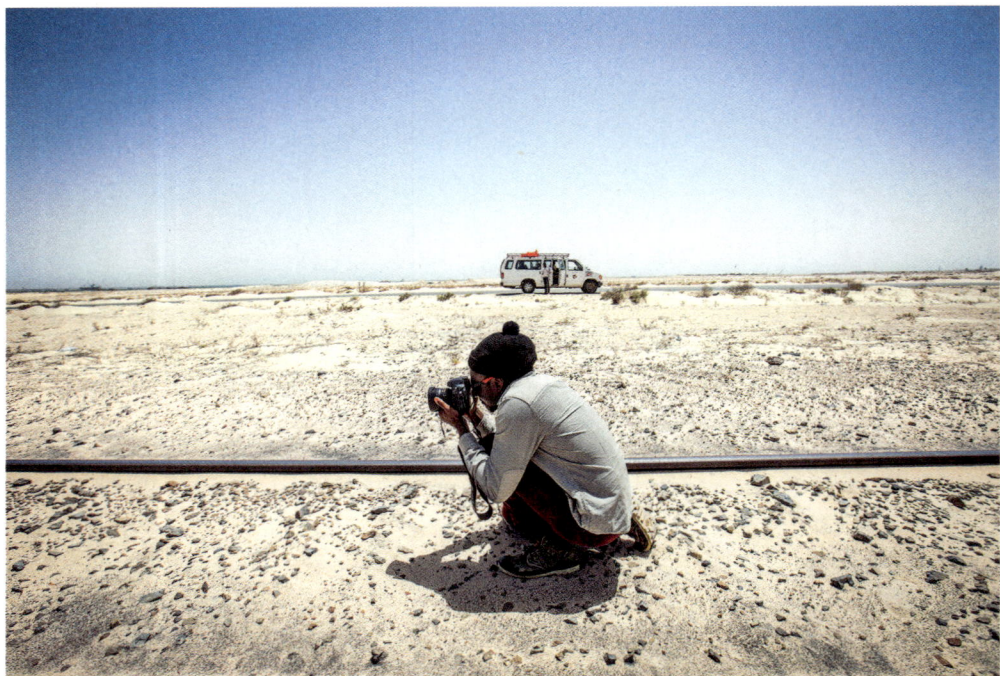

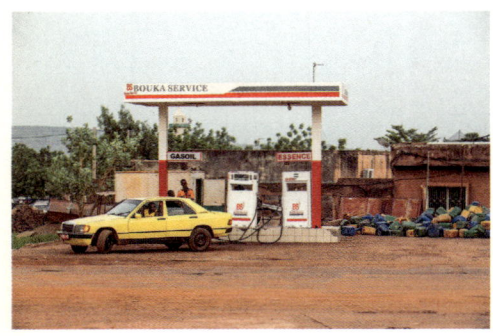

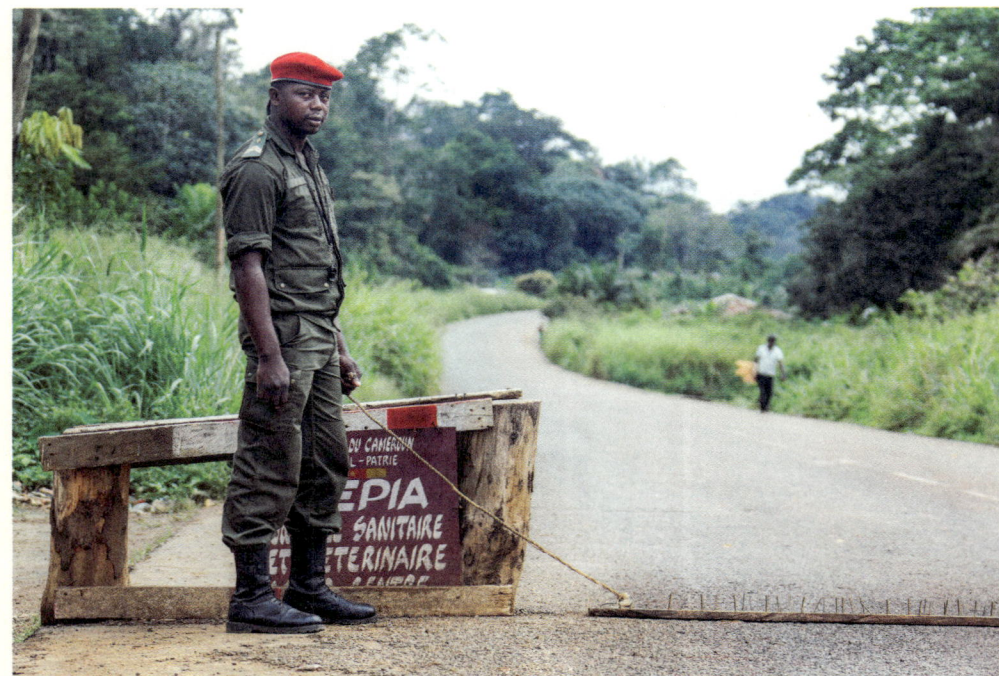

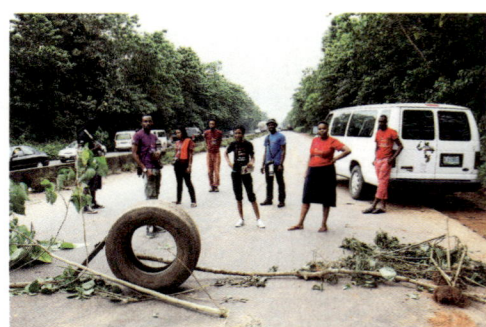

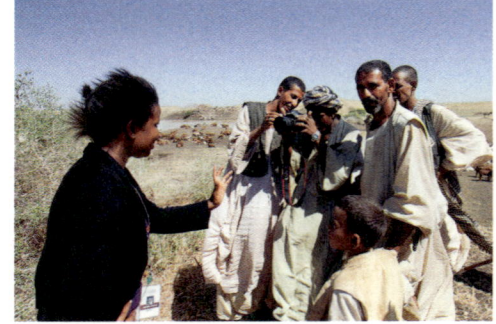

Since 2009, a photography collective has embarked on five road trips across West and Central Africa, creating a kaleidoscopic portrait of everyday life. For their latest trek, the group drove from Lagos to Sarajevo, a bold endeavor that would test their resolve.

Open Roads & Invisible Borders

Sean O'Toole

In early November of 2009, a group of ten Nigerian friends—among them photographers Uche Okpa-Iroha, Amaize Ojeikere, Emeka Okereke, and Ray Daniels Okeugo—piled into a black VW van christened "Black Maria" and headed east out of Lagos on the coastal expressway toward neighboring Benin. Their plan: to spend four days driving a 1,400-mile route from their home city to Bamako, the capital of Mali, where they intended to catch the opening of the eighth edition of the Bamako Encounters, Africa's most important photography biennial. Four days to drive roughly the same distance separating New York from Miami. Plotted on a map it looks easy. But maps don't account for muddy quagmires that sometimes pass as roads in the tropics, nor do they anticipate delays posed by lethargic and corrupt immigration officials staffing West Africa's many border checks. Maps simplify reality; they can make the foolhardy seem doable.

A week after they embarked on their overland journey across Nigeria, Benin, Togo, Ghana, and Burkina Faso to Mali, the group of travelers participating in the inaugural road trip of the Invisible Borders Trans-African Photographers Organisation, an artist-led nonprofit that has now coordinated five completed expeditions, arrived in Bamako by interstate bus. Despite a breakdown in Accra, the Ghanaian capital, they had made it, albeit three days late. Bamako's collegial photography biennial, which that year was thematically concerned with material and symbolic borders, was, however, still in full swing.

Unbeknownst to the travelers, during their journey their episodic blog had gained a small reading public among the photographic community gathered in Bamako. Predating the launch of the photo-sharing app Instagram by a year, their blog, which is still accessible online, is surprisingly text heavy. Updated by various members, notably the poet and writer Nike Adesuyi-Ojeikere, it detailed the group's various encounters with feckless moneychangers and helpful strangers. It also chronicled the group's cumulative frustrations as it navigated spatial and temporal thresholds, and crossed political and psychological boundaries. "We took off like a bunch of novices and thought we would be allowed to cross borders without a thorough explanation," Okereke told me in 2012. The group's idealism was dashed at Seme, a border post between Nigeria and Benin, where, Adesuyi-Ojeikere writes, they were held up for two hours and paid "official and unofficial taxes" before continuing.

By the time their van broke down in Accra, the group's enthusiasm for observing Africa's diverse realities, a core tenet of the project, waned as the "why not?" attitude that kick-started the inaugural journey ceded to the actuality of life on the road. "With no van, and living from minute to minute in the hope that the repairs would soon be done and we would hit the road again, we did not dare venture far from base," remarked Unoma Giese, a former stockbroker turned artist, of the layover in Accra.

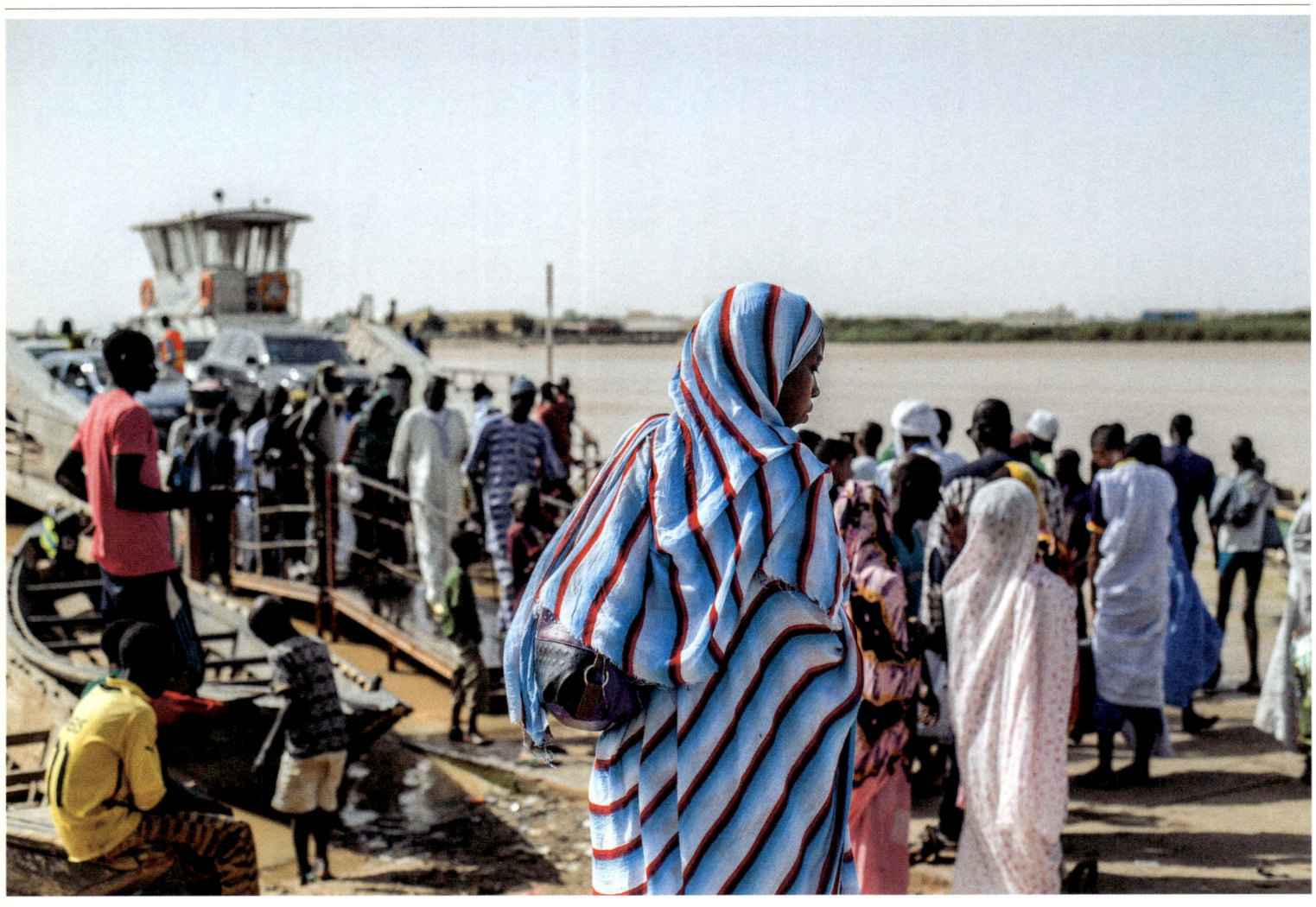

Page 44, clockwise from top left: Emeka Okereke, *À La Frontière*, Ngueli, Chad, 2011; Emeka Okereke, *A Third Screen*, Bamako, Mali, 2014; Tom Saater, *Emeka Okereke at Port-Bouët*, 2014; Emeka Okereke, *Borders of Road Blocks*, Ore Benin Expressway, 2012; Ala Kheir, *Jumoke and Nomads of Sudan*, 2011; Emeka Okereke, *Gendarmerie*, Minkok, Cameroon, 2012; Tom Saater, *Gas Station*, Bamako, Mali, 2014; Emeka Okereke, *Frontière Mali-Senegal*, Kidira (Mali–Senegal border), 2014

This page: Emeka Okereke, *Waiting*, Rosso (Mauritania–Senegal border), 2014

Opposite: Ray Daniels Okeugo, *Nna Olopa*, Lagos, Nigeria, 2011

Invisible Borders is a gregarious project. It is also a durable, Afrocentric, mobile photography platform.

The constraints of travel, she continued, demanded a continual regrouping and rearranging of priorities.

Invisible Borders is a gregarious project. It is also, notably, a durable, Afrocentric, mobile photography platform that has outgrown its early origins as an informal Lagosian thing. At heart, though, it is a sociable aggregation of like-minded photographers. Named by photographer Uche James-Iroha, a participant in the first trip, this organization traces its origins back to an earlier photographic collective. In 2001, following their participation in that year's edition of the Bamako Encounters, four Lagos-based friends—including James-Iroha and Ojeikere, son of the famed Nigerian portrait photographer J.D. 'Okhai Ojeikere—founded Depth of Field (DOP), a loose affiliation of individuals rather than an aesthetic movement bounded by a common style. The collective later expanded to include Emeka Okereke, the current artistic director of Invisible Borders.

The remit of DOP's photography was diverse, ranging in subject from James-Iroha's allegorical portraiture to Ojeikere's abstracted documentary studies of market goods and Okereke's more naturalistic observations of urban soccer. After a brief flurry of exhibitions in Berlin, London, and New York in the mid-aughts, the collective's momentum dissipated, prompting Okereke to act. "He felt that they were not doing enough artistically and project-wise to further their initial success," says Akinbode Akinbiyi, a Berlin-based Nigerian photographer who is a key mentor and ally of the group. "Initially he launched the idea of the intercontinental travels to his closest colleagues in DOP." They liked his idea. The maiden journey of Invisible Borders included three DOP members.

The warm response to the 2009 road trip project prompted Okereke to develop it into an annual event. In 2010, a journey was undertaken from Lagos to Dakar, the Senegalese capital city and host, since 1992, of Dak'Art, a visual arts biennial. Departing once again along the trans–West Africa coastal highway, the road trip included visits to Cotonou, Lomé, Accra, and Abidjan, before detouring inland to Bamako, bypassing the troubled states of Liberia and Sierra Leone. At Diéma, a Malian settlement between Bamako and Dakar, the group met three Nigerian women operating a roadside eatery, which they had opened after a smuggler abandoned them while en route to Spain. As was custom early on, a group portrait was produced of the Nigerian adventurers with their enterprising compatriots.

In its earliest iterations, Invisible Borders was overwhelmingly Nigerian in its makeup. Since 2011, however, when the group navigated overland from Lagos to Addis Ababa in Ethiopia to join the Addis Foto Fest (with one flight connection between N'Djamena, Chad, to the Sudanese capital city of Khartoum), they have taken on a more pan-African appearance. "It began with what seemed like a Nigerian collective, but the main idea is to make it a platform for artists from different parts of the African continent," Okereke explained in 2012.

At the time, he was planning a fourth trip: from Lagos to Lubumbashi, a mineral-rich city in the south of the Democratic Republic of Congo and site of the Lubumbashi Biennale. This southerly trip, which included participants from Equatorial Guinea, Mozambique, Rwanda, and South Africa, was marked by an epic five-day struggle on muddy roads between Calabar, a city in southern Nigeria, and Mamfe, in neighboring Cameroon. Encountering roads of thick, golden-brown clay, they hired "mud workers" to aid their passages, and later argued with officials who imposed a fine when a vehicle owned by a Chinese construction outfit collided with them. The last-minute

postponement of the Lubumbashi Biennale saw the trip rerouted to the port city of Libreville, Gabon, where participant Jide Odukoya, from Nigeria, made a portrait series of his expatriate countrymen living in this oil-rich state. By this time only Okereke and Ray Daniels Okeugo, a photographer and Nollywood actor who died in October 2013, remained of the original group of ten Nigerian friends who founded Invisible Borders.

The group's malleable membership is less important than its modus operandi, which by 2011 had matured from spontaneous adventurism into a sustained exercise in transcontinental networking and photographic encounter. The latter action, to photograph, is an important facet of the collective, but also possibly the hardest thing to coherently track. Their work is widely and consistently exhibited—including appearances in *The Idea of Africa (re-invented)*, a 2010 photography exhibition at Kunsthalle Bern, Switzerland; *The Ungovernables*, the 2012 New Museum Triennial in New York; and *All the World's Futures*, curator Okwui Enwezor's exhibition at the 2015 Venice Biennale—but it is somewhat misleading to speak of an Invisible Borders style.

Often thought of as a photographic collective, Invisible Borders has evolved to include video, site-specific performances, and a good deal of writing. Although diverse, this creative output is linked by an impressionistic and sensorial thread, exemplified by Nigerian author Emmanuel Iduma's blog posts and South African filmmaker Lesedi Mogoatlhe's short web clip of Cameroon-based singer Danielle Eog Makedah. However, for the group's career-defining Venice showcase, Okereke— assisted by Akinbiyi, Iduma, and photographer Jumoke Sanwo— emphasized the group's lens-based work. Multiplicity and diversity trumped the discrete image in their photographic

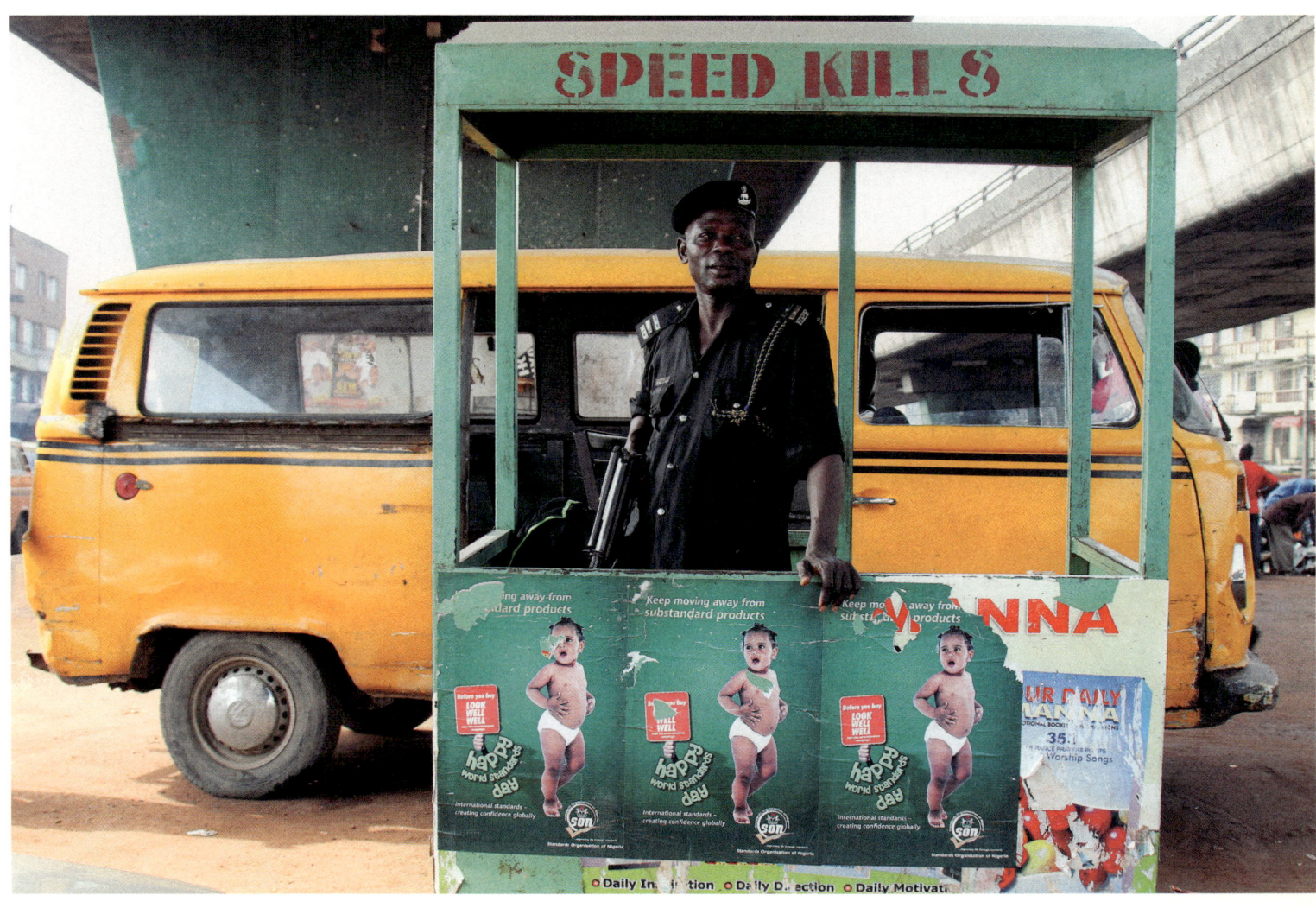

This page:
Ray Daniels Okeugo,
Smuggler, Koussiri
(Cameroon–Chadian
border), 2011

Opposite:
Ala Kheir, *Equilibrium*,
Addis Ababa, Ethiopia,
2011
All photographs ©
the artists and courtesy
Invisible Borders

selection: a collage of densely clustered reportage, documentary, and pictorial images represented Invisible Borders.

Looking past the collective imprimatur of the group, it is nonetheless possible to intuit traces of individual style. The overriding subject of Okereke's and Okeugo's photography, for instance, is the human figure in the city. Street scenes and frontal portraiture predominate in their work. Okeugo especially is deft at isolating individual figures, at work and at rest. Rather than sensationalize or criticize the makeshift and unfinished rudiments of the African city, their photographs describe its quotidian factuality and great diversity. However, this emphasis on the visible—on photography as legible artifact—elides a central function of the Invisible Borders project.

"Invisible Borders is not so much about this residue," insists Okereke. "We began the project thinking it is about photography, or outcomes like that, but at some point we realized what is much more important is the process within the journey, rather than the outcome." The ambition of each road trip, he says, is to "affect perception, rather than produce works that will hang on a wall."

Okereke has a habit of describing the experiential methodology of the road trip project as without precedent in Africa. This is not entirely true. In 1991, a group of art students at the University of Nigeria, Nsukka, founded the Pan-African Circle of Artists (PACA) as a mobile forum to create and exhibit art. A decade later, PACA initiated the first of three transnational road trips under the banner *Overcoming Maps*. Similarly, in 2006, Cameroonian artist Goddy Leye organized a traveling exhibition and networking tour that conveyed a small collective of artists from Douala, Cameroon, to Senegal by public transport. He later described his *Exit Tour* as a "pleasant trek" by "a band of happy, lightheaded companions." This cheerful reckoning sits at odds

Rather than sensationalize or criticize the makeshift rudiments of the African city, their photographs describe its great diversity.

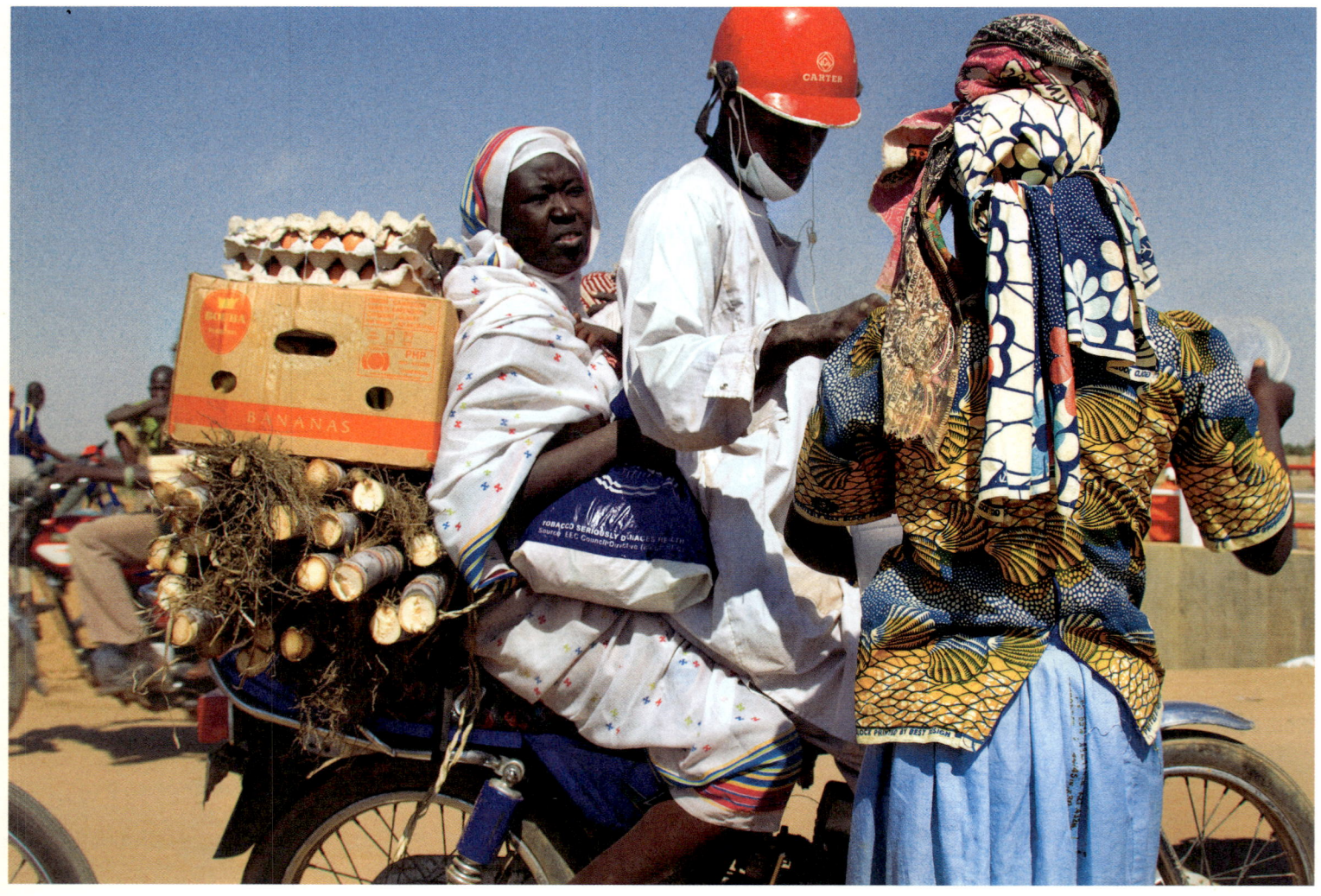

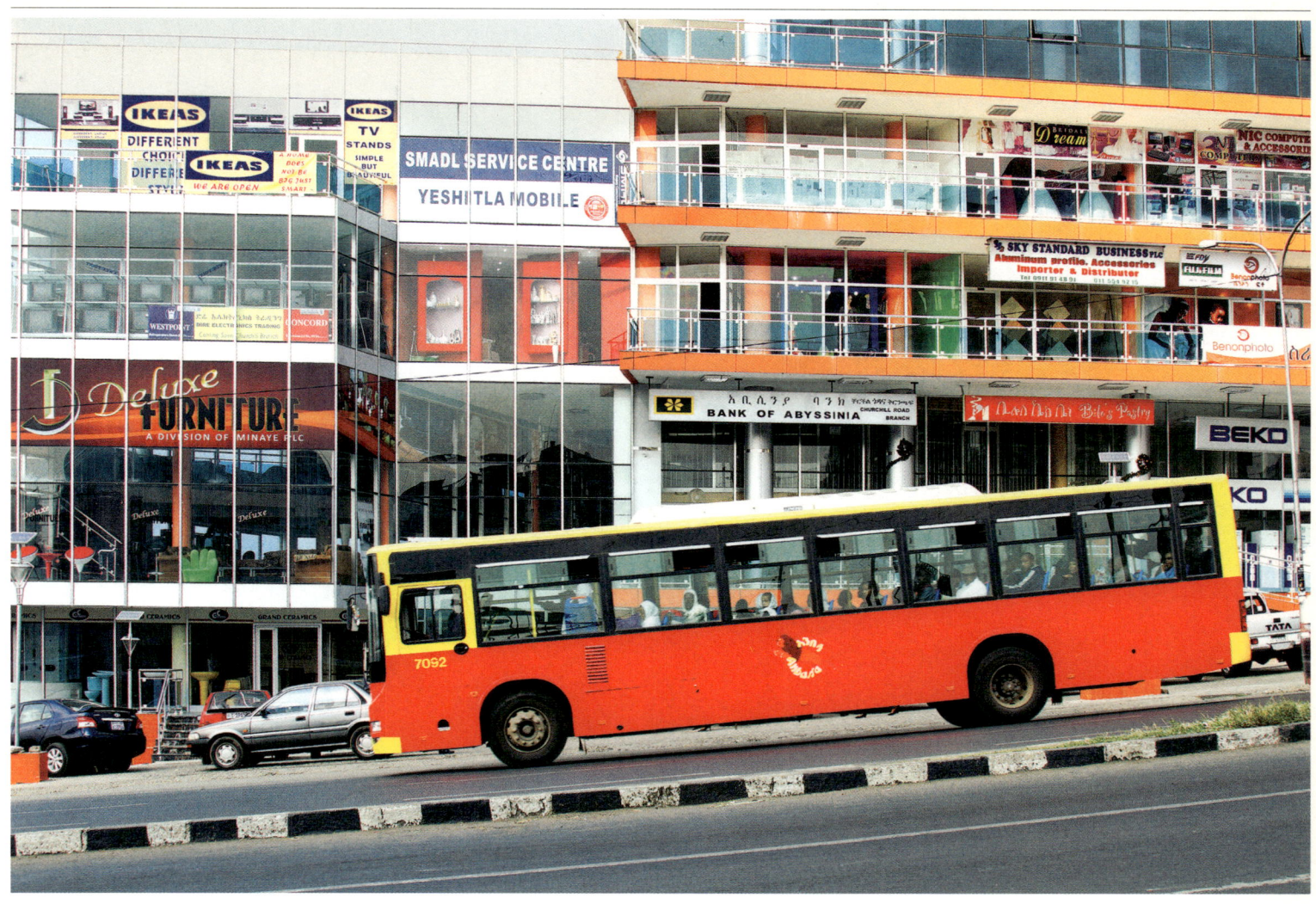

with the experiences of participants in the 2014 Invisible Borders road trip, an ambitious twenty-two-week journey from Lagos to Sarajevo that ended acrimoniously when six of the ten participants withdrew from the project in Amsterdam, where Invisible Borders exhibited at the Prince Claus Fund Gallery. Three weeks later, and 142 days after leaving Lagos, Okereke and Iduma arrived in Sarajevo, much to the excitement of local children. As Iduma noted, "The black body is still a source of unpretentious wonderment."

Dawit L. Petros, an Eritrean-born photographer based in the United States, known for his conceptually bold photographic installations, cites the restrictive discursive and visual framework of the project as a key obstacle. "The reality is that we were expected to adhere to, rather than question, politically and culturally constructed categories of subjectivity, artistic practices, and conventions," says Petros, who together with Cairo-based artist and fellow road-trip participant Heba Amin founded the Black Athena Collective, a collaborative platform for engagement with African political discourse around migrancy and territory.

The complexities of the 2014 trip are not easily glossed over. Okereke's response is pragmatic rather than vexed. The multiple strains of a road trip, he says, in particular the tensions between subjective and collective consciousness, often prompts participants to "fall back on what they're used to." Akinbiyi, who has known Okereke since 2001, ascribes the "rupture" that defined the 2014 trip to the lengthy travel time, clash of "unbending egos," as well as the project's "lack of good, solid leadership." "As a movement based very much on the road, it finds itself often in the position of learning while doing and this can be precarious," adds Akinbiyi. His emphasis on the road is germane.

The road is a recurring theme in postcolonial Nigerian literature, notably in the works of Cyprian Ekwensi, Ben Okri, and Wole Soyinka, whose feverish play *The Road* (1965) ends with its dying protagonist saying, "Breathe like the road, be even like the road itself …" It is a logic that undergirds Invisible Borders, which posits the road not singularly as a tangible fact but as a mechanism to explore the diverse subjectivities of the African continent in a collective framework. "The purest form of the project is while we are on the road," says Okereke, who is working on the next iteration, "and while we are sharing it on our everyday online platforms." It is a strikingly contemporary diagnosis, one that emphasizes an embodied experience in space, while photographically speaking to an intangible network of followers across borders.

Sean O'Toole is a writer and editor based in Cape Town, South Africa.

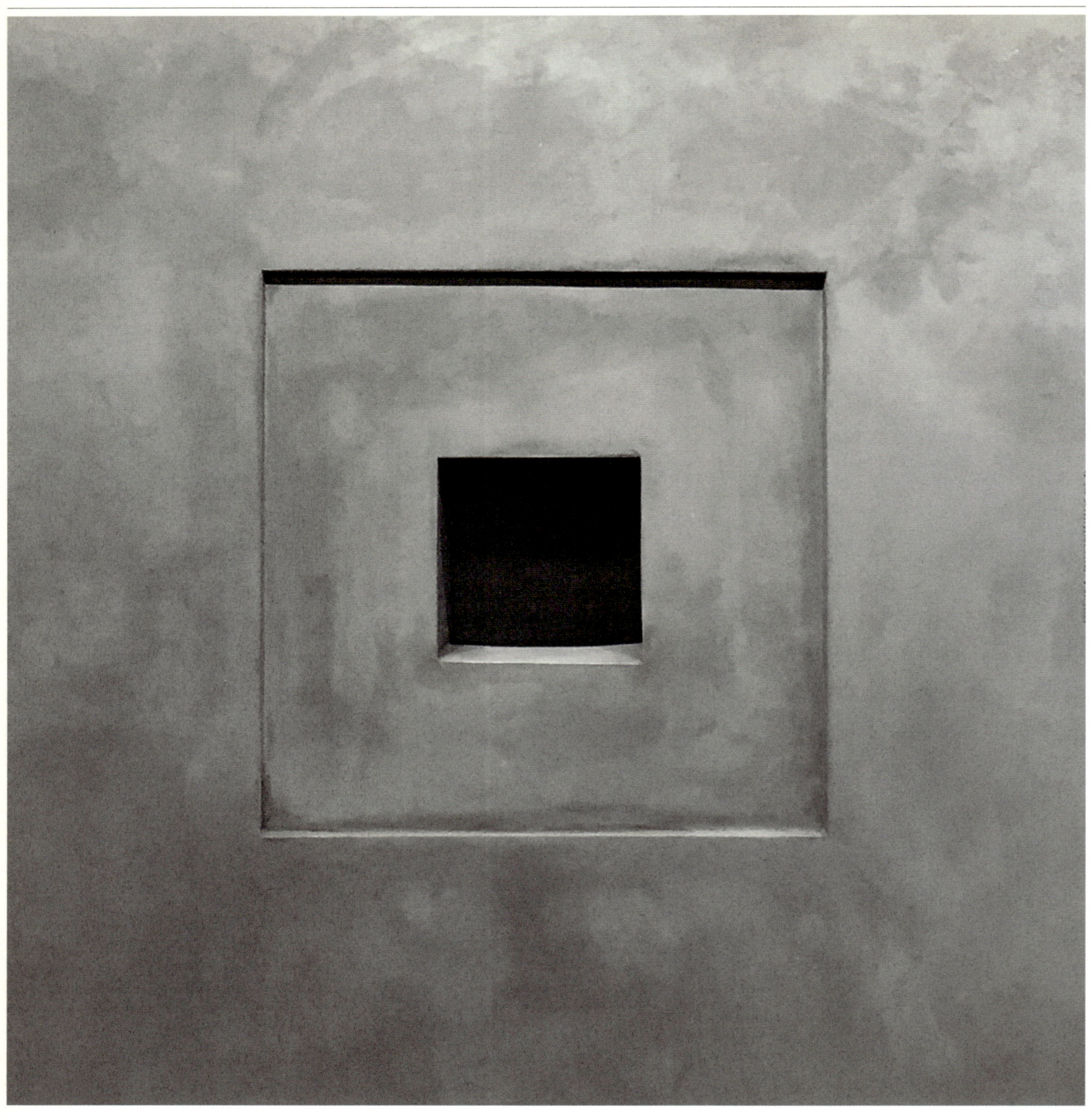

Black Square XVII.

In the year 3015, approximately one thousand years after its creation, a black square made from vitrified nuclear waste will occupy this space. Fabricated on May 21, 2015, the black square is currently being stored in a concrete reinforced steel container, within a holding chamber surrounded by clay-rich soil, at the Radon nuclear waste disposal plant in Sergiev Posad, located 72 km northeast of Moscow. It will reside at the Radon facility until its radioactive properties have diminished to levels deemed safe for human exposure and exhibition. Cast within the black square is a two-ply cylindrical steel capsule holding a letter to the future written by Taryn Simon.

The process of vitrification converts radioactive waste from a volatile liquid to a stable solid mass resembling polished black glass. It is considered to be one of the safest and most effective methods for the long-term storage and neutralization of radioactive waste. *Black Square XVII* was created in collaboration with Russia's State Atomic Energy Corporation (ROSATOM), during the centenary year of the debut exhibition of Kazimir Malevich's *Black Square* painting. Simon's *Black Square XVII* is composed of medium-level, long-term nuclear waste containing organic liquids, inorganic liquids, slurries, and chemical dusts from a nuclear plant in Kursk, and from pharmaceutical and chemical plants in the greater Moscow region.

Black Square, 2006–
Void for artwork
Permanent installation
at Garage Museum of
Contemporary Art, Moscow

Into the Void

**Taryn Simon in Conversation
with Kate Fowle**

"There are multiple truths attached to every image," Taryn Simon said in her 2009 TED talk. Known for her obsessive, painstaking research and immersive installations, Simon is concerned with the uneasy pact between photographic evidence and public knowledge. Skeptical of the image as definitive fact, she hinges her photographs to precise texts, which form her own apparatus of classification. Several of her series explore the underside of science, communication, criminal justice, and government intelligence in the United States. For *A Living Man Declared Dead and Other Chapters I–XVIII* (2011), she ventured across the world seeking to profile cultural mythologies through the narrative of bloodlines. Simon's works to date are collected in *Rear Views, a Star-Forming Nebula, and the Office of Foreign Propaganda*, published by Tate in 2015.

In this issue, Simon speaks with Kate Fowle about her project *Black Square*. Since 2006, Simon has collected objects and documents in a black field measured to the exact dimensions of Kazimir Malevich's painting *Black Square* (1915). Set to end on May 21, 3015, and created in collaboration with Russia's State Atomic Energy Corporation, Simon's newest iteration of the project, a journey into the future, is the ultimate homage—a black square of vitrified nuclear waste. *Black Square XVII* is now a permanent installation at Garage Museum of Contemporary Art in Moscow, where the ongoing series will be presented in spring 2016. With *Black Square XVII*, Simon explained, "I wanted to make a work not for my generation, nor my children's generation, but for a distant future to which I have no tangible relationship."

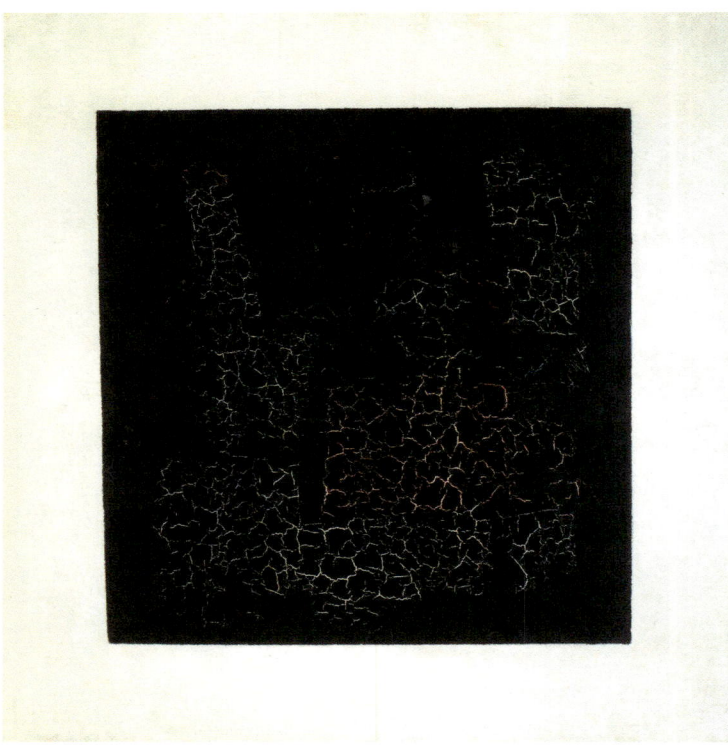

Kazimir Malevich,
Black Square, 1915
Courtesy HIP/Art Resource,
New York

The goal was to construct a black square made from vitrified nuclear waste that would hold within it a letter that I had written to the future.

Kate Fowle: ***Black Square*** **began in 2006 and is ongoing, making it the longest running project you have embarked upon so far. At the same time, it has never been exhibited as a series, or perhaps it's better to say not exhibited as a complete story. Does this project enable you to structure, or think out loud, about various subjects and ideas that become important to you during your research for other series?**

Taryn Simon: It was a needed liberation from the tight margins of my projects. I've worked for so long in very closed and serial projects—ones that take consecutive years to produce. The *Black Square* series has allowed me to think and work differently.

KF: **It's "action research."**

TS: I make the individual works for *Black Square* whenever I feel like it—not in a controlled time slot. Within the "black" I'm able to dig into the lists I collect of singular ideas. I guess the irony is that I couldn't escape my taxonomic instinct, as I put all of these distinct subjects in the repetitive void of the black square. But, for me, it's the messiest I've been.

KF: **Let's talk about the premise of this series. Why did you choose to use Kazimir Malevich's painting *Black Square* (1915) as an organizing principle? What is your own story in relation to this work?**

TS: The *Black Square*—or the great nothing, a zero form, as Malevich described it—was the first icon without an icon in Russian painting. This average shape, size, and color was inscribed with countless political and mystical dimensions. A very simple, dull gesture became revolutionary. For years I've used the shape, color, and scale of Malevich's square as background to a number of representations of man's inventions, or man's disruptive marks. Then the great nothing became a big something—researchers using X-rays have recently discovered that beneath the paint of the *Black Square* lay secret messages and earlier paintings. Ironically, the painting itself suddenly takes on overtly secretive and hidden characteristics, like many other subjects of my work. On a more personal note, Malevich's *Black Square* was created during a period of Russian history that led to my family's departure from the country.

KF: **The works share a format, but their contents are all very different.**

TS: The subjects of the black squares come from my imagination, things I'm reading or lists I've made through the years of ideas to consider for projects. There's no real reason behind them, just things that have a certain solitude or inherent contradiction.

KF: **Can you describe a couple of the works and how they came about?**

TS: *Black Square IV* pictures "The Blaster," an anticarjacking system installed beneath vehicles in South Africa. It's a flamethrower activated by a driver or passenger of a car under attack. *Black Square V* includes a shadowed image of Henry Kissinger. *Black Square XII* documents *The Protocols of the Learned Elders of Zion*, which purports to be the minutes of a meeting between Jewish leaders outlining their plan to control the world. Despite having been exposed as a false document, it continues to be reproduced in many languages and distributed throughout the world. *Black Square XIII* pictures a functional 3-D handgun printed in my studio in nine hours and forty-eight minutes, using black ABS plastic. *Black Square XVIII* looks at the variations in dust from different nations.

KF: **The most recent iteration of the *Black Square* is a sculpture.**

TS: Yes, its start was a fantasy that developed into a long-term project with Garage Museum of Contemporary Art in Moscow. The goal was to construct a black square made from vitrified nuclear waste that would hold within it a letter that I had written to the future. The process of vitrification converts radioactive waste from a volatile liquid to a stable, solid mass resembling polished black glass. It is considered to be one of the safest and most effective methods for the long-term storage and neutralization of radioactive waste. At long last, in 2015, we began fabricating the black square, which will be stored in a steel container reinforced with concrete, situated within a holding chamber surrounded by clay-rich soil, and then placed at the radon nuclear waste disposal plant in Sergiev Posad, located seventy-two kilometers northeast of Moscow. It will reside at the radon facility until its radioactive properties have diminished to levels deemed safe for human exposure and exhibition—approximately one thousand years after its creation.

KF: **I have to say I was skeptical at first that it was ever going to be possible to make the project happen.**

TS: I was, too. I don't think I, or the people I was collaborating with, believed it could happen. But, after two years of conversations by proxy with agencies, scientists, nuclear physicists, and nuclear laborers in various regions in Russia, the project started becoming real. Suddenly we were gaining access and even collaborating with Russia's State Atomic Energy Corporation (ROSATOM). In this iteration of *Black Square*, the fantasy was a piece in and of itself—and the process of entertaining it, through the research program at Garage, allowed for the collection of data and visual material along the way. For example, I love that a physicist at Mayak nuclear facility in Russia sent me an illustration of the black square I was proposing to build positioned at the bottom of a lake in the sun. It came with instructions to take a blank piece of paper from the package and hold it beneath a sheet of lead to reveal a secret message written to me by a finger dipped in lake water with radioactive properties from the nuclear waste stored in its surroundings.

KF: **Is there currently a logical or conceptual end to this series? In terms of your practice, which normally has defined limits, what does it mean for you to have a project that's ongoing—perhaps even beyond your control?**

TS: It's the one project in which I don't crave a close. With the radioactive black square, I've even tried to have it keep unfolding after my death and my children's death and their children's death. So far, I've imagined it to the year 3015, into a future of machines, or even very large rats—lost amongst them or maybe cracked open if the documentation evidencing its innards survives, and if English is understood or decipherable.

KF: **Your most recent addition to *Black Square* also takes the form of institutional critique. You have constructed a permanent installation at Garage Museum of Contemporary Art's new building, but it will take between eight hundred to a thousand years for the piece to really come to fruition. The research and development of *Black Square XVII* was**

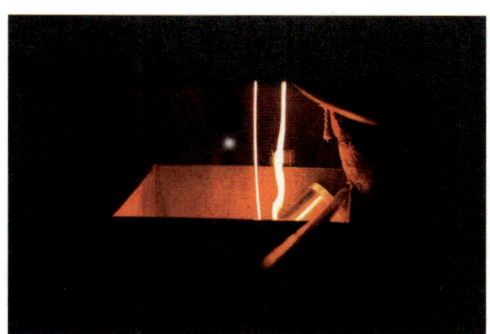
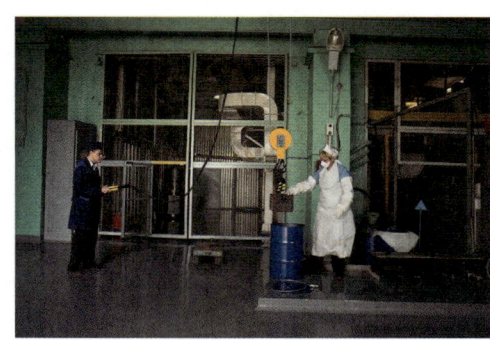

Film stills, Radon nuclear waste disposal plant, Sergiev Posad, Russia, 2015–ongoing

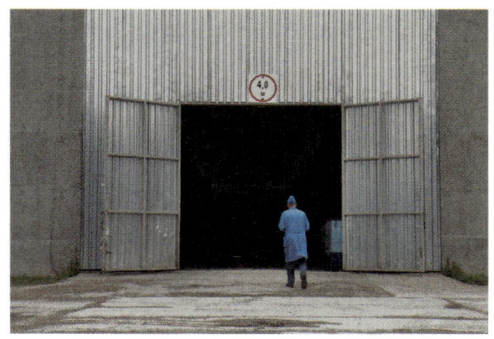

Black Square VI.

Blue buckets were
mounted atop civilian
vehicles in Moscow to
protest the misuse of
emergency blue rotating
lights by VIP businessmen,
celebrities, and officials
to bypass Moscow traffic.

Black Square, 2006–

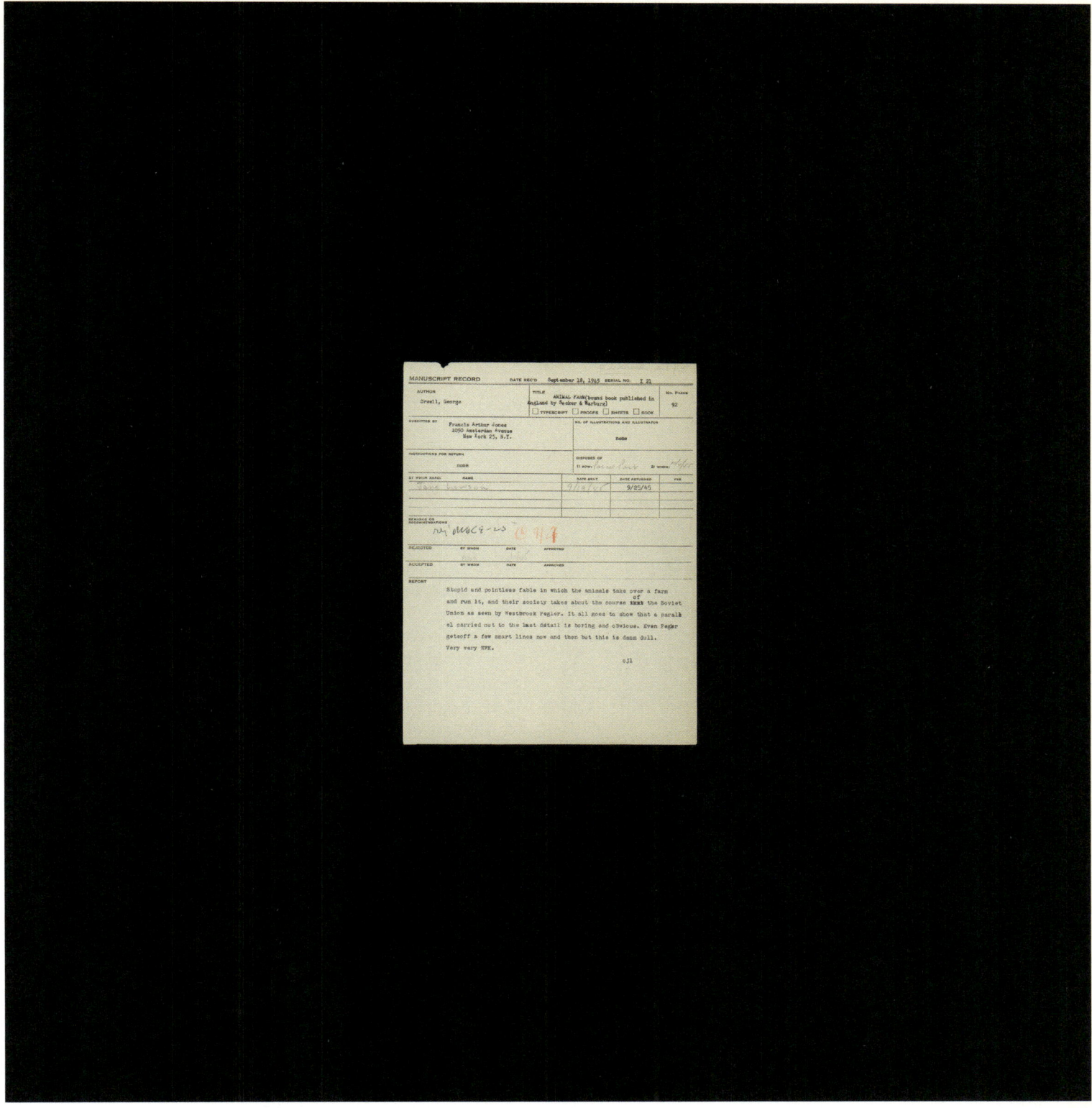

Black Square XVI.

George Orwell's *Animal Farm* was rejected by Knopf Publishing Company on September 18, 1945. The manuscript was described as a "[s]tupid and pointless fable in which the animals take over a farm and run it, and their society takes about the course of the Soviet Union as seen by Westbrook Pegler. It all goes to show that a parallel carried out to the last detail is boring and obvious. Even Pegler gets off a few smart lines now and then but this is damn dull. Very very NFK."

Black Square, 2006–

created as part of the museum's Field Research program and has been undertaken, in collaboration with ROSATOM, in 2015, the centenary year of the debut exhibition of Malevich's *Black Square* painting. Can you describe how this iteration came about? What *is* this work exactly?

TS: My *Black Square* was constructed in collaboration with ROSATOM. It does not take photographic form but instead is a physical incarnation of the black square that will eventually fit into the wall of the museum with a frame that is the same dimensions as the original white surround of Malevich's *Black Square*. The concrete wall permanently installed at Garage has a void within it that is the exact shape of the black square I made from vitrified nuclear waste. The void is awaiting my black square's arrival in one thousand years. Until then it stands as a nothing that is sometimes filled with objects inserted by visitors, or dust. In order to retrieve the letter to the future, protected in a specially designed steel container within the black square, someone in the future would need to decide whether or not to break it—in which case it wouldn't fit seamlessly into its home built one thousand years earlier.

KF: Although *Black Square XVII* will take many years to finally manifest itself for audiences, the project is spawning other works, such as a film. How does this project relate to the original series?

TS: The film is its own work: a surreal story of an American citizen constructing an object with a Russian nuclear agency that she can only see or understand through film, photography, or the written word—never in reality. Many scenes are shot by individuals following my very specific instructions, as only Russian citizens can physically be on the site of its creation according to the rules of the facility. It is directed by everyone involved including myself, and no one. I'm shooting by proxy as the film records areas to which I'm not allowed to travel. By this and all the psychological sludge it confronts, it's becoming something that doesn't make sense in logical film terms. Its authorship, ownership, and story are in many ways up for grabs—much like the object itself. A major component of my exhibition at Garage is an active film set where we will be collecting footage for the film.

KF: What does it mean to be developing a project in Russia—to be working not just with the metaphorical histories and imaginaries of Malevich's most famous work, but also in the country surrounded with the conceptual legacies of the artist?

TS: This work will be buried in a country that I'm bound to by blood and history, but to which I have very little living relationship. Its black glass is beautiful, yet fatal to touch or behold. It contains a message that would require breaking the form to read. As for ownership, it's mine, but really it's the States'. It represents a collaboration between the United States and Russia operating above and outside of differences. It's preserved through things designed to wait for it. But they may wait forever or it may all just get lost or forgotten.

Black Square XI.

In captivity many birds develop Feather Destructive Behavior as a result of conditions including lack of psychological and emotional stimulation, stress, lack of companionship, and limited freedom. "Amiga" is a blue and gold macaw suffering from this condition.

Black Square, 2006–
All photographs courtesy the artist and Gagosian Gallery

Kate Fowle is the chief curator at Garage Museum of Contemporary Art in Moscow and Director-at-Large at Independent Curators International in New York.

Pictures

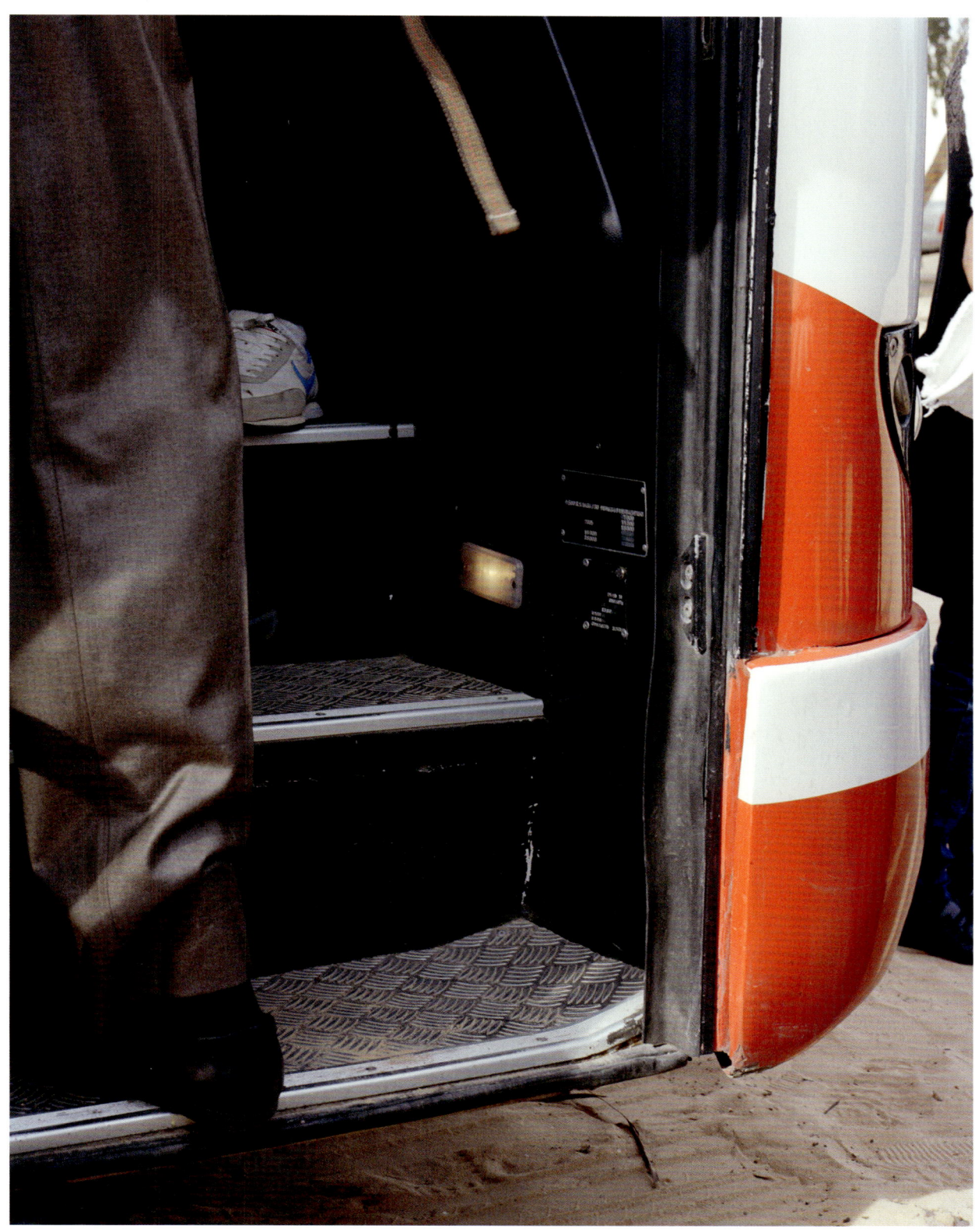

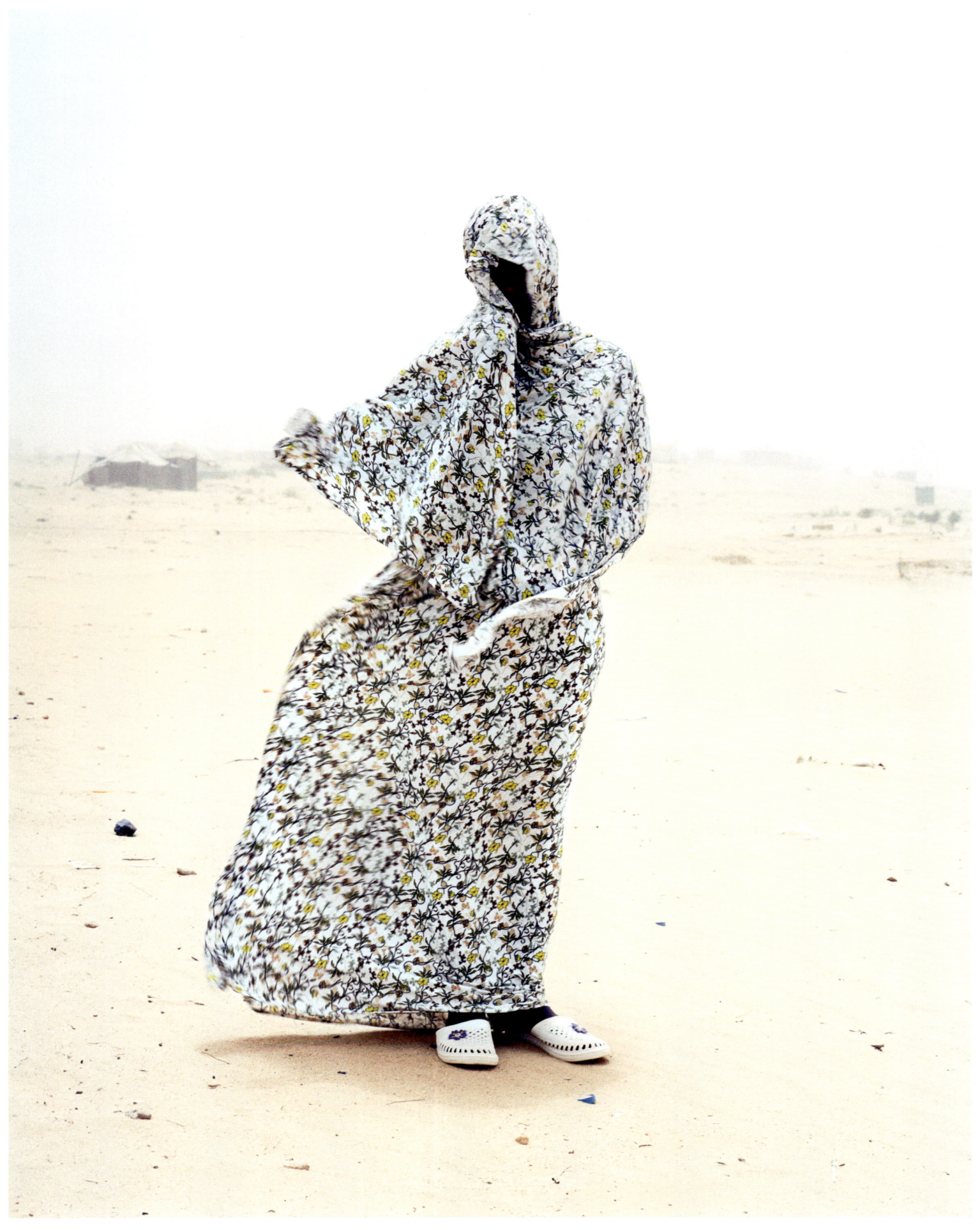

Close to the port of Ben Guerdane in Tunisia is the site of Choucha Camp, a refugee center operated from 2011 to 2013 by the United Nations Human Rights Council. A few miles from the Libyan border, it was the recipient of thousands fleeing the Libyan crisis, which began in 2011 and has evolved into a protracted civil war. But since Ben Guerdane is itself a city along the route to Europe for displaced people from sub-Saharan Africa, many other groups populated the camp after it opened: Nigerians, Darfurians, Chadians, Ivorians, even people from the Asian subcontinent—Pakistanis, Bangladeshis. This transit zone, where French photographer Samuel Gratacap's *Empire* (2012–14) is set, must be, like other such camps on the continent, emblematic of our time. Choucha, however, is extreme: wild, desolate, inhospitable, and now abandoned by the world. During its three years of official operation, it held more than 200,000 people, but these numbers dwindled to a few hundred in 2014 as supplies, water, and electricity were cut off and the camp was ostensibly closed. Dozens have stayed because their applications for refugee status were stamped REJECTED and they simply have nowhere else to go.

Samuel Gratacap Empire

Bronwyn Law-Viljoen

Bronwyn Law-Viljoen
is an Associate Professor
of Creative Writing
at University of the
Witwatersrand,
Johannesburg, and editor
of Fourthwall Books. Her
first novel will be published
in 2016.

Gratacap's project is partly an attempt to grasp what it means, physically and psychologically, to be entirely rejected. In Choucha, it means that one must make one's bed in a tent since there is no departing, and no belonging. In Gratacap's photographs, the makeshift shelters with their fading blue UNHRC logos are almost obscured by dust and sand. Inside them, blankets and sleeping mats are neatly made up. Floors are swept, as though neatness will keep back hunger and thirst. Here, in the hot, dry, four-year *moment* of the camp, migration reaches stasis. The migrants are suspended inside the swirling dust, and Gratacap's photographs give us some sense of the quality of their waiting—for asylum, for supplies, or for some way out of this terrible impasse. In one image, Somali men read a list of names of asylum seekers summoned for one last interview with UNHRC. Their anxiety is palpable.

Tempting as it surely was for Gratacap—and as it is for the viewer who has never been there—to see Choucha as a *terrain vague*, a metaphor for migrancy and statelessness, a no-place in which human beings drift outside of all boundaries, emblematic rather than real, he seems to want to fully grasp this limbo territory as a terrifying place in which people do live, albeit meagerly. There is beauty in his images, but also an attempt to understand the bare-life *fact* of Choucha, and to avoid consigning the camp's inhabitants to the realm of the poetic.

Empire is part of Gratacap's long investigation into the Mediterranean migration crisis. Begun in 2007, it encompasses interviews, community involvement, filmmaking, the collection of ephemera, and, finally, photography. This immersion is reflected in the photographs: they suggest at once a respectful distance and a desire for a slender connection, achieved through acute observation of gestures: the pervasive, knuckle-biting anxiety; the young man clasping two cellphones, holding up the edge of his jacket to listen; the exquisite improbability of three men in immaculate suits walking away into a blown-out horizon. Gratacap notices that the men are trying, with almost comic delicacy, to keep the hot, insistent sand out of their shoes.

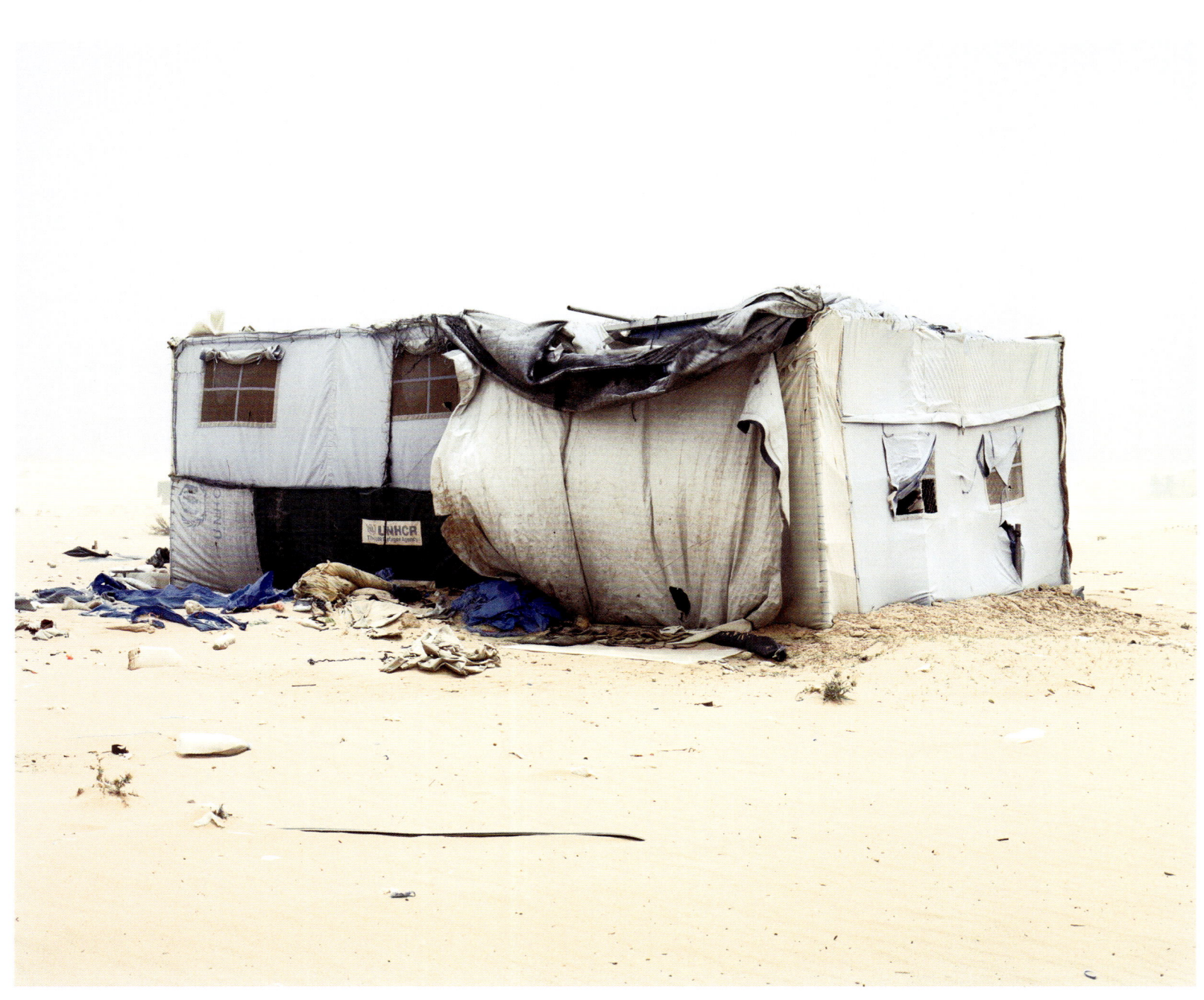

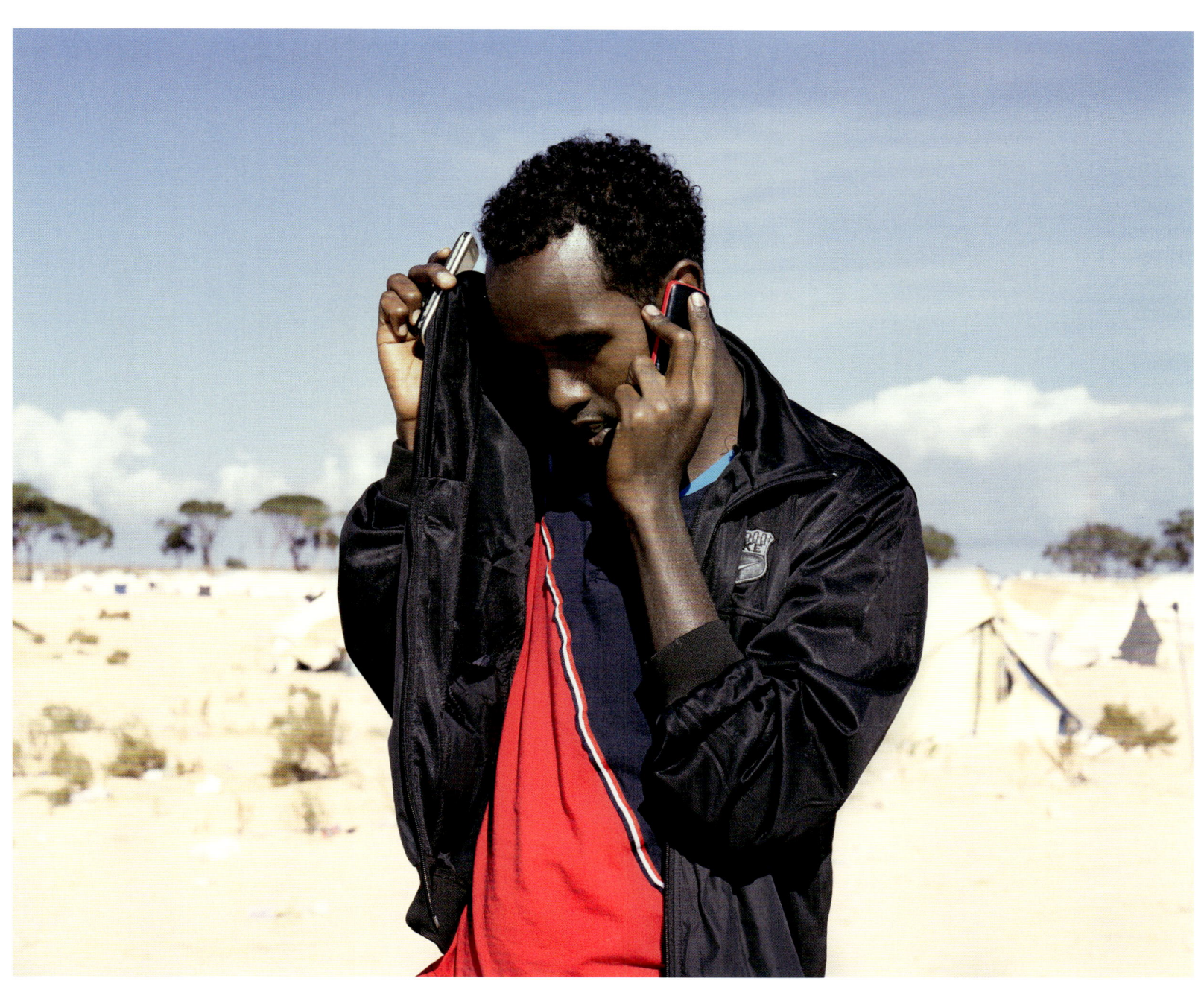

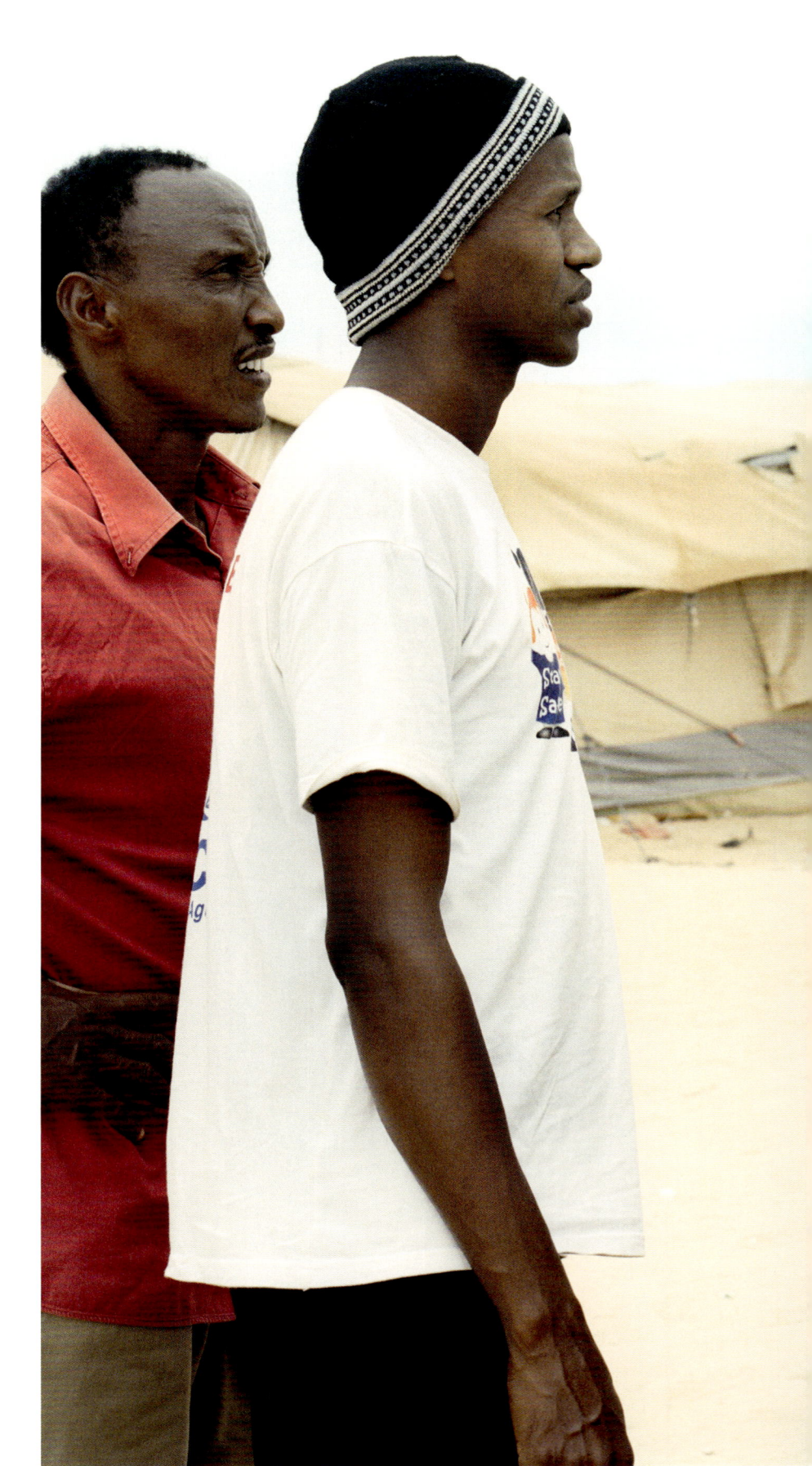

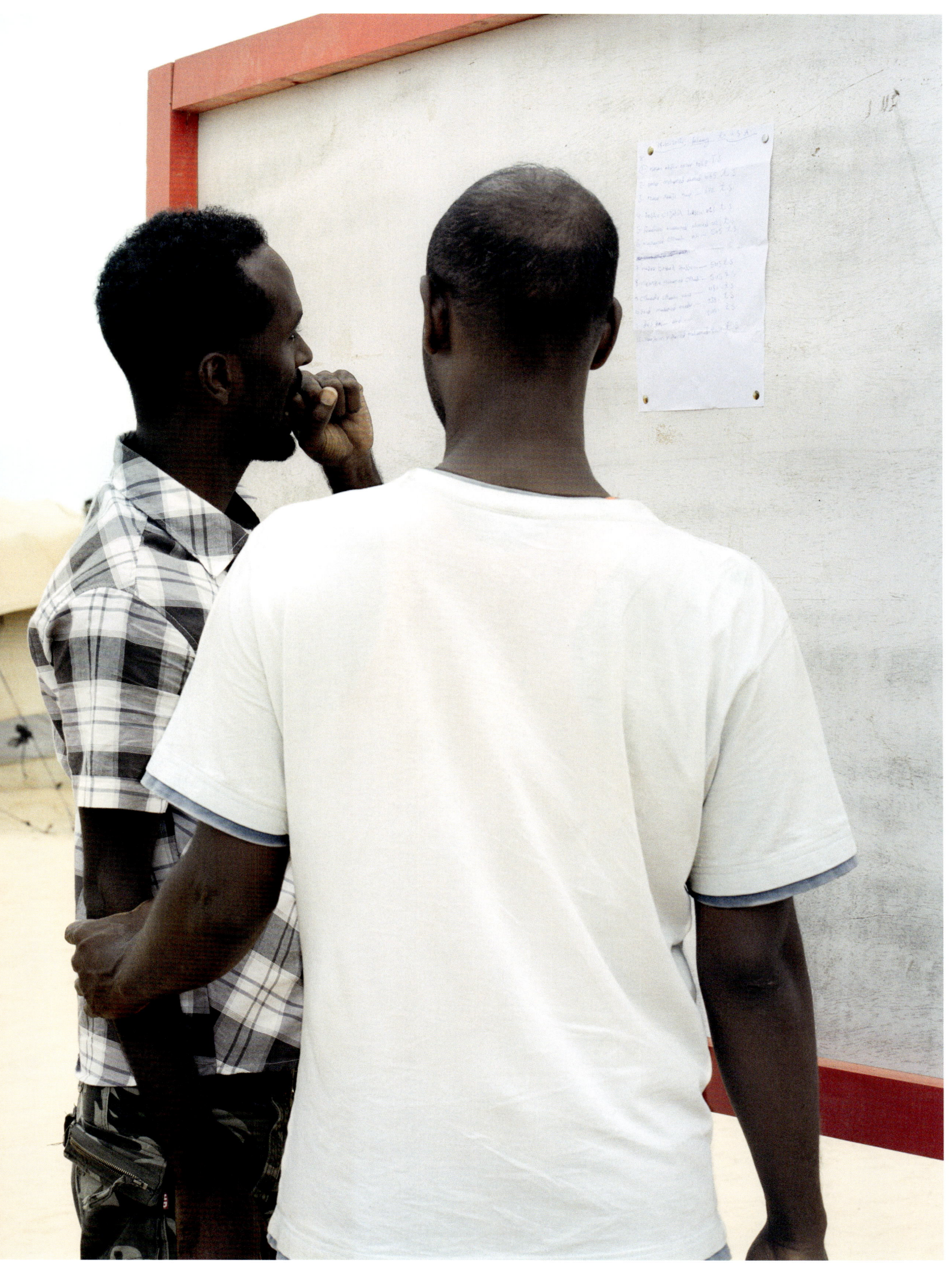

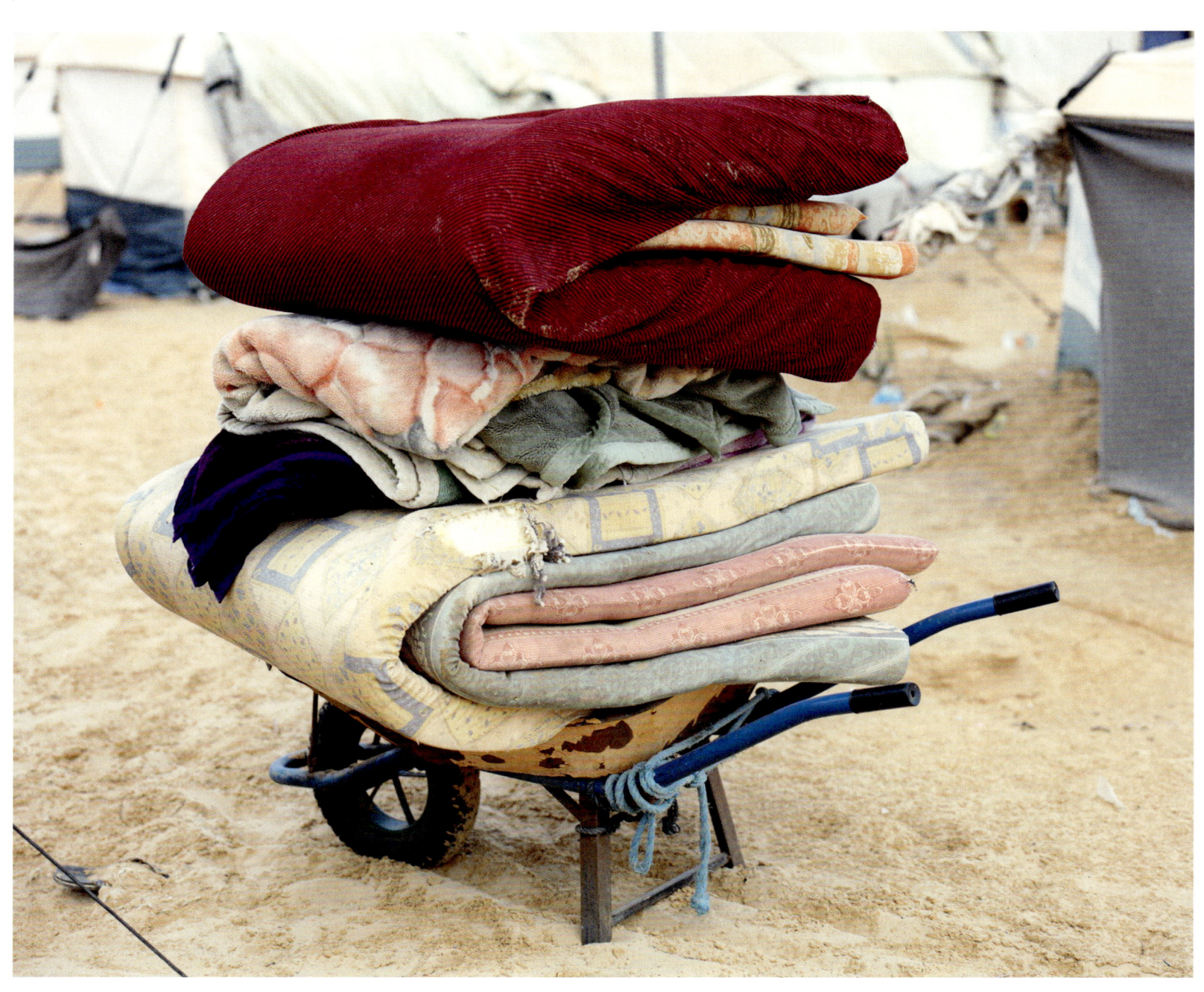

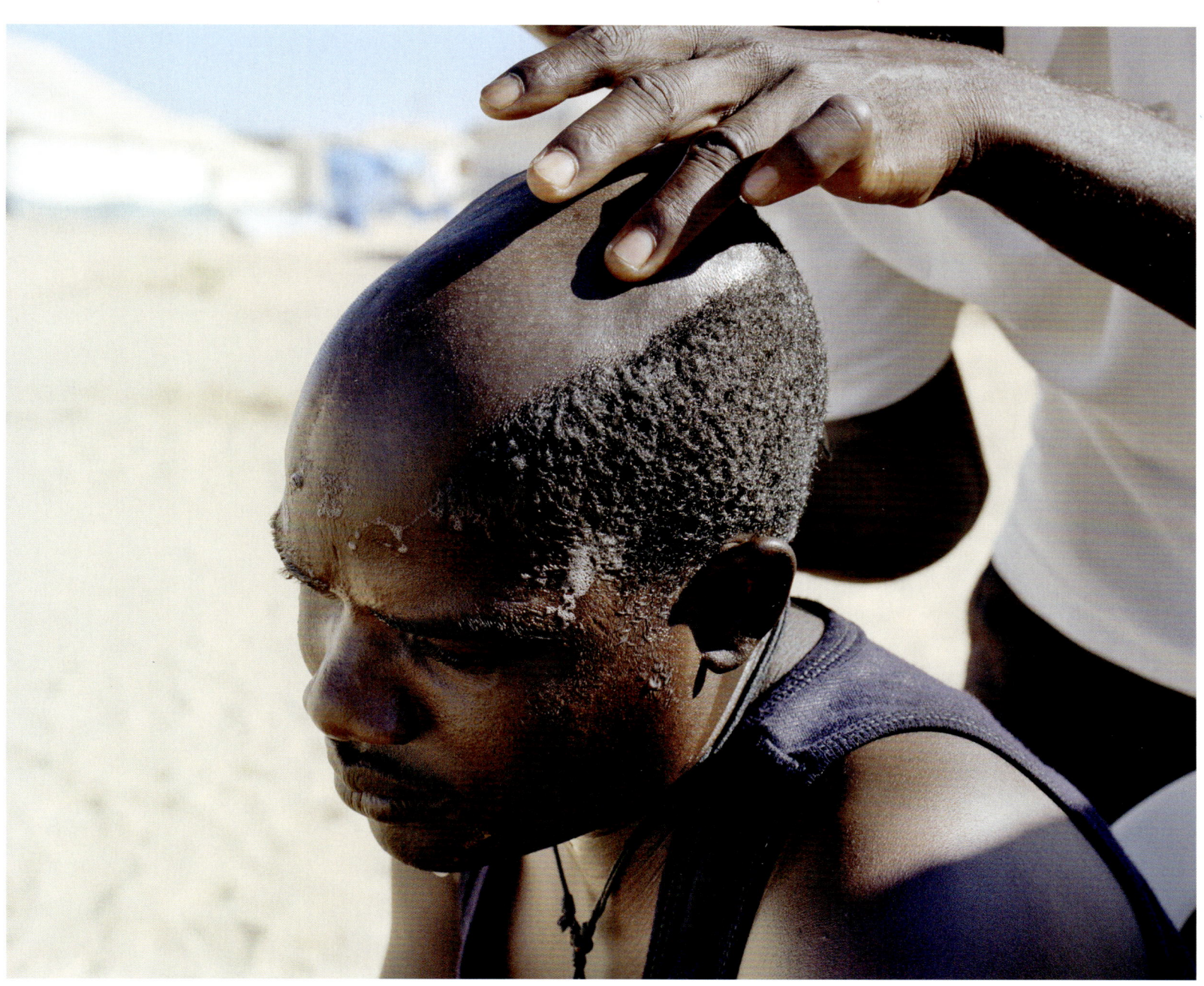

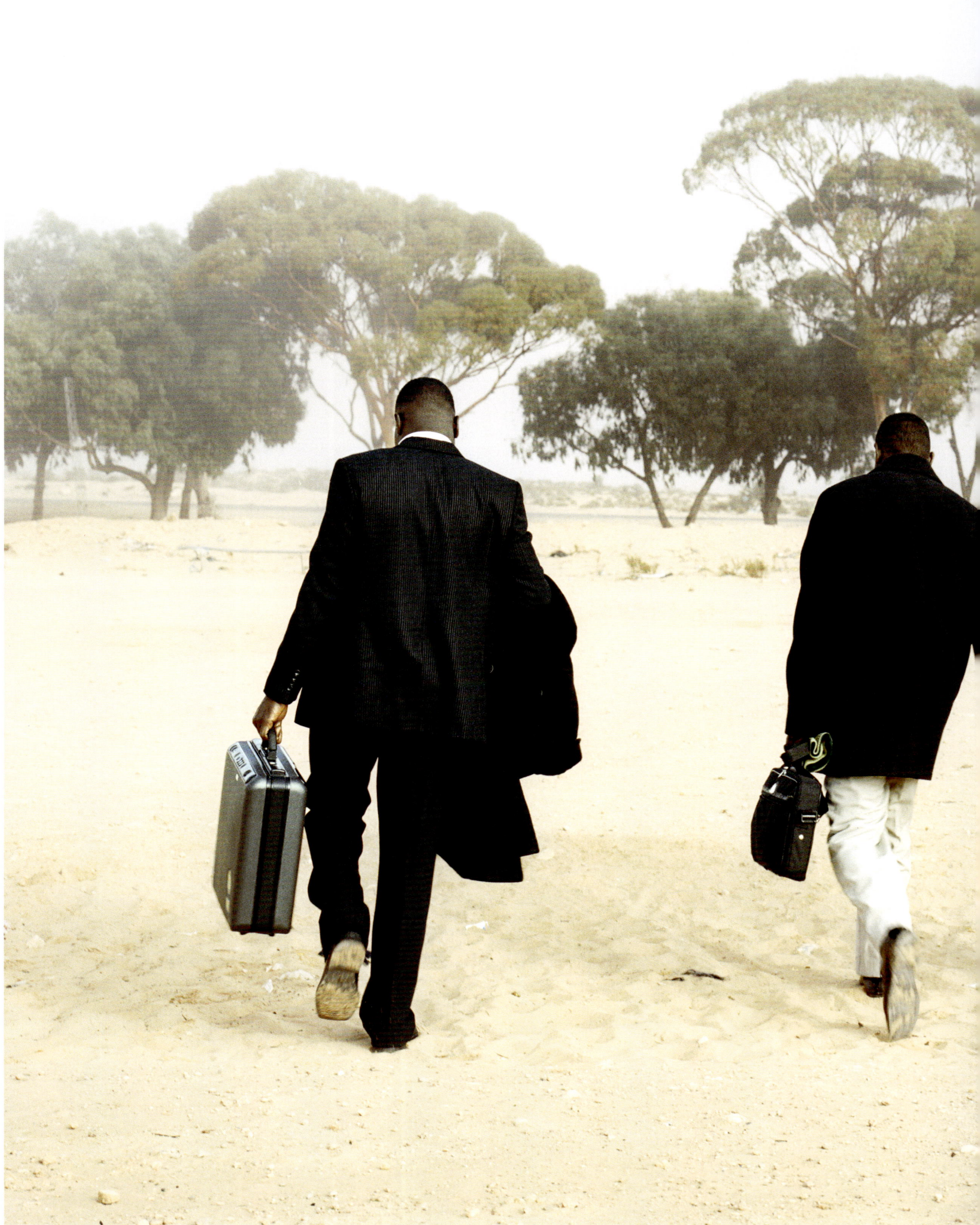

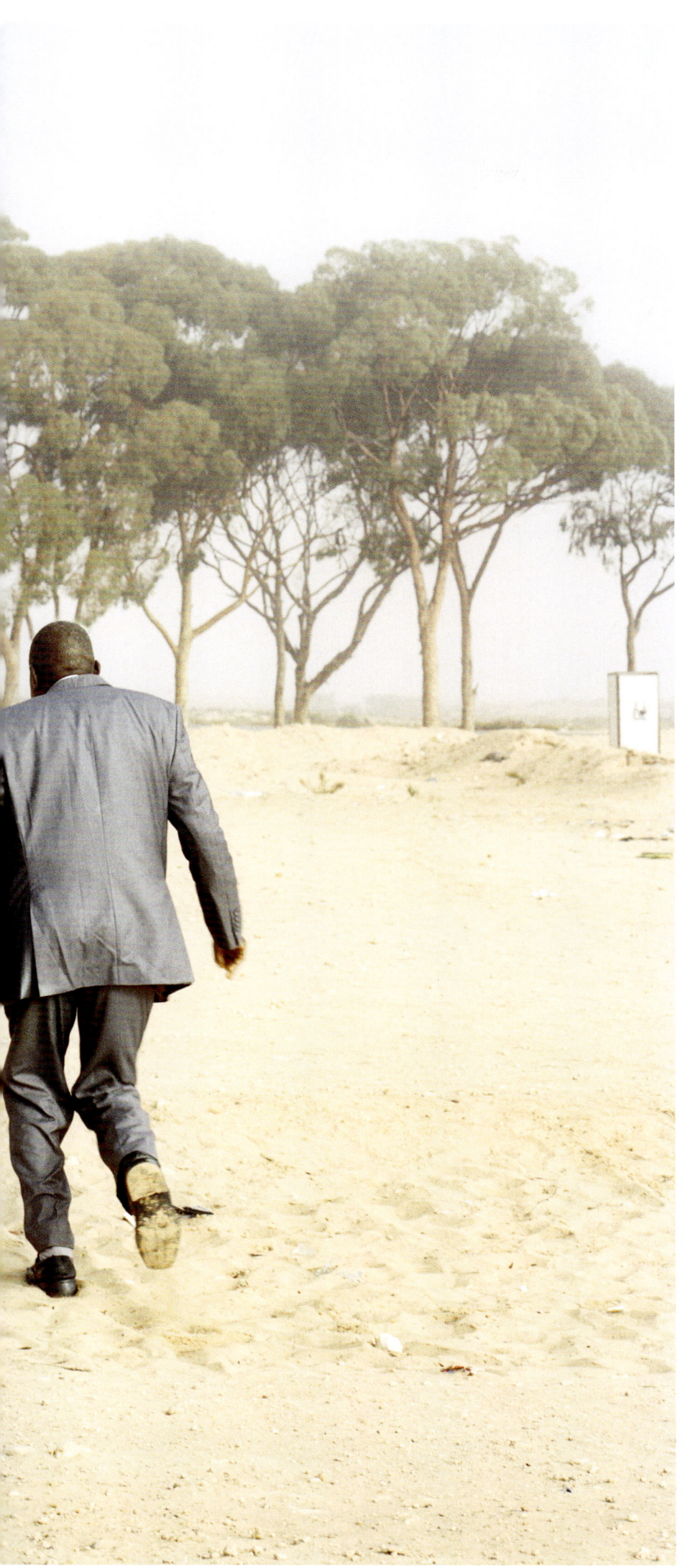

All photographs from the series *Empire*, Choucha Camp, Tunisia, 2012–14
Courtesy the artist and Galerie Les Filles du Calvaire, Paris

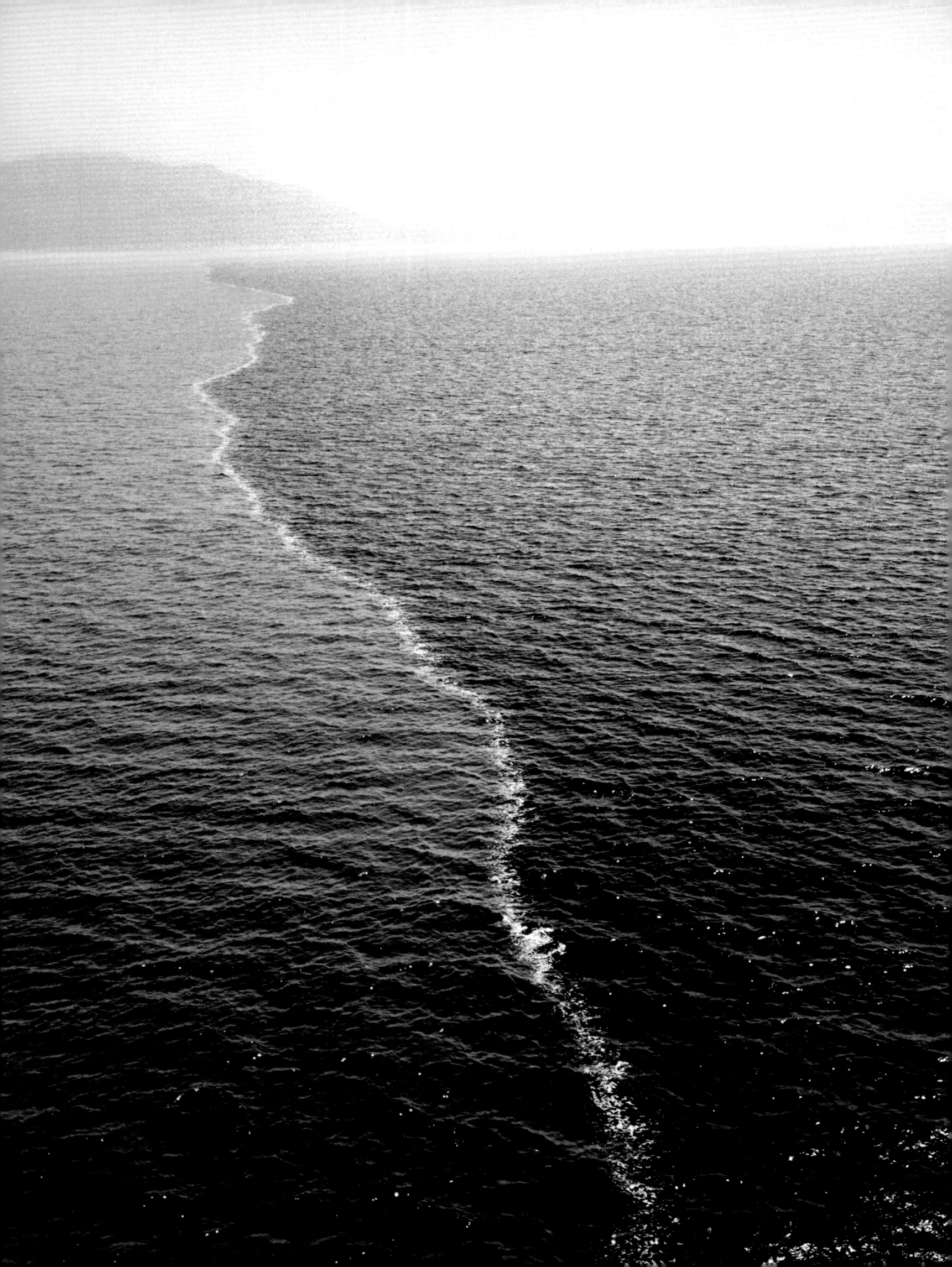

In 2009, the Swiss artistic duo Taiyo Onorato & Nico Krebs released their celebrated body of work *The Great Unreal*, a collaborative project based on several road trips the two had taken throughout the United States over the previous three years. More than a direct investigation of the country's geography, society, or culture, *The Great Unreal* involved various forms of image manipulation and intervention, which Onorato & Krebs used to both reflect upon and toy with the vast inventory of American visual iconography.

More recently, Onorato & Krebs set off on another set of extended trips, spanning from 2013 to 2015. This time they drove east, from Switzerland to Mongolia, in an attempt to explore the vast region that straddles Eastern Europe and Central Asia. Encompassing both photographic works and several 16mm short films, Onorato & Krebs's resulting body of work, *Eurasia* (2013–15), is in part an expedition through countries that are generally unfamiliar or underrepresented in the West—former Soviet republics, such as Georgia, Kazakhstan, Turkmenistan, and Uzbekistan, and elsewhere—but it is also an unconventional celebration of exploration itself, of curiosity, and, most of all, the adventure of encountering the unfamiliar in a manner that is unmediated and unfiltered. "In the States, there's so much imagery and iconography to work with," Onorato notes, "but Eurasia was almost like a black hole for us, in terms of visual references."

Instead of engaging with, playing with, or subverting a broad catalog of preexisting imagery for places where, arguably, a limited one currently exists, Onorato & Krebs formed *Eurasia* as a meditation on the search for the "unknown" within the twenty-first century and the surreal fluctuations and uncertainties that occur when one experiences something seemingly "new" today. In their photographs, the historical and the contemporary merge in compelling ways: a nomadic shepherd on horseback brandishes a high-powered chainsaw; a traditional samovar is grotesquely enlarged and hewn in marble as a nationalist symbol; a bank of high-tech, mirror-plated solar panels both reflects and camouflages itself within a pillow-clouded Caucasian landscape. "As soon as we left 'the West,' so to speak," Krebs explains, "we started to notice that everything was in an extreme state of flux. There's a different pace—an enormous will to go forward—especially in urban environments, yet many rural regions remain static, or even seem to be going backwards. This shifting, backwards and forwards, becomes surreal."

Rather than tap into the conventional documentarian's sense of knowingness, or the romantic traveler's sense of sentimentality or nostalgia, many of the works in *Eurasia* are simply baffling— a plastic bottle atop an iron-oxide red rock formation spews viscous white liquid onto the shallow riverbed below; new monumental architecture shimmers in barren and underdeveloped desert landscapes. "As an onlooker, you often can't figure out what's going on," Krebs says, "and that's partly what this work is about—the incompleteness, or the lack of in-depth understanding that we experienced while we were traveling." When questioned further about how the project might be perceived as antidocumentary compared with more traditional ideas of the genre, Krebs responds: "We're artists, and the artistic imagination can, and should, allow itself to be selective and incomplete."

In this sense, Onorato & Krebs's *Eurasia* embraces not only the spirit of discovery that can be found in a relatively unfamiliar region, but also a freewheeling artistic spirit. "In a country like Mongolia, the dirt roads themselves are nomadic," Onorato says, "constantly moving, shifting, and changing." And in many ways, the duo's project relishes the precious absence of certainty experienced when a place itself feels as though it is moving, shifting, and changing at a pace faster than those who travel through it.

Taiyo Onorato & Nico Krebs
Eurasia

Aaron Schuman

Sea Division, 2013

All photographs from the series *Eurasia*, 2013–15
Courtesy the artists, RaebervonStenglin, Sies+Höke, and Peter Lav Gallery

Aaron Schuman is a London-based writer and curator.

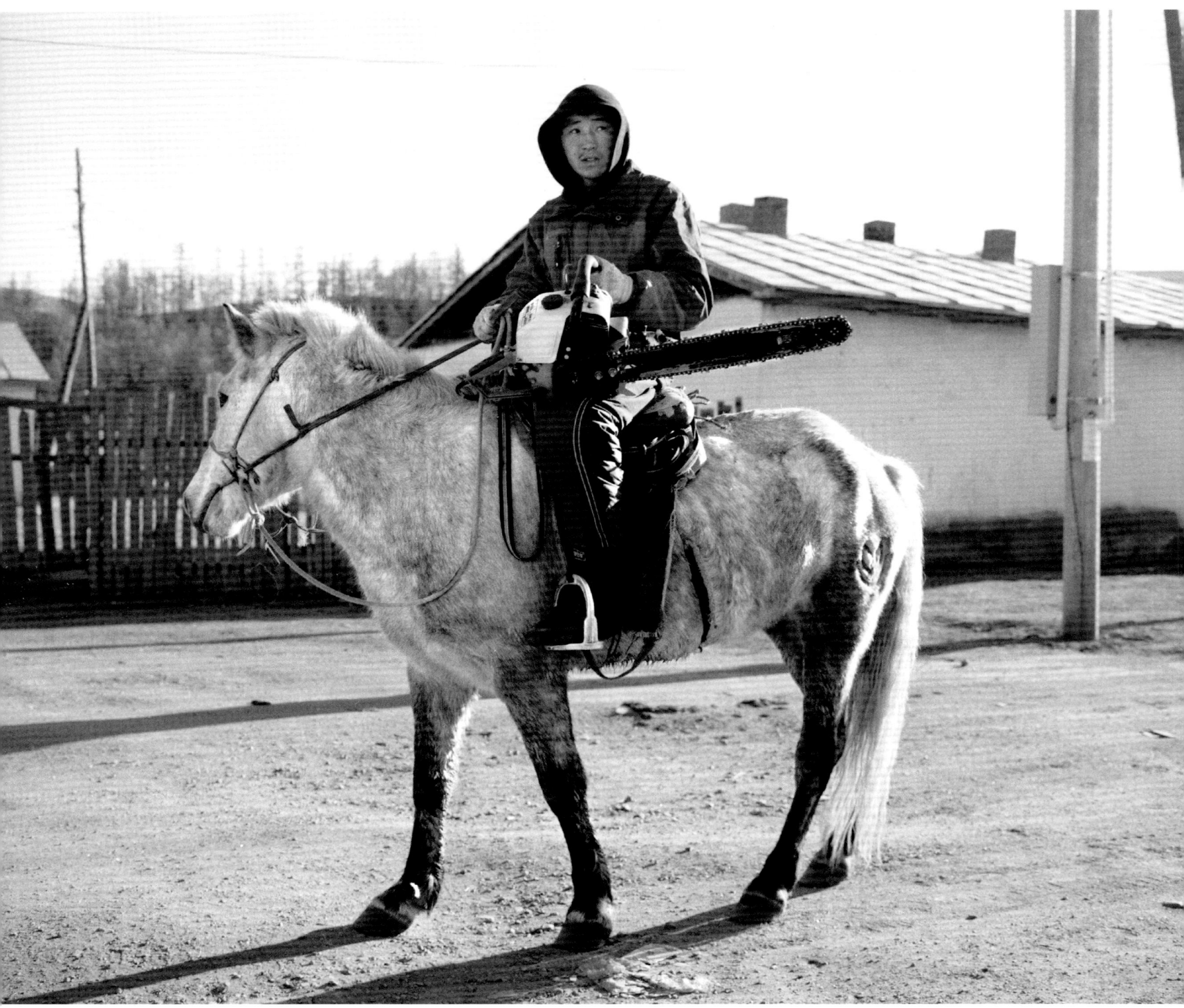

This page:
Fish, 2013

Page 72:
Samovar, 2013

Page 73:
Well, 2013

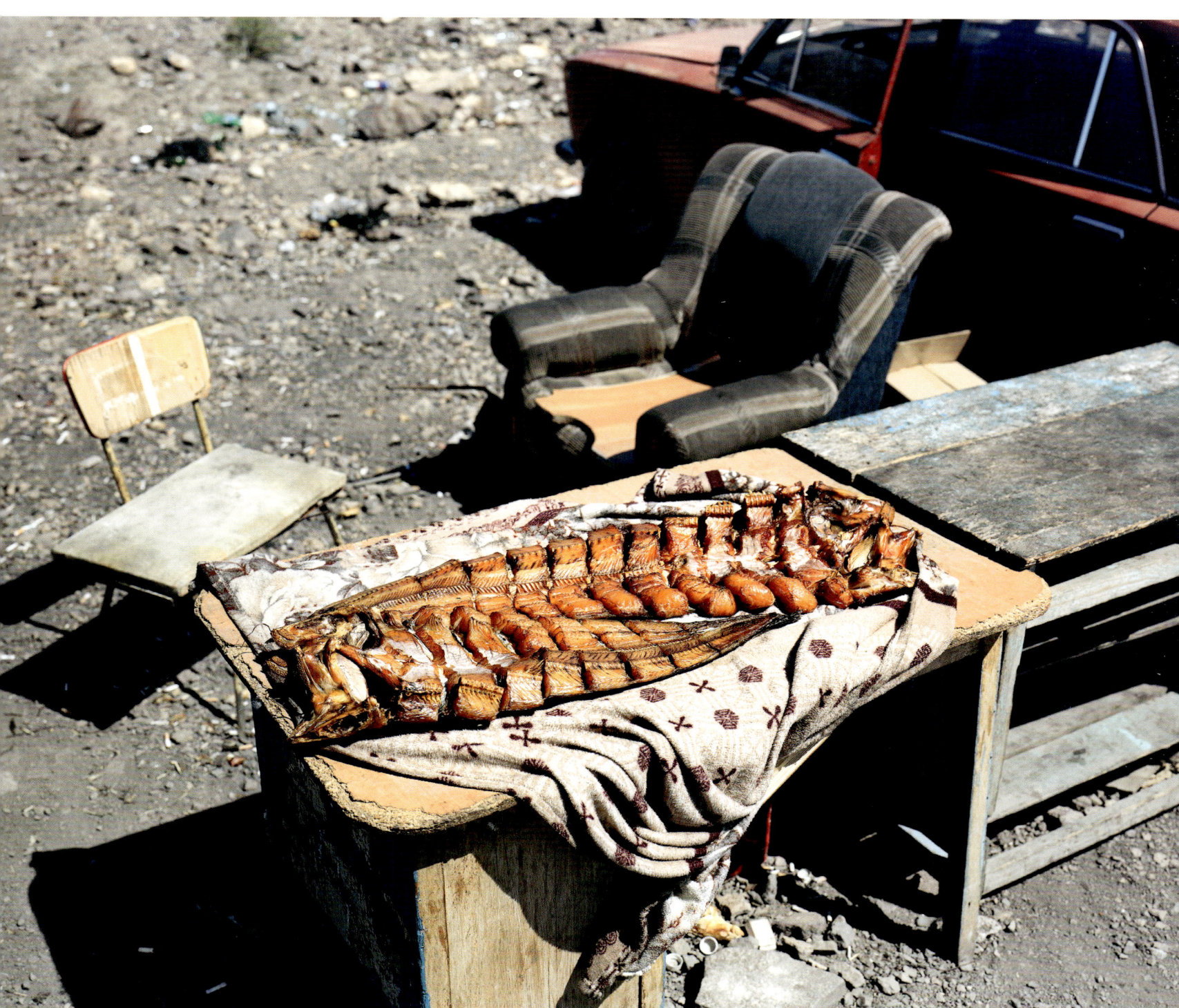

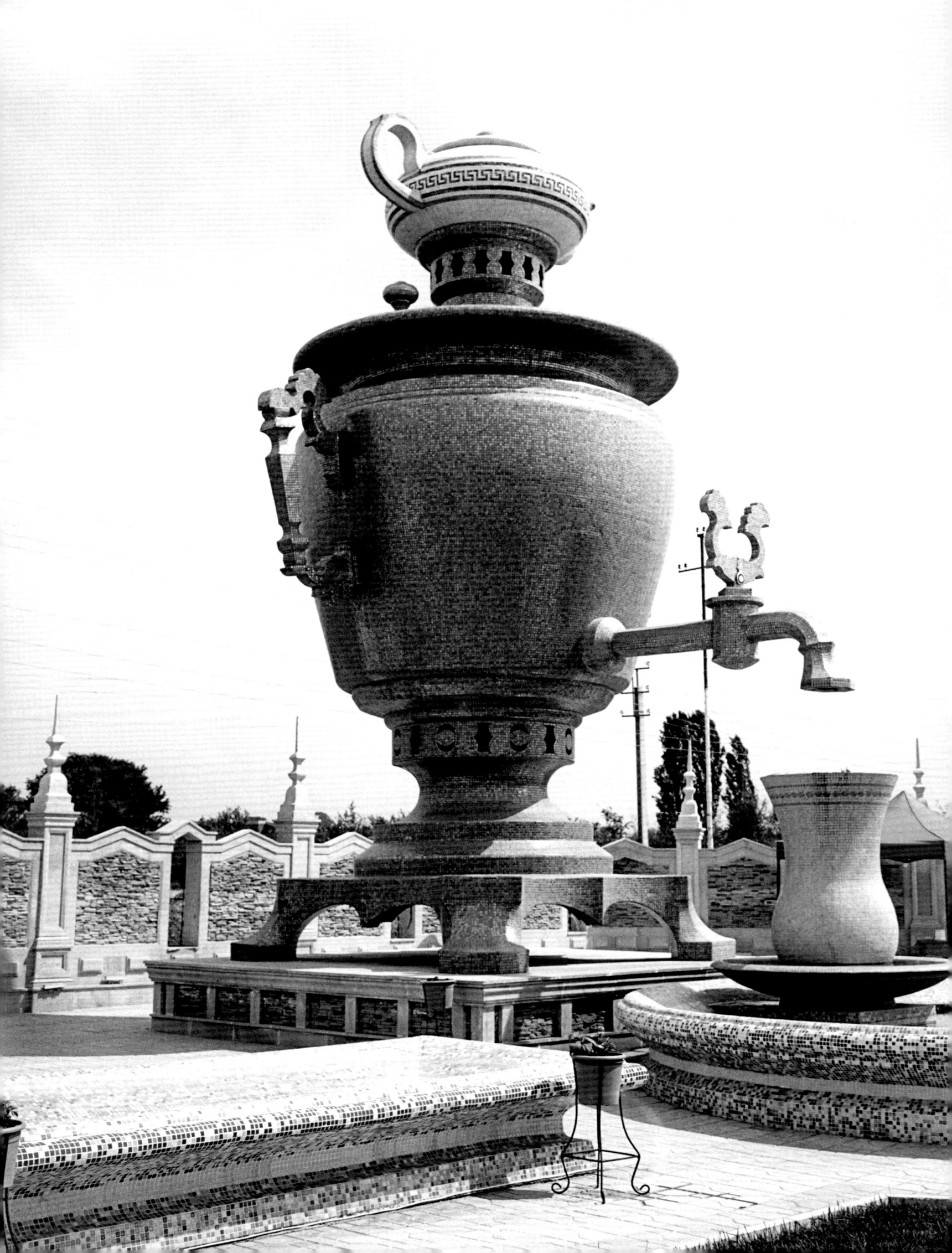

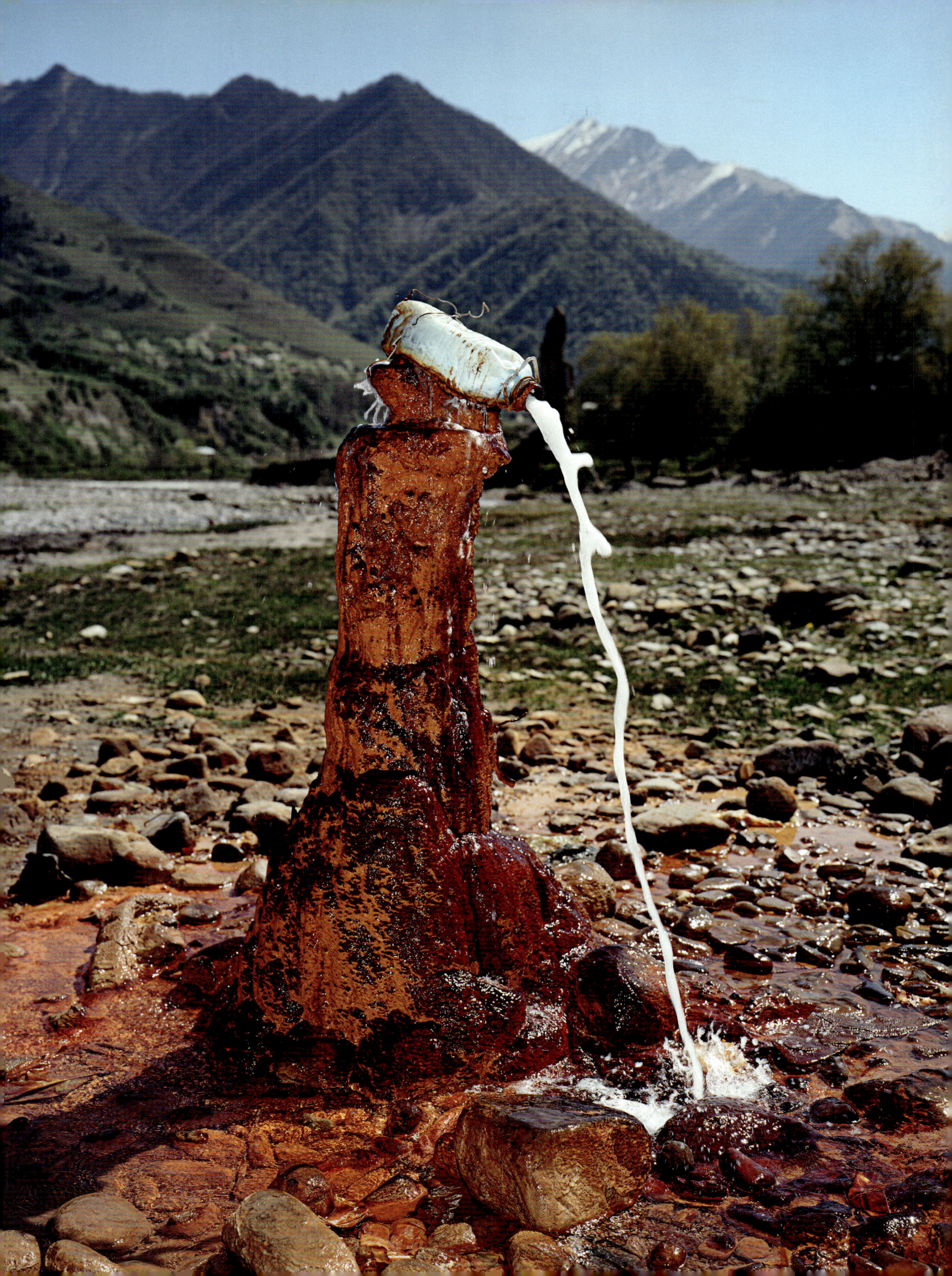

White City, 2013

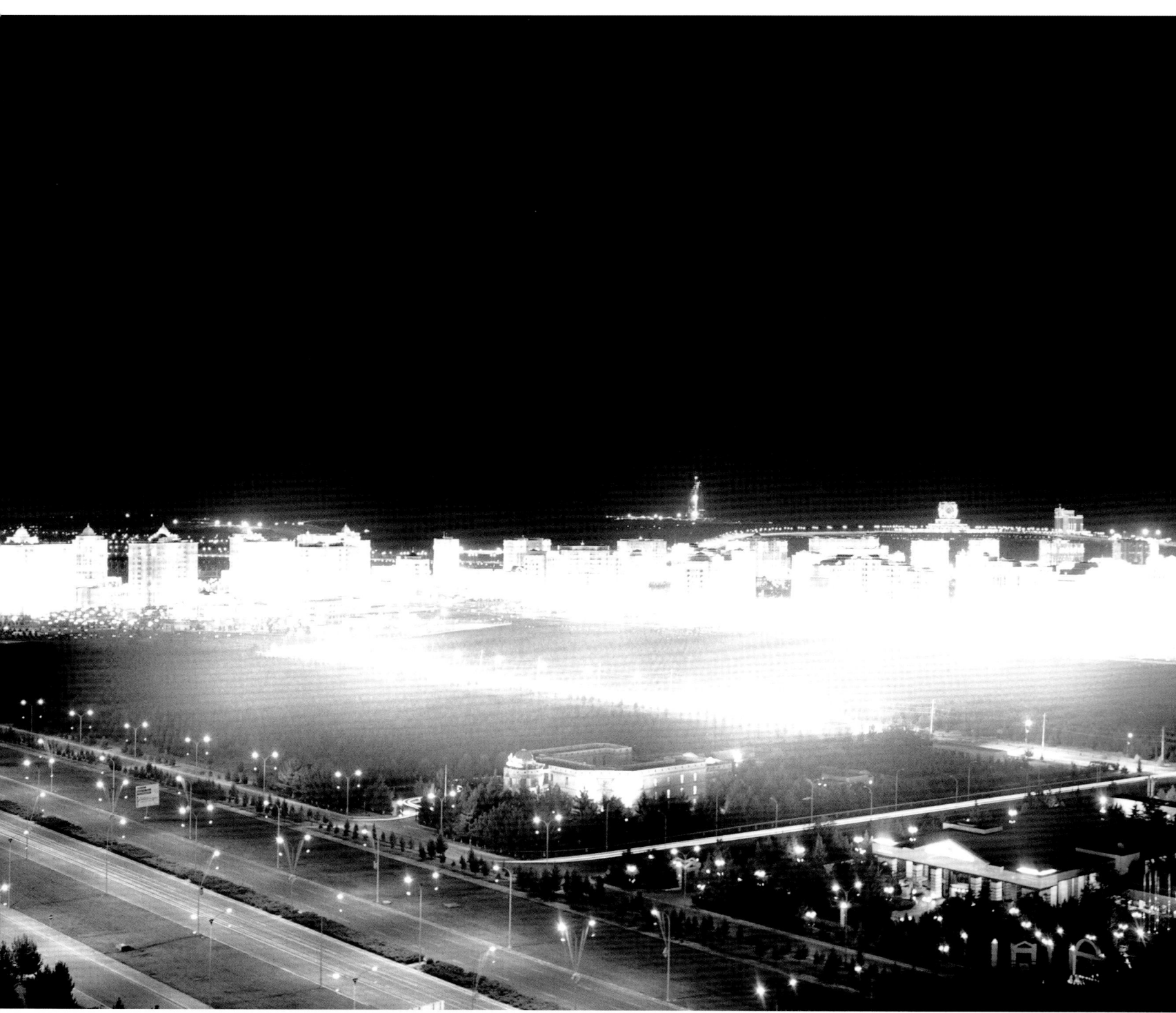

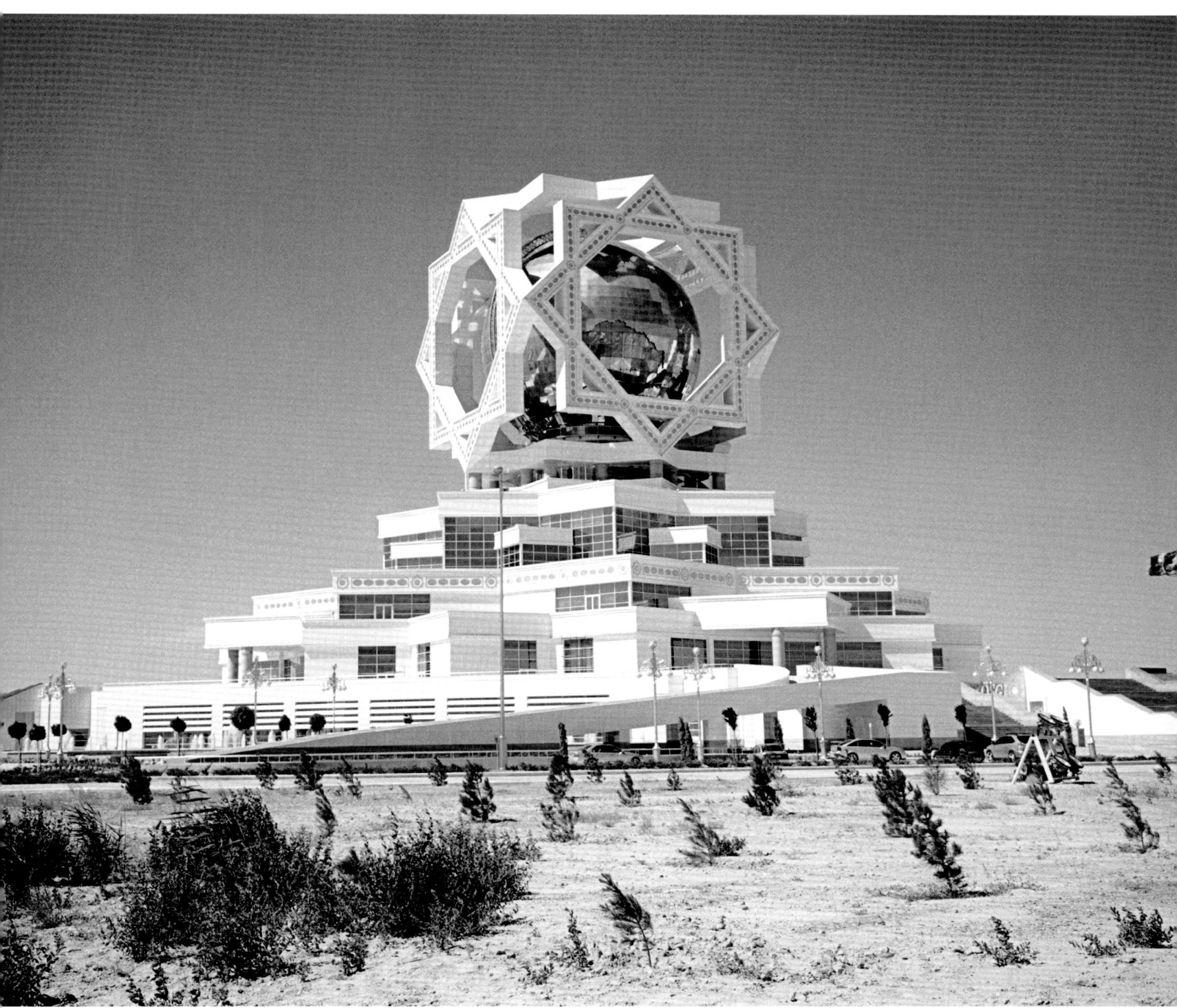

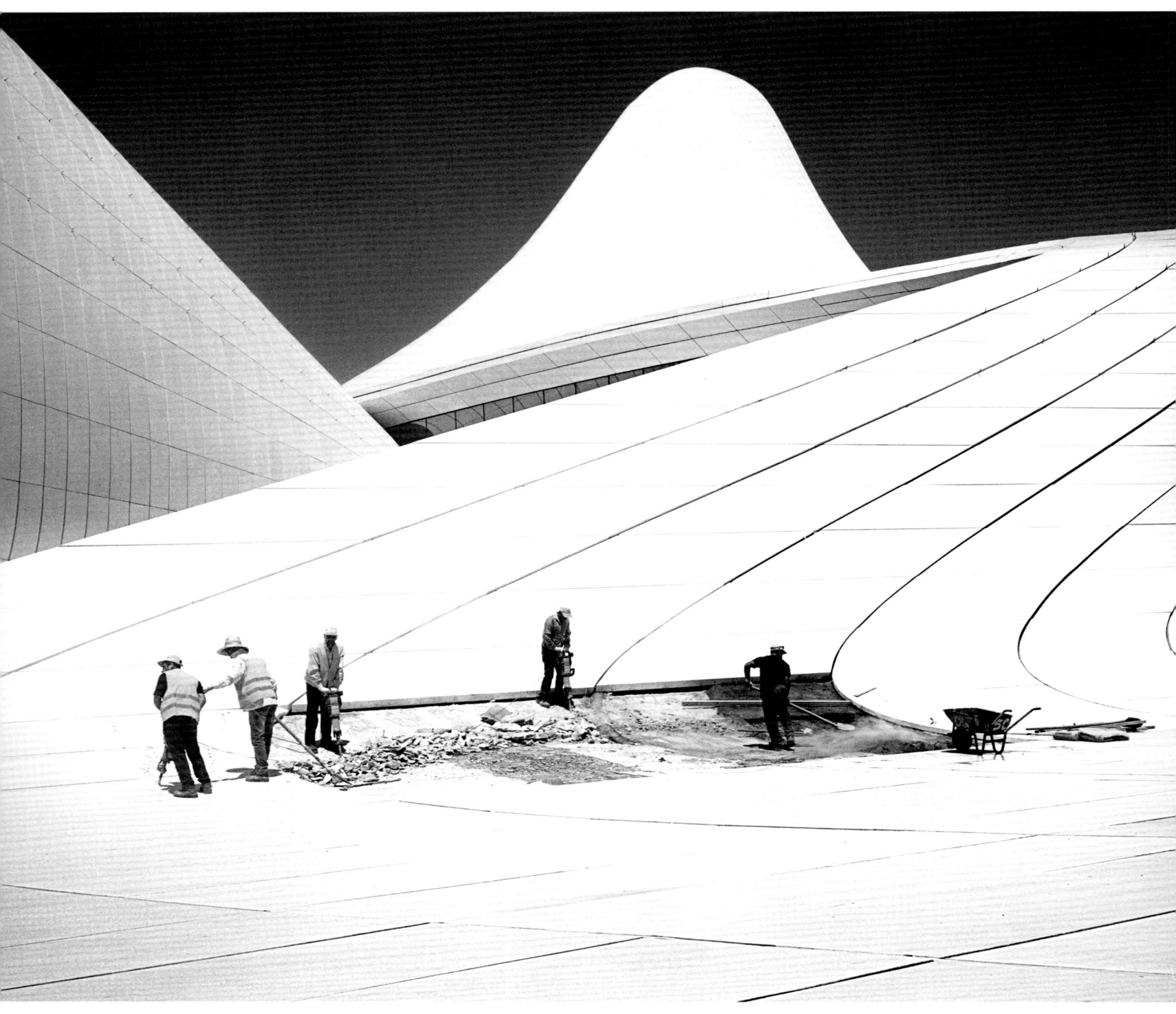

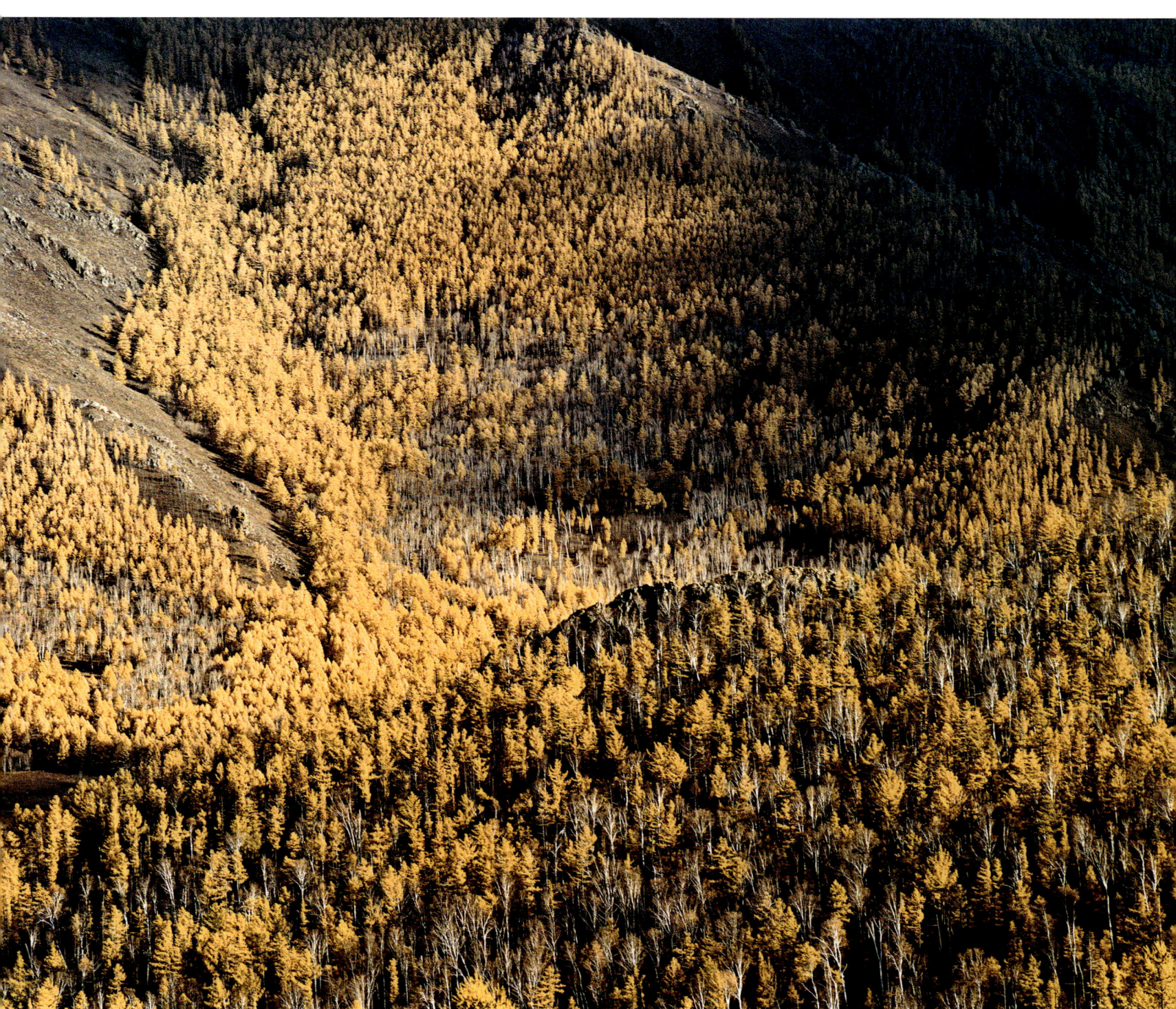

Bahamas Internet Cable
System (BICS-1) NSA/
GCHQ-Tapped Undersea
Cable, Atlantic Ocean,
2015

If you saw *Citizenfour*, Laura Poitras's Oscar-winning 2014 documentary about National Security Agency whistleblower Edward Snowden, you may have noticed Trevor Paglen's extraordinary cinematography: blurry telephoto shots of NSA headquarters and some of the most secret military installations on the planet. To gather these images, Paglen had to research the facilities, camp out at vantage points ten or more miles away, and film the complexes through ultra-high-focus lenses generally used for astrophotography. Paglen later exhibited these grainy sequences as a large, dual-channel video perversely titled *Eighty Nine Landscapes* (2015). But his earlier title for this video series, *Limit Telephotography*, better suggests the true subject of Paglen's project: the limits of seeing—and of photography itself—in our age of extreme secrecy and techno-surveillance.

The challenge implicit in Paglen's work is to represent something that is by its very nature unrepresentable: the rhizomes of digital communications that govern both global commerce and everyday life, as well as the ultrasecret methods used to tap this network for countering terrorism and for domestic spying. Snowden's NSA revelations, along with those of Julian Assange, WikiLeaks, Anonymous, and even North Korean hackers, have demonstrated the vulnerabilities and potential civil liberties violations that are rampant within this system, where complicities between paramilitary governmental agencies and commercial telecommunications providers are pervasive. But plotting the coordinates of this vast and uncharted "black world" and mapping the psychology of its cohorts require a different strategy than conventional documentary photography or photojournalism.

Paglen refers to his recent series as "postrepresentational," an adjective that seems to fit the way his work moves beyond the conventions of photographic realism. Trained as an experimental geographer, Paglen uses precise navigational charts and imprecise photographs to expose the highly vulnerable undersea cables that carry much of the global Internet traffic through certain chokepoints on the East and West Coasts of the United States—networks that the NSA has tapped. To uncover this digital communications complex, Paglen conducted extensive research into secret documents, conferred with numerous experts, charted the histories and locations of the conduits, and even learned to scuba dive so he could photograph the tubes himself. The investigatory process, which seems to be the only way to comprehend the enterprise of cyber warfare Paglen documents and pieces together, is key. In this respect, the models, maps, videos, and photographs that he exhibits are not ends in themselves, but rather by-products, presented as evidence of his research and as hypothetical tools for further inquiries.

As visible manifestations of a largely invisible and seemingly limitless communications and surveillance grid, Paglen's photographs and videos suggest a sublime banality. They are compelling images that by themselves show nothing at all, and seem to ignore debates about the beauty or veracity of photography. The algae-encrusted cables, the innocent-looking shorelines, the faraway, top secret facilities shimmer with ordinariness—such everyday scenes are relevant primarily as fragments of evidence. Like the millions of hypervisible images on Instagram or the metadata prizes of contemporary electronic surveillance, these postrepresentational photographs gain meaning not through aesthetics or pointing but rather through the steady, critical buildup of disturbing revelations.

Trevor Paglen Landing Site

Brian Wallis

Brian Wallis is the former
Director of Exhibitions
and Chief Curator of the
International Center of
Photography in New York.

This spread and overleaf:
*NSA-Tapped Fiber Optic
Cable Landing Site,
Miami Beach, Florida,
United States*, 2015

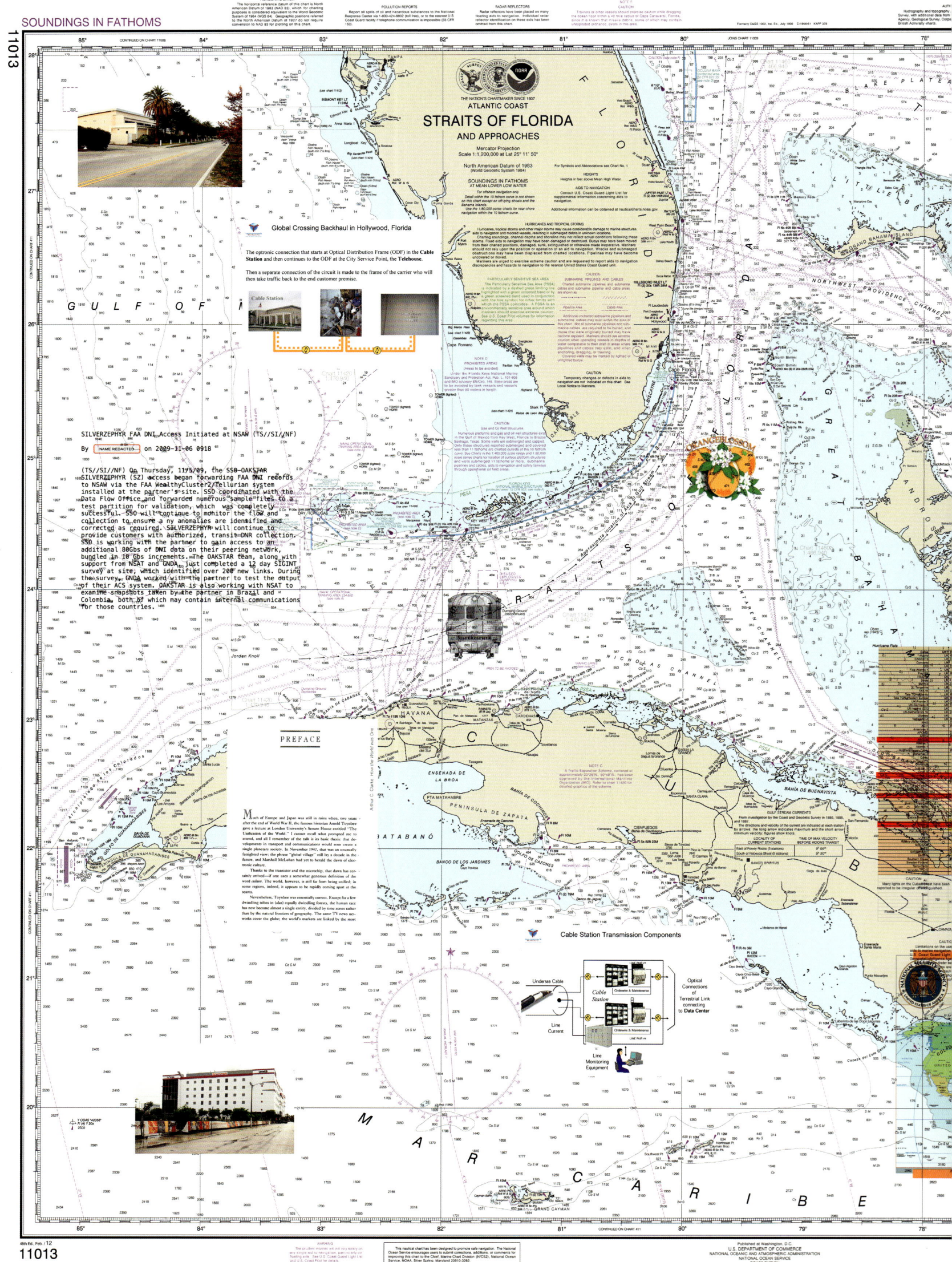

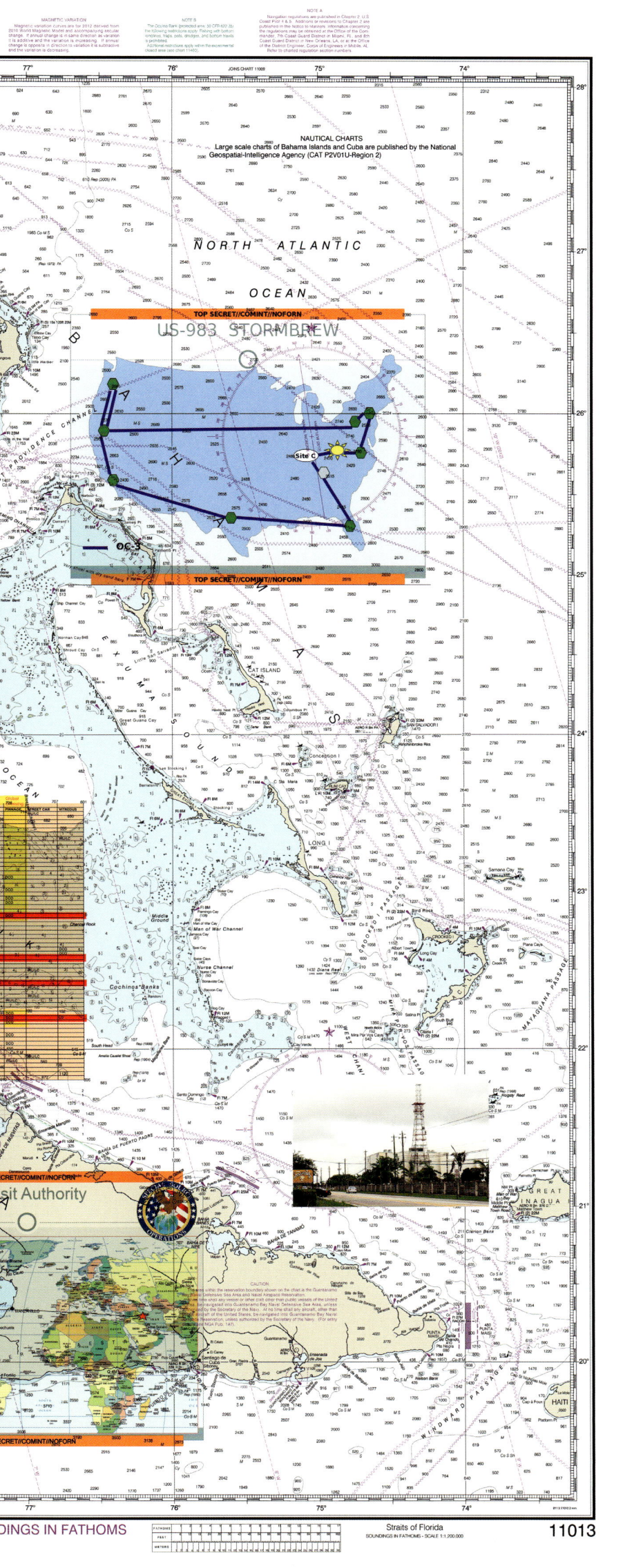

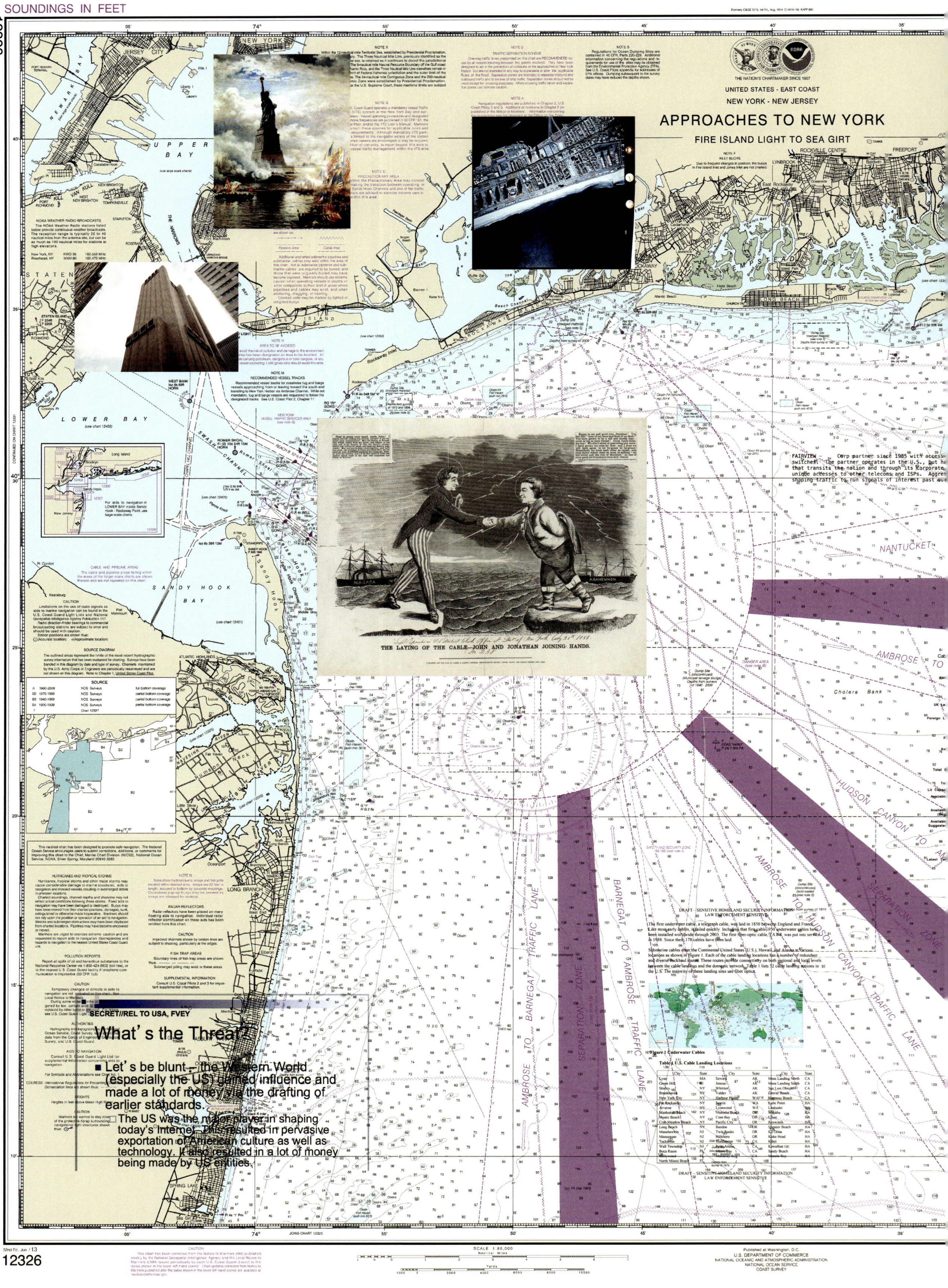

12326

UNITED STATES - EAST COAST
NEW YORK - NEW JERSEY

APPROACHES TO NEW YORK

FIRE ISLAND LIGHT TO SEA GIRT

THE LAYING OF THE CABLE—JOHN AND JONATHAN JOINING HANDS.

SECRET//REL TO USA, FVEY

What's the Threat?

■ Let's be blunt - the Western World (especially the US) gained influence and made a lot of money via the drafting of earlier standards.

☐ The US was the major player in shaping today's Internet. This resulted in pervasive exportation of American culture as well as technology. It also resulted in a lot of money being made by US entities.

SCALE 1:80,000

Published at Washington, D.C.
U.S. DEPARTMENT OF COMMERCE
NATIONAL OCEANIC AND ATMOSPHERIC ADMINISTRATION
NATIONAL OCEAN SERVICE
NATIONAL OCEAN SURVEY

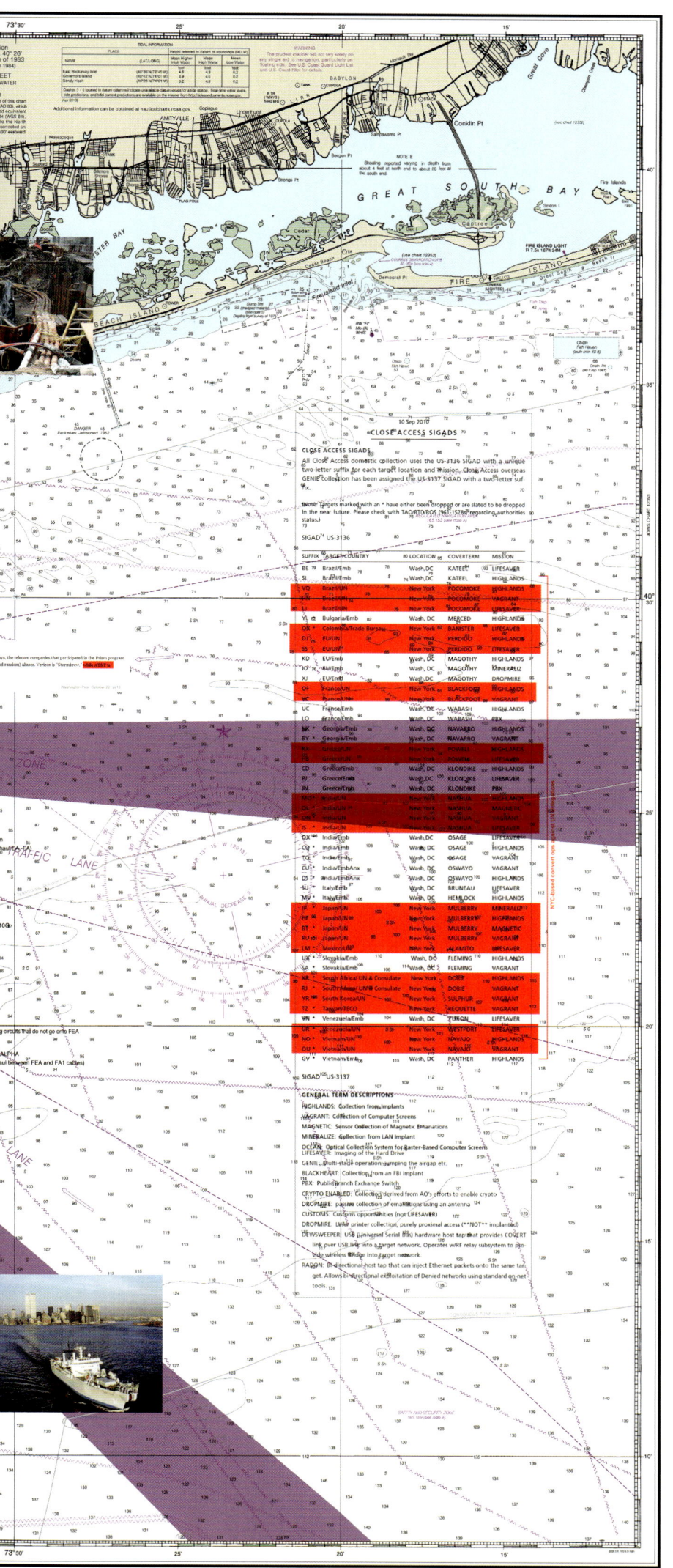

10 Sep 2010

CLOSE ACCESS SIGADS

All Close Access domestic collection uses the US-3136 SIGAD with a unique two-letter suffix for each target location and mission. Close Access overseas GENIE collection has been assigned the US-3137 SIGAD with a two-letter suffix.

(Note: Targets marked with an * have either been dropped or are slated to be dropped in the near future. Please check with TAO/RTD/ROS (961-15780 regarding authorities status.)

SIGAD: US-3136

SUFFIX	TARGET/COUNTRY	LOCATION	COVERTERM	MISSION
BE	Brazil/Emb	Wash, DC	KATEEL	LIFESAVER
SI	Brazil/UN	Wash, DC	KATEEL	HIGHLANDS
VO	Brazil/UN	New York	POCOMOKE	HIGHLANDS
	Brazil/UN	New York	POCOMOKE	VAGRANT
LI	Brazil/UN	New York	POCOMOKE	LIFESAVER
YL	Bulgaria/Emb	Wash, DC	MERCED	HIGHLANDS
QX	Colombia/Trade Bureau	New York	BANISTER	LIFESAVER
DJ	EU/UN	New York	PERDIDO	HIGHLANDS
SS	EU/UN	New York	PERDIDO	LIFESAVER
KD	EU/Emb	Wash, DC	MAGOTHY	HIGHLANDS
IO	EU/Emb	Wash, DC	MAGOTHY	MINERALIZE
XJ	EU/Emb	Wash, DC	MAGOTHY	DROPMIRE
OF	France/UN	New York	BLACKFOOT	HIGHLANDS
VC	France/UN	New York	BLACKFOOT	VAGRANT
UC	France/Emb	Wash, DC	WABASH	HIGHLANDS
LO	France/Emb	Wash, DC	WABASH	PBX
NK	Georgia/Emb	Wash, DC	NAVARRO	HIGHLANDS
BY	Georgia/Emb	Wash, DC	NAVARRO	VAGRANT
	Greece/UN	New York	POWELL	HIGHLANDS
	Greece/UN	New York	POWELL	LIFESAVER
CD	Greece/Emb	Wash, DC	KLONDIKE	HIGHLANDS
PJ	Greece/Emb	Wash, DC	KLONDIKE	LIFESAVER
JN	Greece/Emb	Wash, DC	KLONDIKE	PBX
	India/UN	New York	NASHUA	HIGHLANDS
	India/UN	New York	NASHUA	MAGNETIC
IS	India/UN	New York	NASHUA	VAGRANT
QX	India/Emb	Wash, DC	OSAGE	LIFESAVER
CQ	India/Emb	Wash, DC	OSAGE	HIGHLANDS
TQ	India/Emb	Wash, DC	OSAGE	VAGRANT
CU	India/Emb/Anx	Wash, DC	OSWAYO	HIGHLANDS
DS	India/Emb/Anx	Wash, DC	OSWAYO	VAGRANT
SU	Italy/Emb	Wash, DC	BRUNEAU	LIFESAVER
MV	Italy/Emb	Wash, DC	HEMLOCK	HIGHLANDS
	Japan/UN	New York	MULBERRY	MINERALIZE
FF	Japan/UN	New York	MULBERRY	HIGHLANDS
BT	Japan/UN	New York	MULBERRY	MAGNETIC
EU	Japan/UN	New York	MULBERRY	VAGRANT
LM	Mexico/UN	New York	ALAMITO	LIFESAVER
UX	Slovakia/Emb	Wash, DC	FLEMING	HIGHLANDS
SA	Slovakia/Emb	Wash, DC	FLEMING	VAGRANT
HR	South Africa/UN & Consulate	New York	DOBIE	HIGHLANDS
R3	South Korea/UN & Consulate	New York	DOBIE	VAGRANT
YR	South Korea/UN	New York	SULPHUR	VAGRANT
TZ	Taiwan/TECO	New York	REQUETTE	VAGRANT
VN	Venezuela/Emb	Wash, DC	YUKON	LIFESAVER
UR	Venezuela/UN	New York	WESTPORT	LIFESAVER
NO	Vietnam/UN	New York	NAVAJO	HIGHLANDS
OU	Vietnam/UN	New York	NAVAJO	VAGRANT
GV	Vietnam/Emb	Wash, DC	PANTHER	HIGHLANDS

SIGAD: US-3137

GENERAL TERM DESCRIPTIONS

HIGHLANDS: Collection from Implants
VAGRANT: Collection of Computer Screens
MAGNETIC: Sensor Collection of Magnetic Emanations
MINERALIZE: Collection from LAN Implant
OCEAN: Optical Collection System for Raster-Based Computer Screens
LIFESAVER: Imaging of the Hard Drive
GENIE: Multi-stage operation; jumping the airgap etc.
BLACKHEART: Collection from an FBI Implant
PBX: Public Branch Exchange Switch
CRYPTO ENABLED: Collection derived from AO's efforts to enable crypto
DROPMIRE: passive collection of emanations using an antenna
CUSTOMS: Customs opportunities (not LIFESAVER)
DROPMIRE: Laser printer collection, purely proximal access (**NOT** implanted)
DEWSWEEPER: USB (Universal Serial Bus) hardware host tap that provides COVERT link over USB link into a target network. Operates w/RF relay subsystem to provide wireless Bridge into target network.
RADON: Bi-directional host tap that can inject Ethernet packets onto the same target. Allows bi-directional exploitation of Denied networks using standard on-net tools.

SOUNDINGS IN FEET

Fire Island Light to Sea Girt
SOUNDINGS IN FEET · SCALE 1:80,000

12326

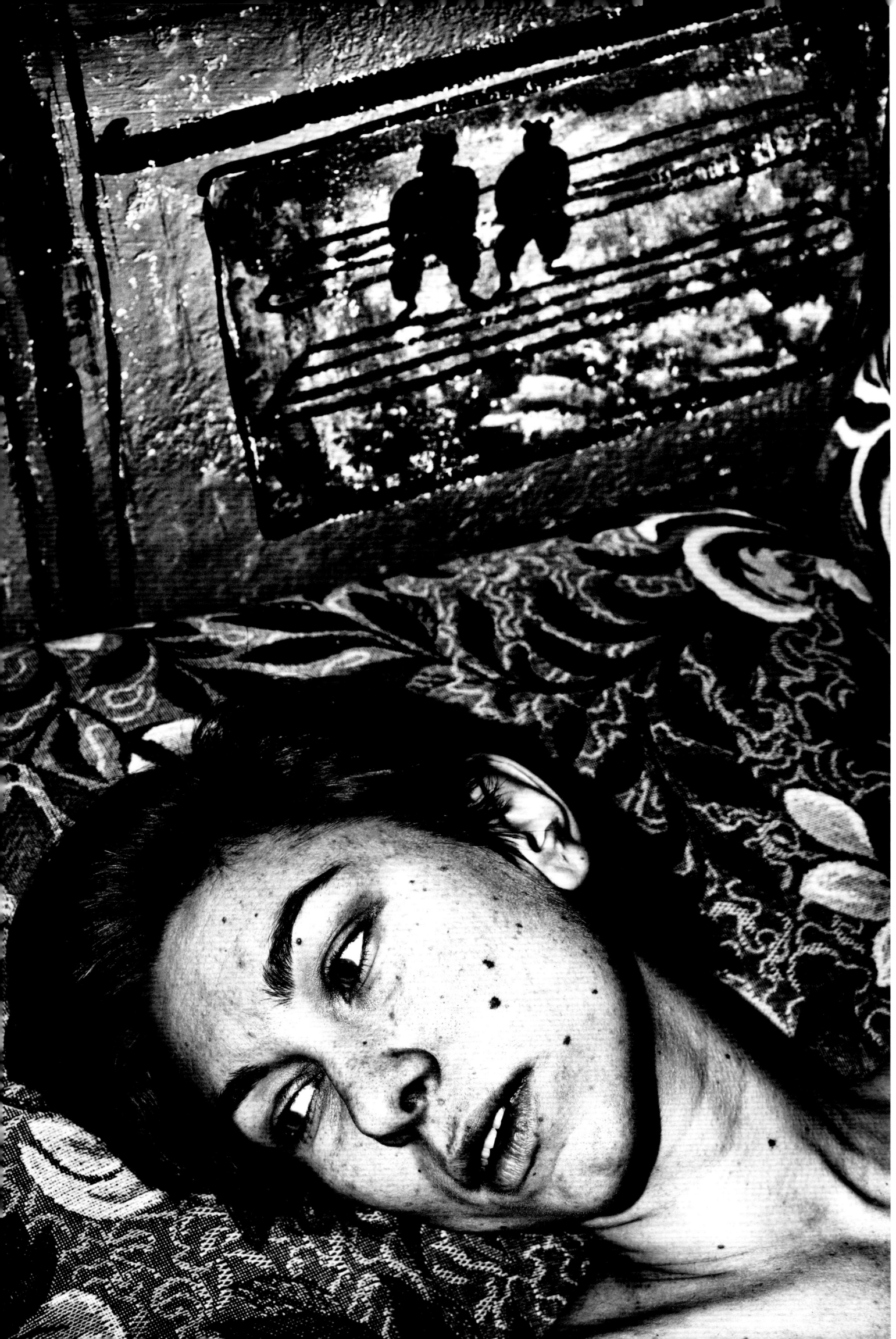

Fierce eyed in their filmy black dresses and off-the-shoulder numbers, the girls of Ulaanbaatar were strutting down the corridors of the gleaming new Shangri-La Hotel last August as if in Bangkok or Shanghai. Some were carrying bags from the shiny Vuitton outlet down the street; others had no doubt been pastoralists on the grasslands just years before. Every time the branch train of the Trans-Siberian Railway stops in the Mongolian capital, fresh faces—new thoughts of faraway worlds—flood out to transform a world of horses and heart-stopping emptiness. "You know," a Mongolian friend said to me just before heading to the bar Naadam, "Genghis Khan was the WTO of the thirteenth century." What he didn't need to say was that what used to be a trade of spices and tea is now very often one of promises and dreams.

As I sauntered among the Thai massage joints and "Vegas" nightclubs of Ulaanbaatar last summer, I might have been in the stark and sometimes unsettling world that Jacob Aue Sobol has made his own. Since 2012, on one month-long trip after another, the Danish wanderer has been opening up a boldly contemporary Asia, as he rides the Trans-Siberian and its branch lines, taking us into Chinese, Russian, and Mongolian lives. At every stage, we feel not just the textures of societies in transition, but something inward and very private on the far side of the tracks. The mixed feelings of a traveler slipping out after a quickie, the unease of arriving in a place that is itself on the move (or even, in Mongolia, on the hunt). The view not through the window of the celebrated train, but from within a shuttered room, looking back.

It's easy—perhaps too easy—to say that the tourist wants to go somewhere while the traveler likes to linger. The tourist hopes to catch something through his lens, while the traveler seeks to surrender, even to be claimed by a surprise in very real life. Yet Sobol's work goes even deeper than most travelers, by seeing what is left behind when the train pulls out, and by seeking out the shadows, the unintended consequences, of a journey that leads not just to discovery but confrontation. Though the title of his ongoing series is *Arrivals and Departures*, he clearly has little interest in the names and times listed on railway-station announcement boards. Destinations are less important to him than those feelings—of guilt, of disquiet, of wanderlust—that arise whenever a wayfarer draws close enough to a local to feel (or impart) real hurt. I think of Jackson Browne's haunting line about running for a morning flight "through the whispered promises and the changing light / Of the bed where we both lie." With the emphasis on "lie."

As a traveler through the alleyways of contemporary urban Asia for the past thirty-two years, I've always sought out those scenes that can't be caught on any screen. I've been interested in why, a few miles from the wind-whipped silences of Mongolia, a "Luxury Nail Spa" is opening amid crowds of Dubai-worthy glass towers, and why Mongolian Airlines is showing *Two Night Stand*, of all Hollywood comedies, as we fly into the land of Genghis Khan. But looking at Sobol's work, I'm reminded of how we writers will always lag behind: it's not so much that a picture is worth a thousand words as that it can grasp a thousand silences. The unspoken moment; the impenitent stare; every murmur or grunt or tremor that no words can begin to transcribe. In the age of the selfie, Sobol's camera looks out—and finds a brazenness that conceals at least as much as reticence does.

In China, bullet trains are being built to travel over 300 miles per hour; coming in from the airport in Shanghai, I rode a Maglev train that whisks passengers past avenues of skyscrapers at 268 miles per hour. In Russia, the ghostly gray monuments of Leninism have given way, almost overnight, to over-the-top dance clubs and, in Moscow alone, eight separate Rolex outlets. Even in Mongolia, I found last summer, the memory of the worldly conquerors known as the Golden Horde is being trumped by the prospect of hoarded gold. Yes, Sobol's inky black-and-whites take us past the glitter of the twenty-first-century Silk Road into more uncertain moments that recall the elemental, even predatory street poetry of Daido Moriyama or Jack Kerouac. This comes from having the patience to step off the train and walk slowly into the lives and bewildering landscapes all around.

These images stay with me in part because they give back so little, and what they do give back is not consoling. They're antisnapshots of a kind about the displacing truth of travel—that places are often resistant to our gaze, and the deeper we enter them, the more we lose all sense of where we are. In this context, the stress on Trans-Siberian Railway falls emphatically on "Trans"—the sense of movement, of crossing frontiers, of stepping toward a human contact that will always remain out of reach. Less transcendence, you might say, than transgression. And—as in the most memorable trips—no answers, but questions that keep on turning inside of you, forever.

Jacob Aue Sobol
Arrivals and Departures

Pico Iyer

All photographs China, Mongolia, and Russia, 2012
© Jacob Aue Sobol and courtesy Magnum Photos and Yossi Milo Gallery, New York

Pico Iyer is the author, most recently, of *The Art of Stillness* (2014).

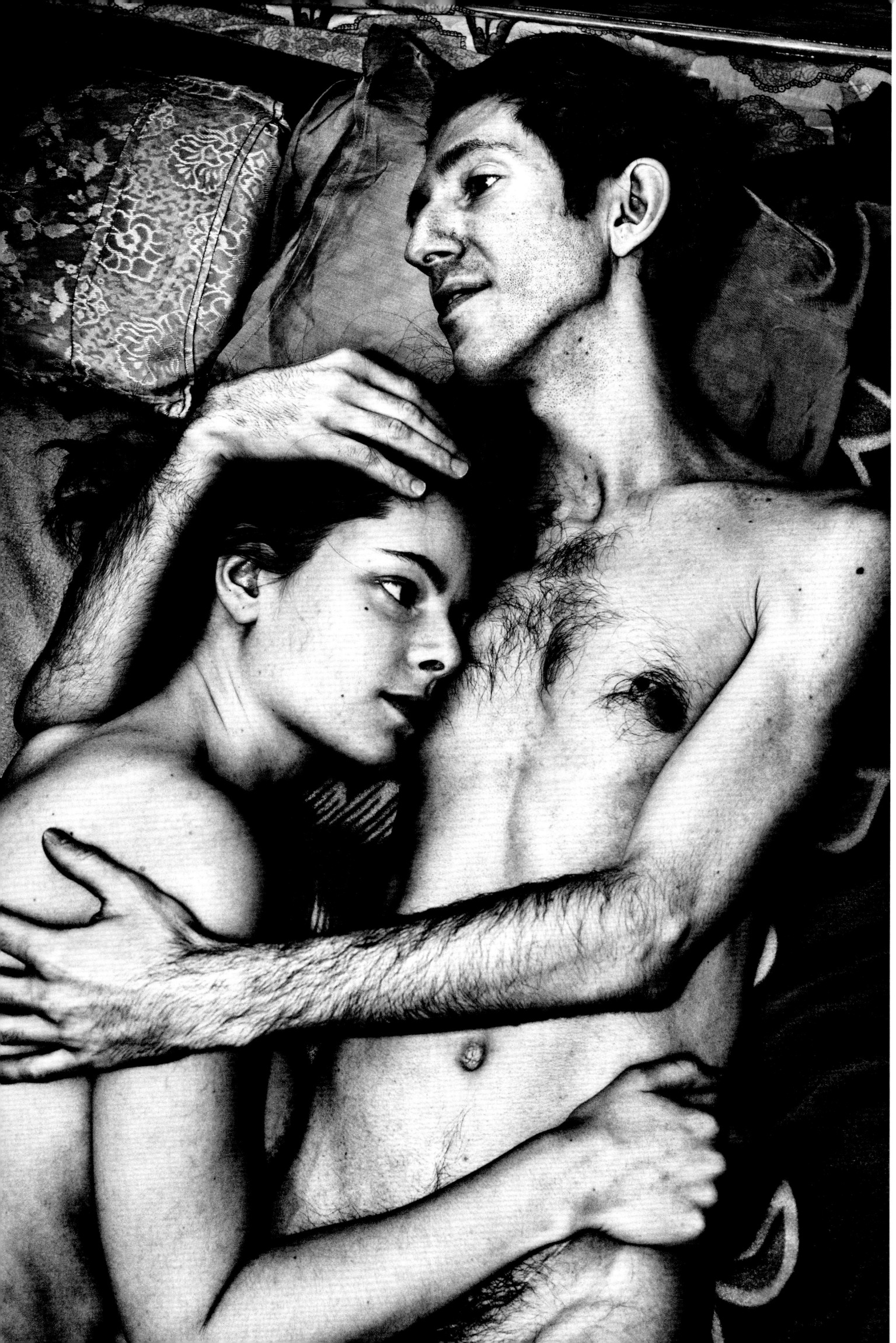

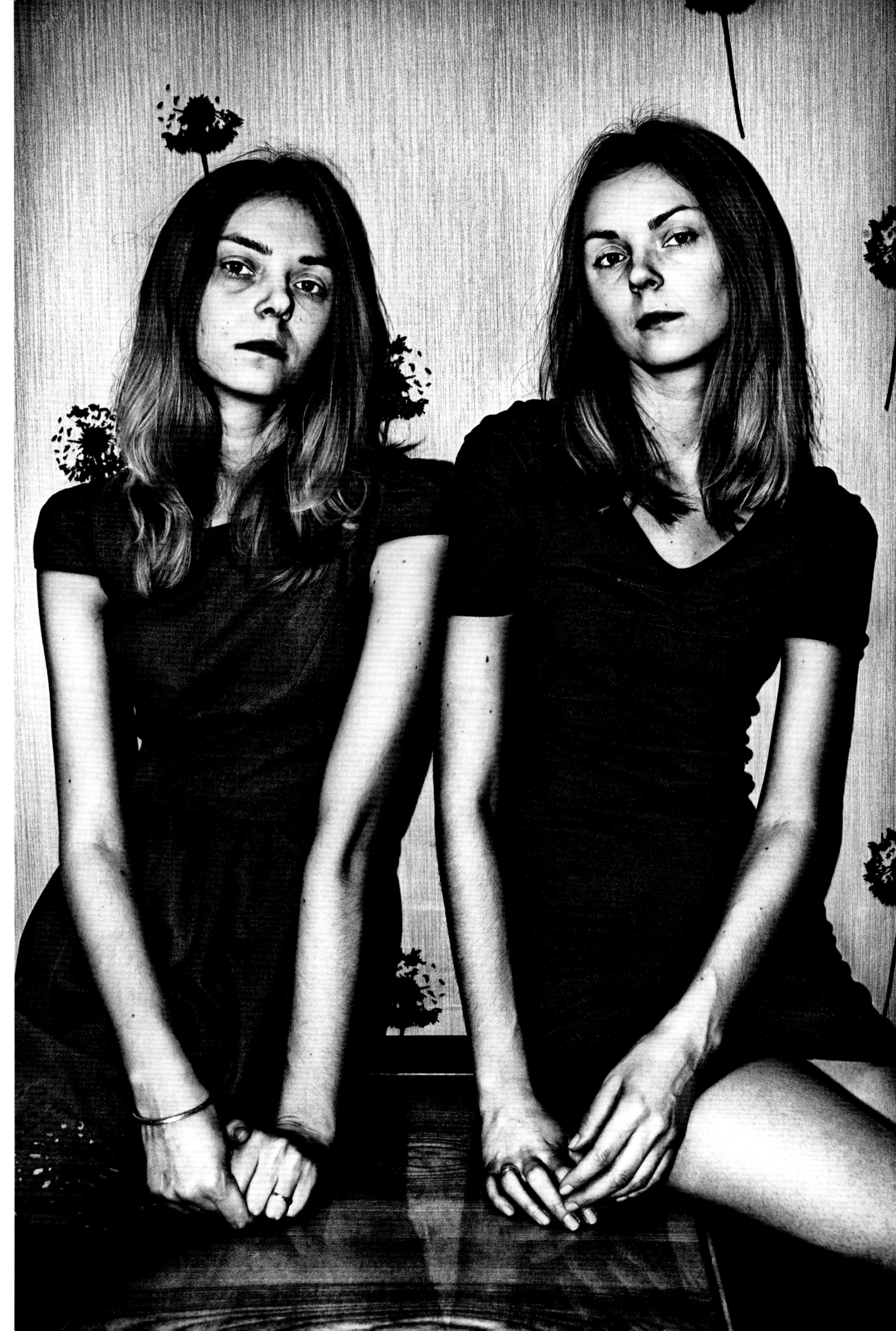

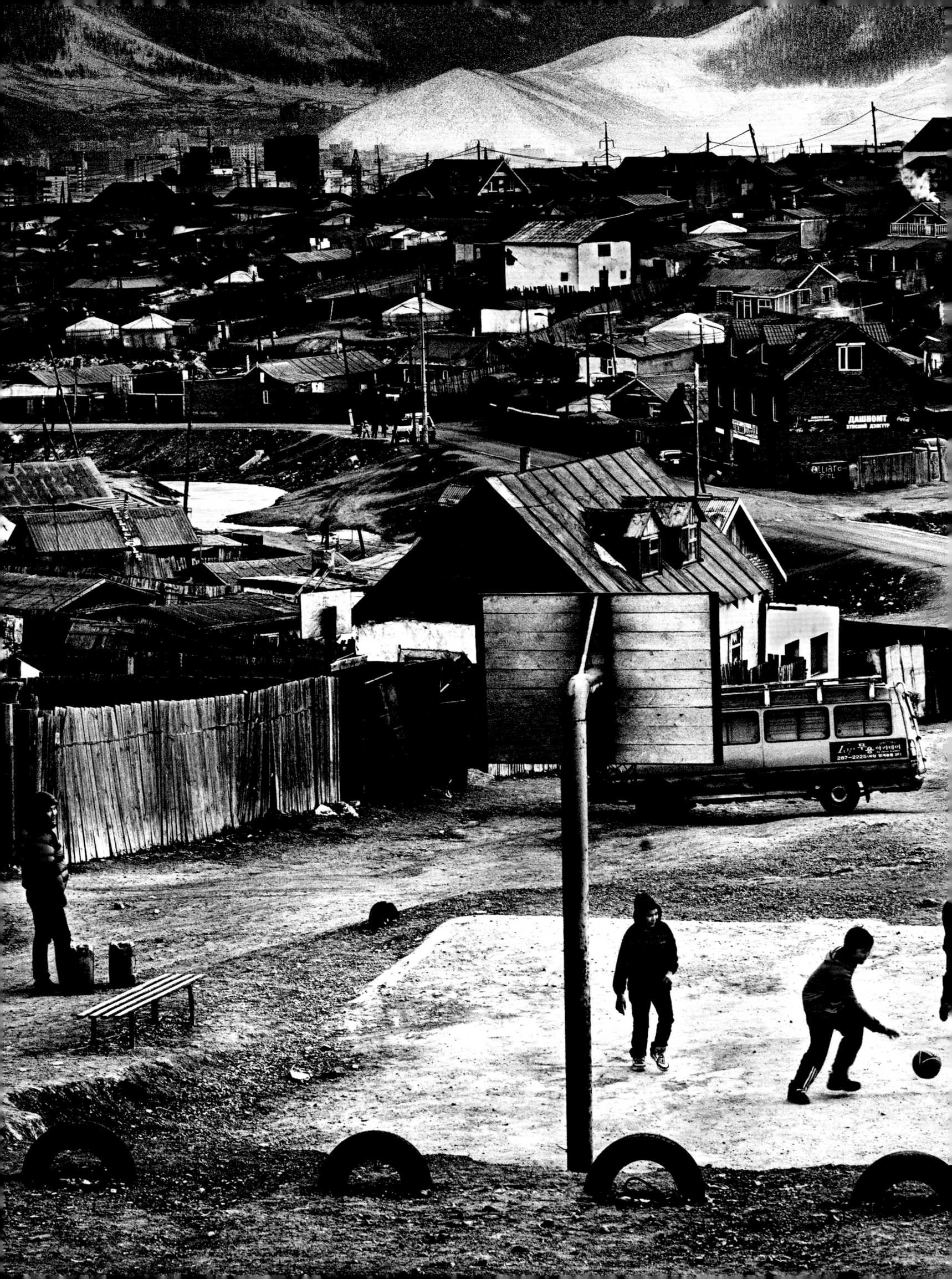

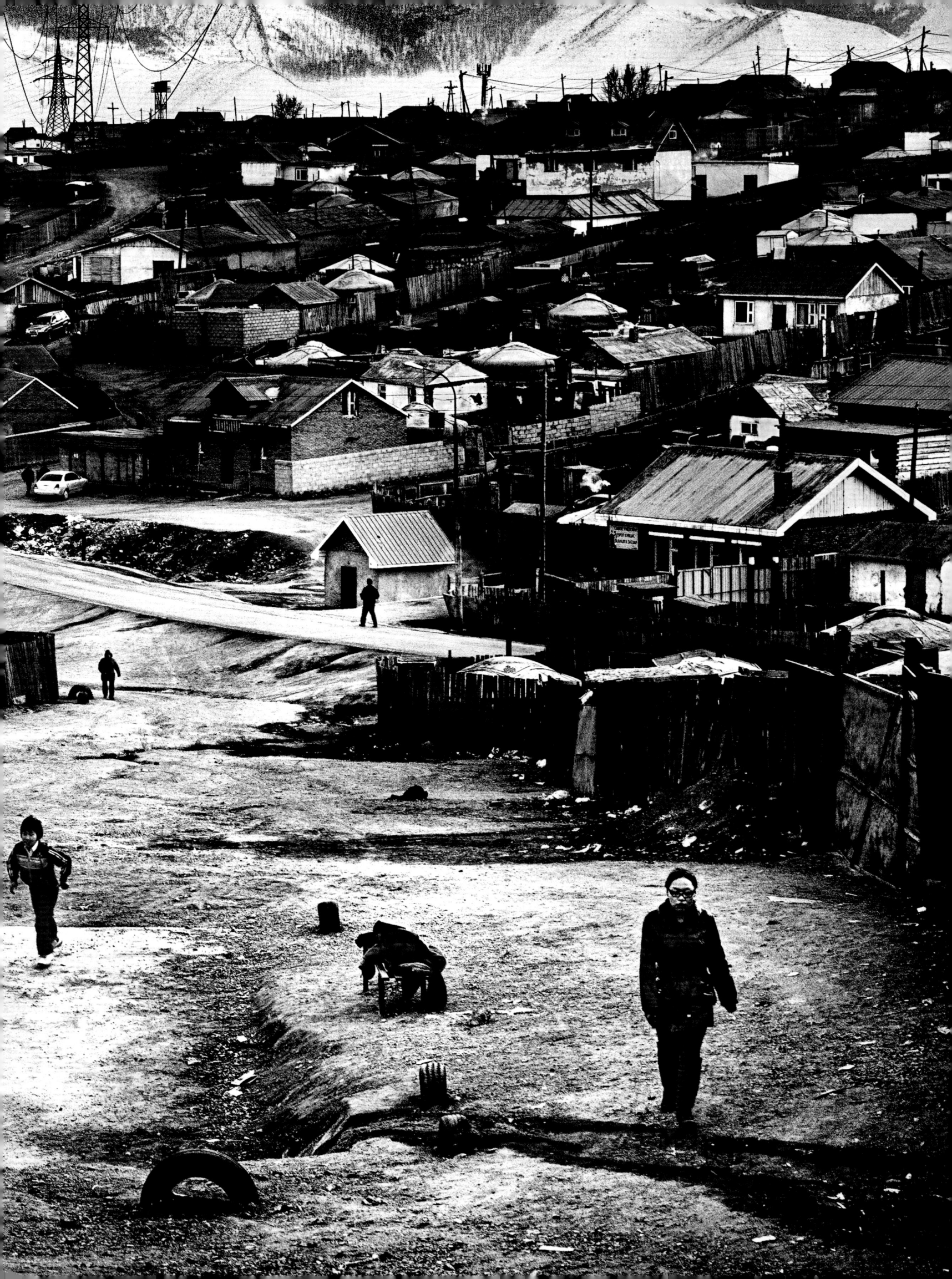

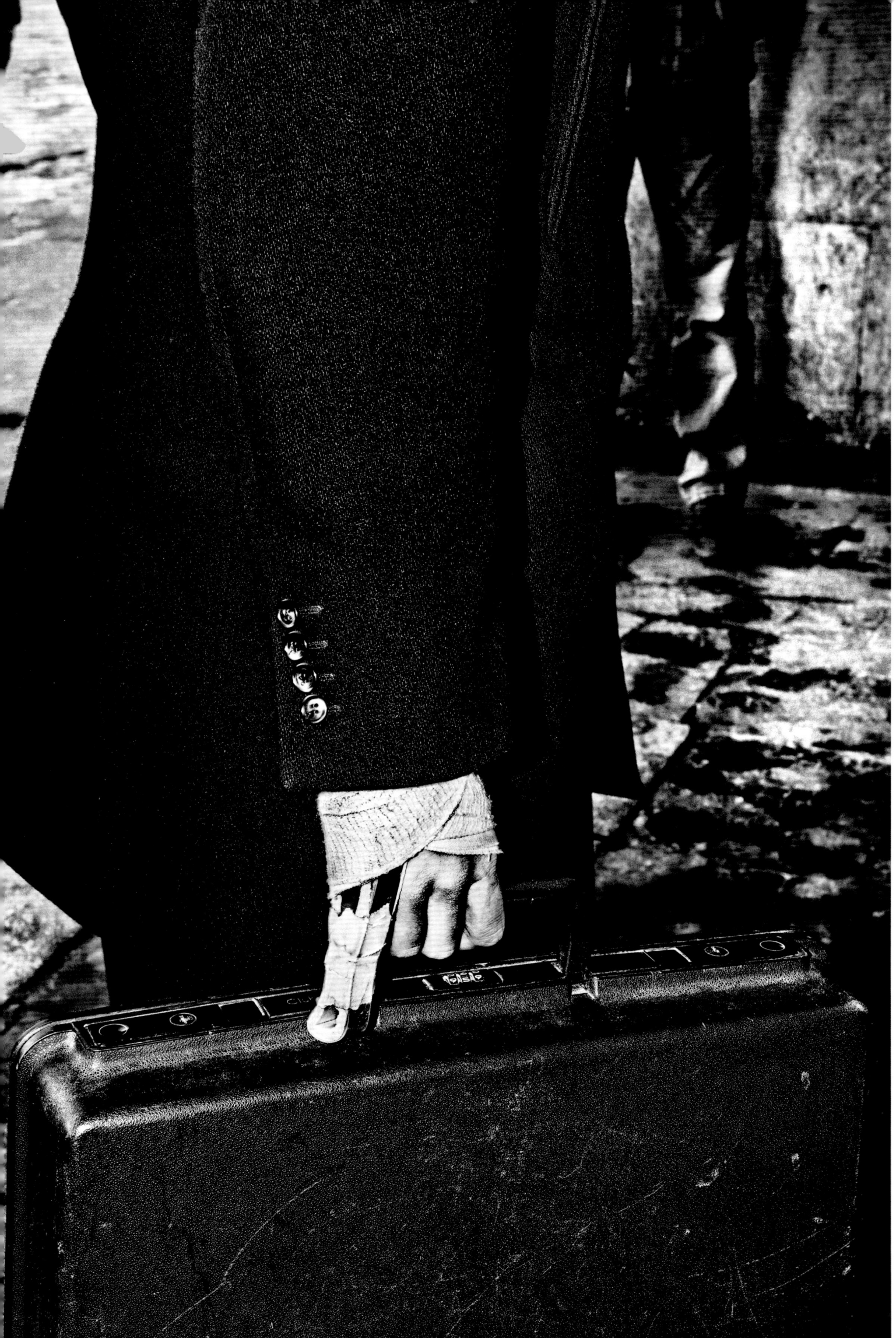

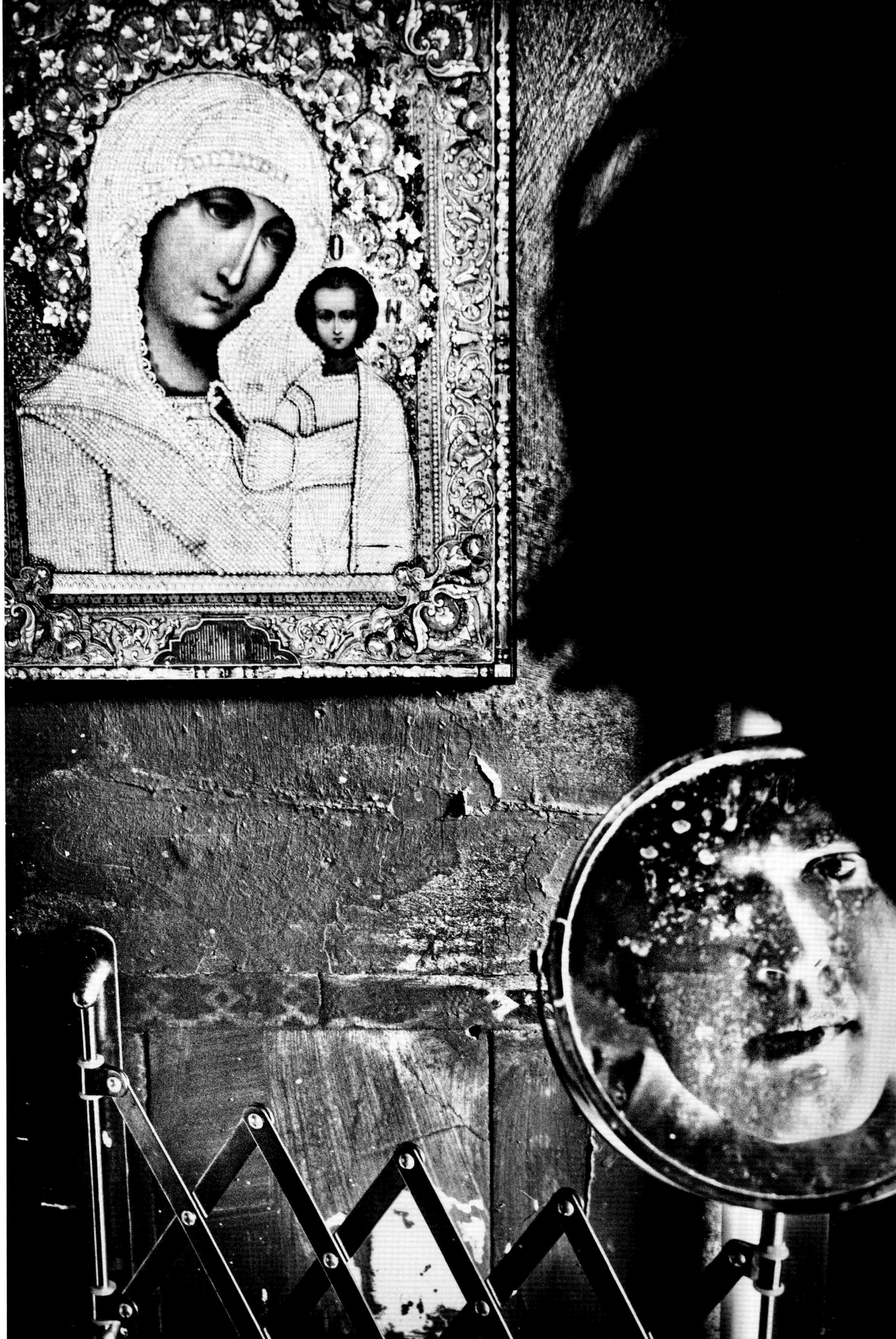

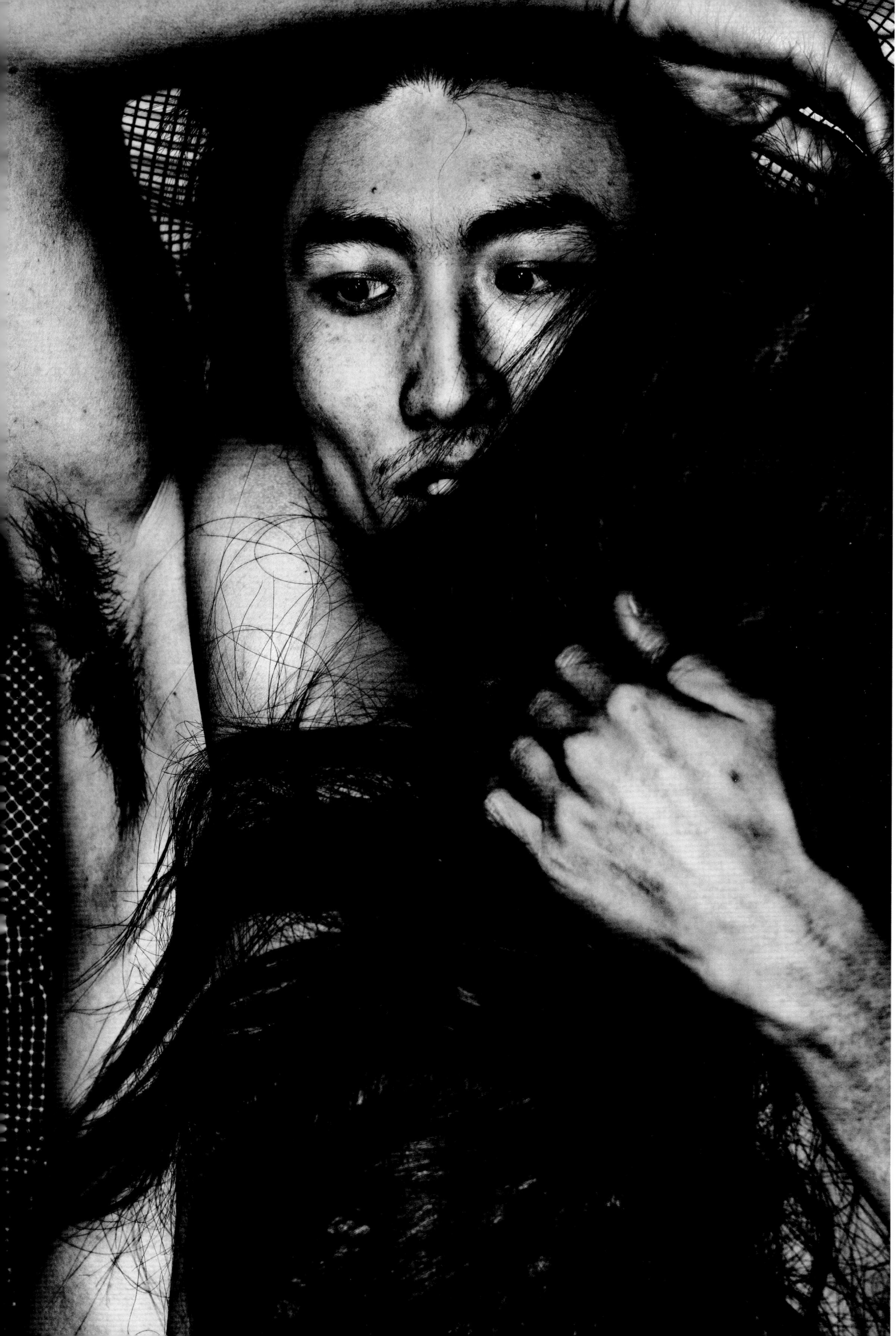

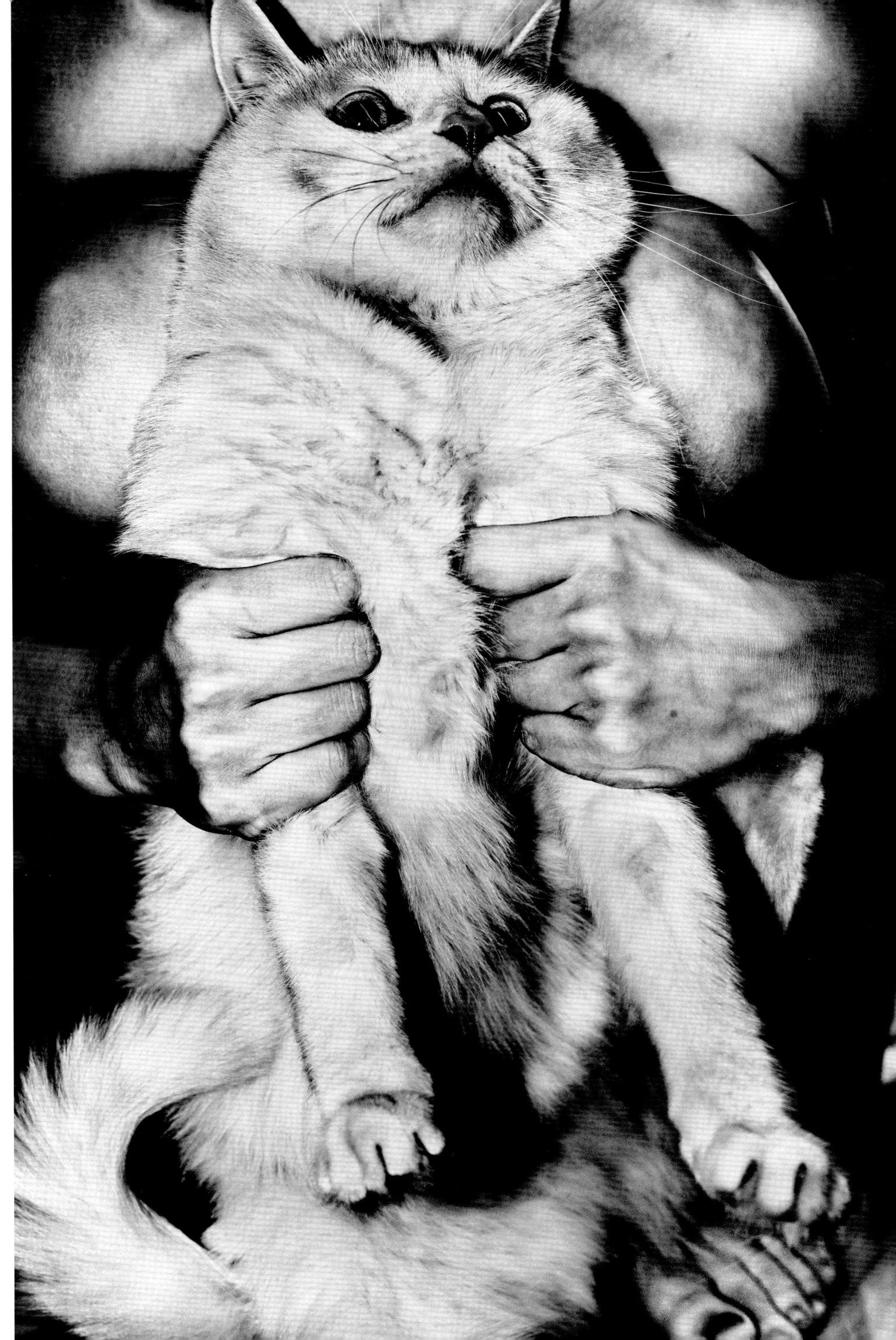

Carly Steinbrunn's *The Voyage of Discovery* begins with a reproduced reproduction of a photograph that shows two brightly lit rocks propped up against a wall. One is a deep gray tending toward black, the other a light gray tending toward creamy white. The two together form a broken compound of separate elements, or represent diametric extremes of light and dark: they are both opposite and integrally related objects under the scrutiny of the camera's lens.

The Voyage of Discovery, published in 2015, comprises appropriated and authored images that deal with the interlinking uses of photography as a means to construct knowledge and as a vehicle for the thrill of escape and discovery. The photographs address photography's historic utility to an exploration of the present that excites changing notions of the future. Thus *Cliffs* depicts the White Cliffs of Dover cropped into the shape of an oval, which figuratively recalls magic lantern slides and stereographs, as well as the relationship of imagery to the expansionism of nineteenth-century Europe. Other photographs have been colorized, or flaunt the pixelation that results from their appropriation; these show stormy tropical scenes, ancient flint heads, traditional costumes, exotic flowers, and the scarred profile of a Bobo tribesman.

Notably, Steinbrunn depicts the English landscape as a site of discovery. This subtle gesture inverts the hierarchy of imperialism and exploration, so that the appetitive gaze of colonial Britain is turned back upon its homeland, suggesting that the photographs might study the centers of power as producers of the exoticism of the periphery.

Steinbrunn develops a subtle critique in measured gestures, titling a landscape of thick foliage *Jungle*, despite the clearly visible grate and tall perimeter fence in the back of the frame. The whiteness of the hand that grasps the tiny foot of a baby gorilla in *Gorilla Foot* intimates the problem of control, the decontextualized nature of observation, and the differentiating function of race as integral to the production of anthropological knowledge. *Iguazu Falls* relays the extraordinary power of natural forces in a dark, compressed landscape view, while its location, at the border between Argentina and Brazil, points toward European imperial history and the Guarani tribespeople who first discovered and named the falls.

With the exception of the caption list and colophon, the only text in the book is a quotation from *Tristes Tropiques* (1955), by the French anthropologist and ethnographer Claude Lévi-Strauss. In his seminal travelogue, Lévi-Strauss laments his historically circumscribed inability to see with sufficient capaciousness, and reproaches himself for that failure while confessing to the pain he is caused "by everything I see." In Steinbrunn's images, each provided with a brief nomenclature, we see specimens of natural history (*Okapi*), ancient scrolls riddled with lost languages (*Parchment*), visionary modernist architecture (*Brasília*), and moments of interplanetary travel (*Rocket*). Such images celebrate the complex beauty of the natural world, while also invoking the hubris of grand ambitions.

These pictures interrogate Eurocentric exploration, pointing up the excision of conquest and slavery from the Western narrative of discovery. This approach brings pivotal erasures into view, but in a tempered fashion that depends (perhaps precariously) on the rigorous attentiveness of the viewer. Steinbrunn's reflexive examination of photography's role in the contested history of exploration requires a willingness to read caption against image, in order to separate implicit metaphor from apparent subject, and address oneself to the underlying critique. In the absence of such effort, *The Voyage of Discovery* risks a repetition of the history it interrogates. We must work to see the gaps pictured in this history of discovery in order to envision a future that includes those who have been historically dispossessed.

Carly Steinbrunn
The Voyage of Discovery

Stanley Wolukau-Wanambwa

Stanley Wolukau-Wanambwa is a photographer, a writer, and the editor of *The Great Leap Sideways*.

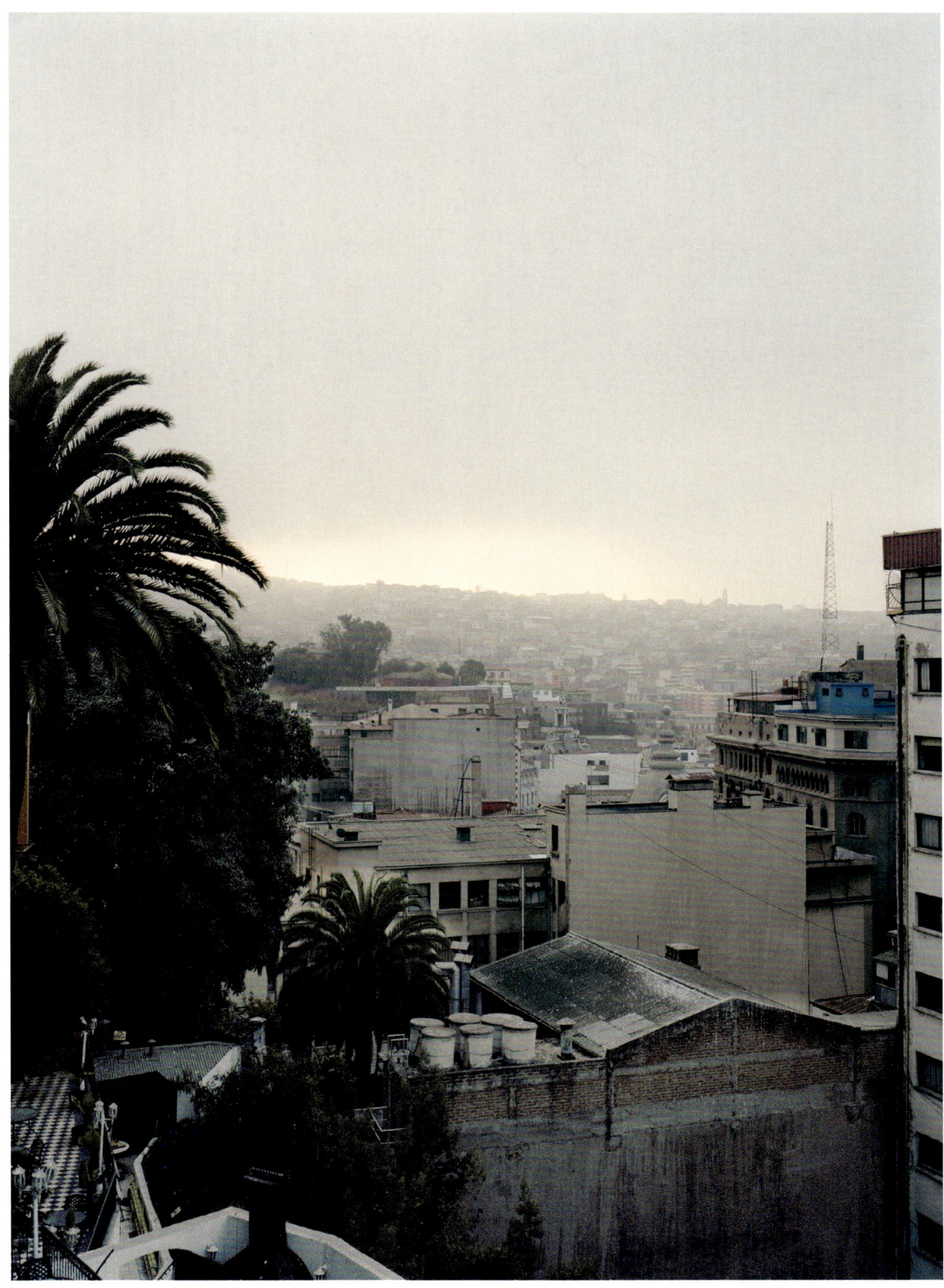

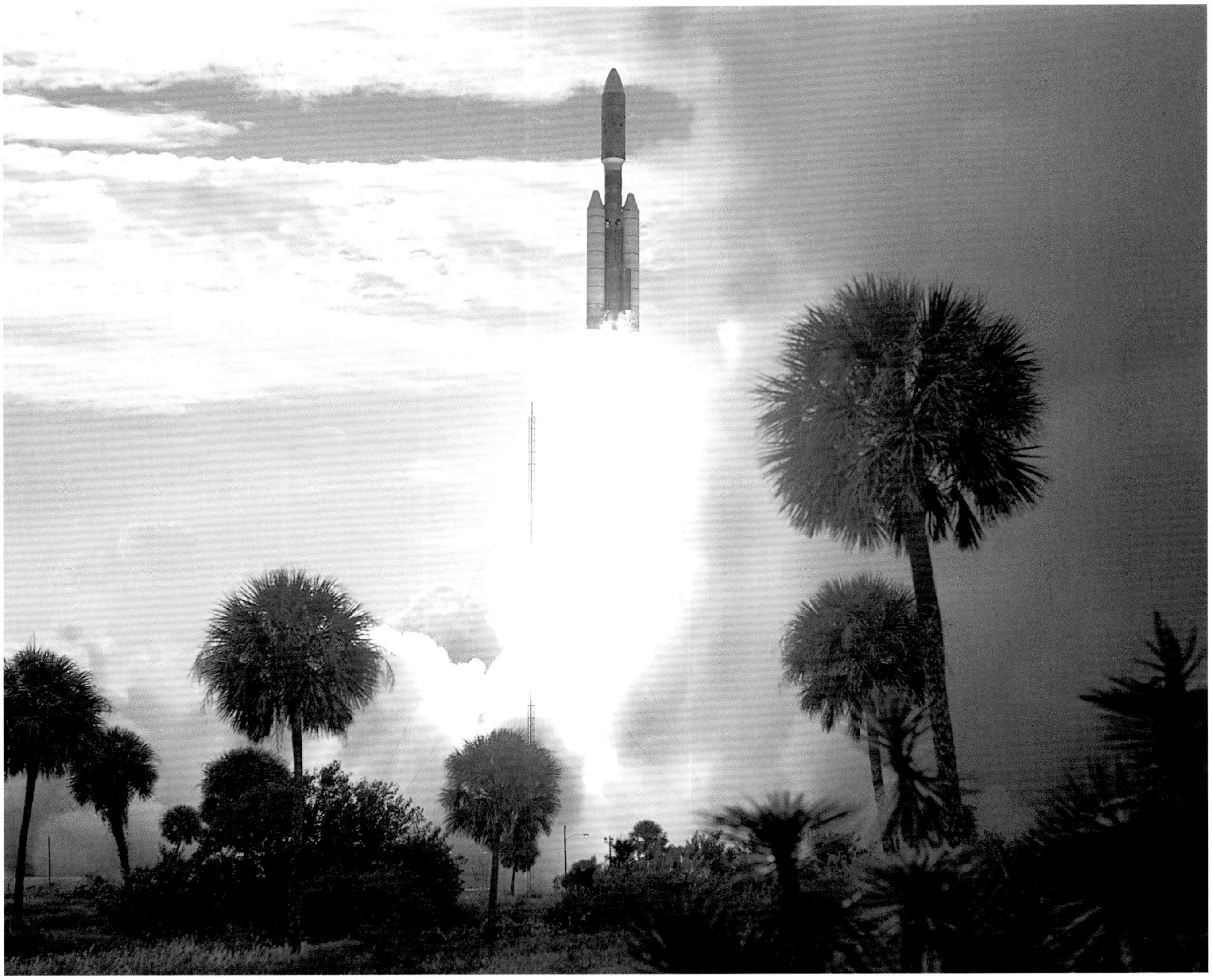

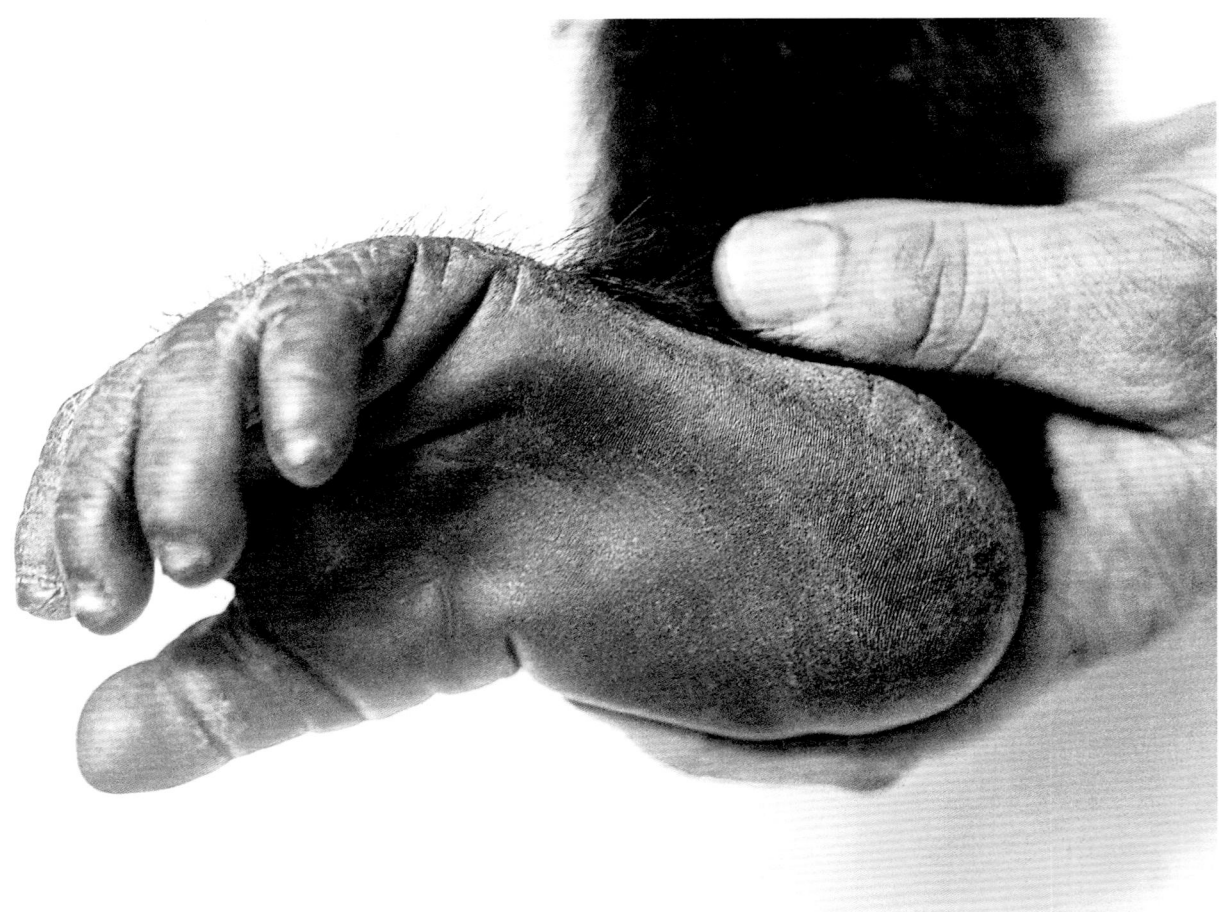

Opposite, top:
Rocket, 2011

Opposite, bottom:
Gorilla Foot, 2013

This page:
Butterfly, 2013

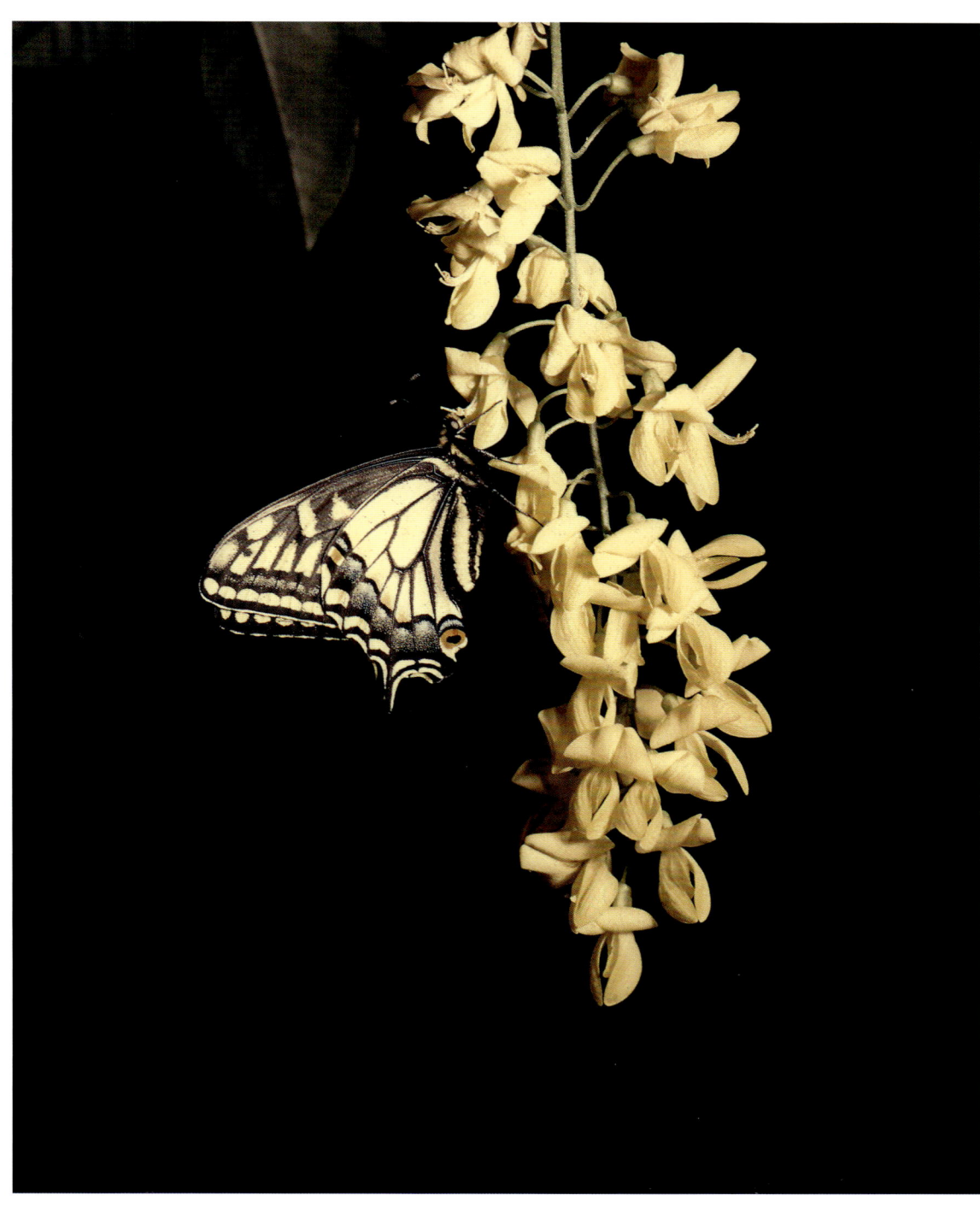

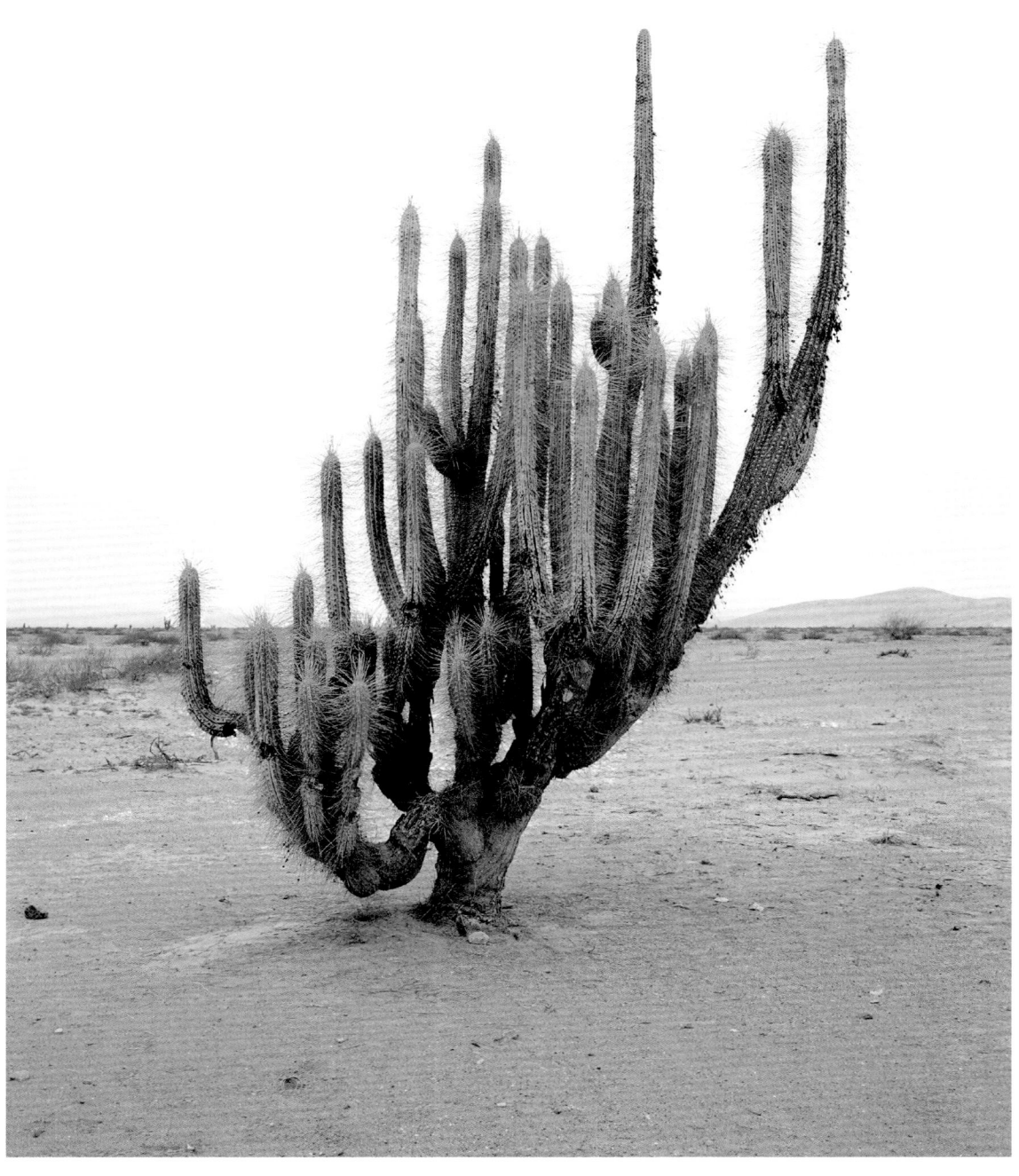

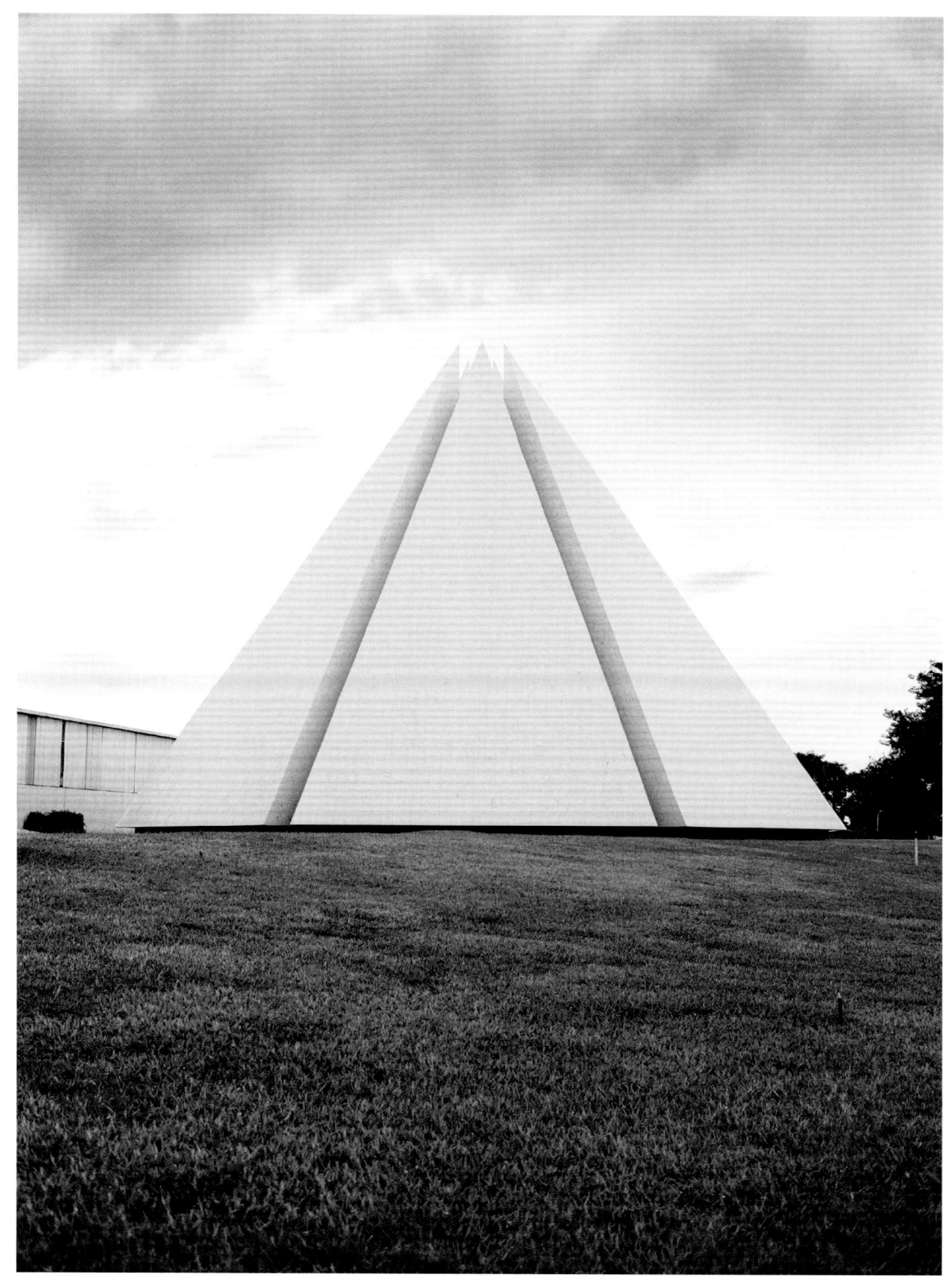

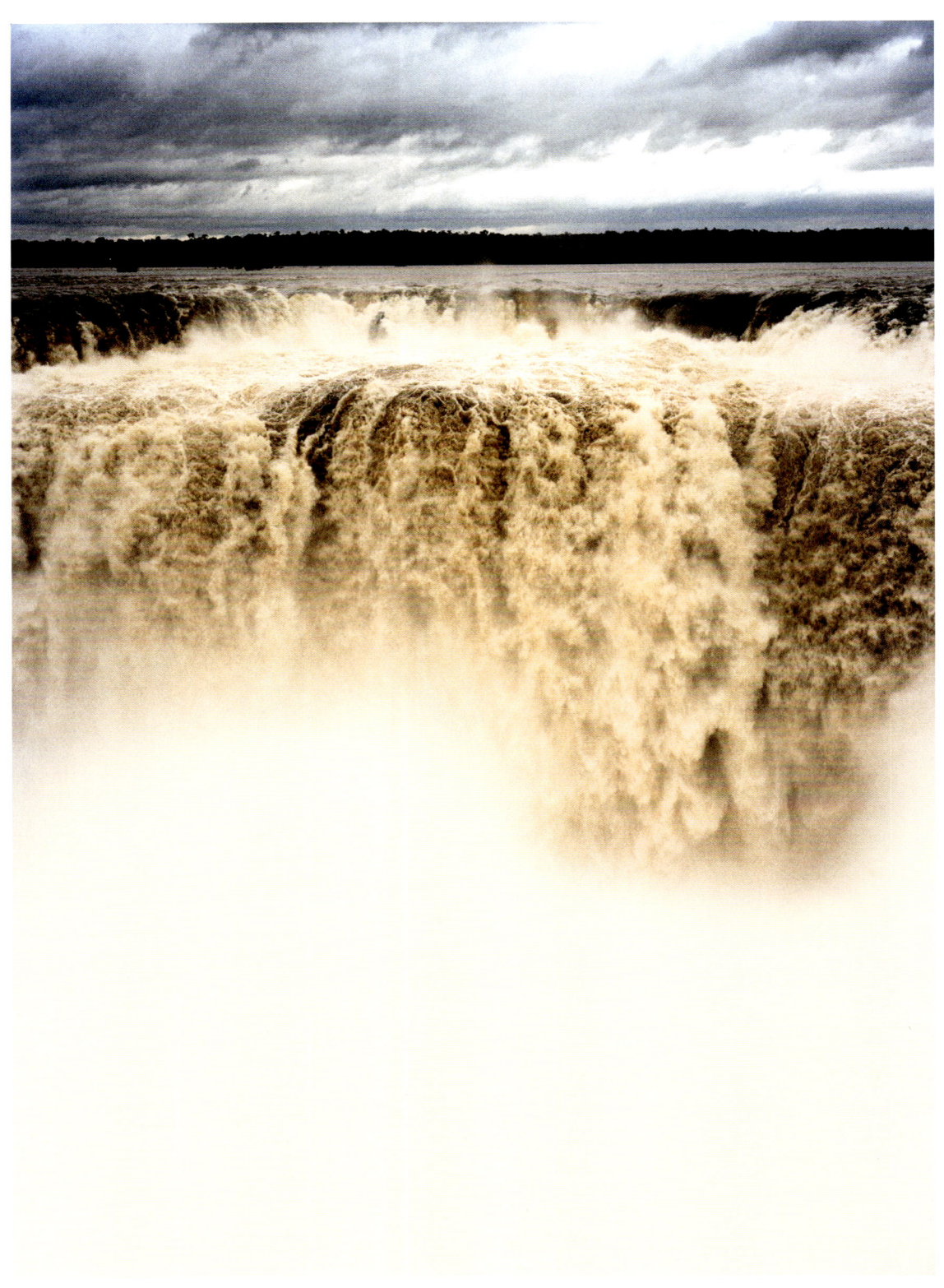

Opposite:
Iguazu Falls, **2013**

This page:
Boeing, **2011**
All photographs from
the series *The Voyage
of Discovery,* 2015
Courtesy the artist
and MACK

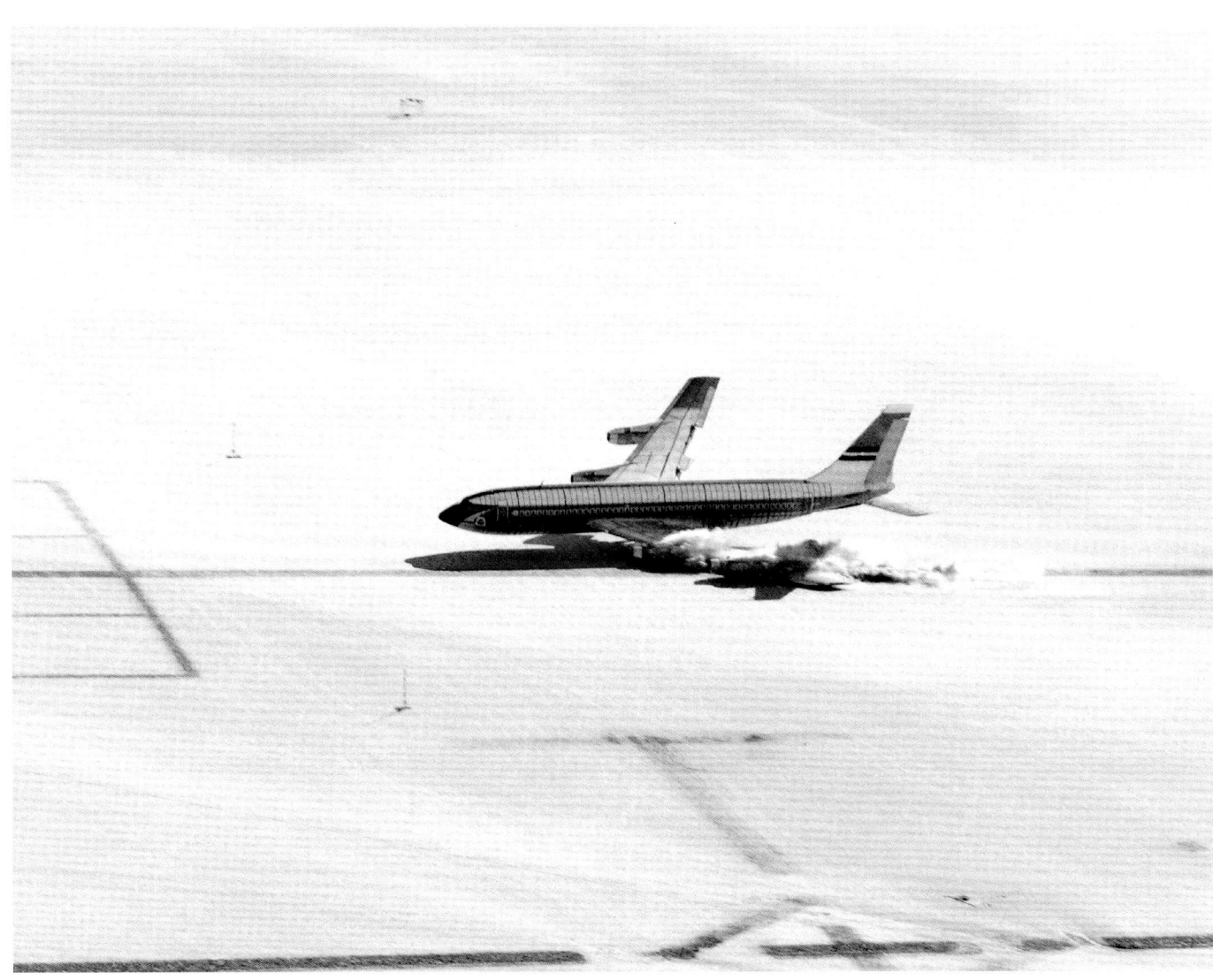

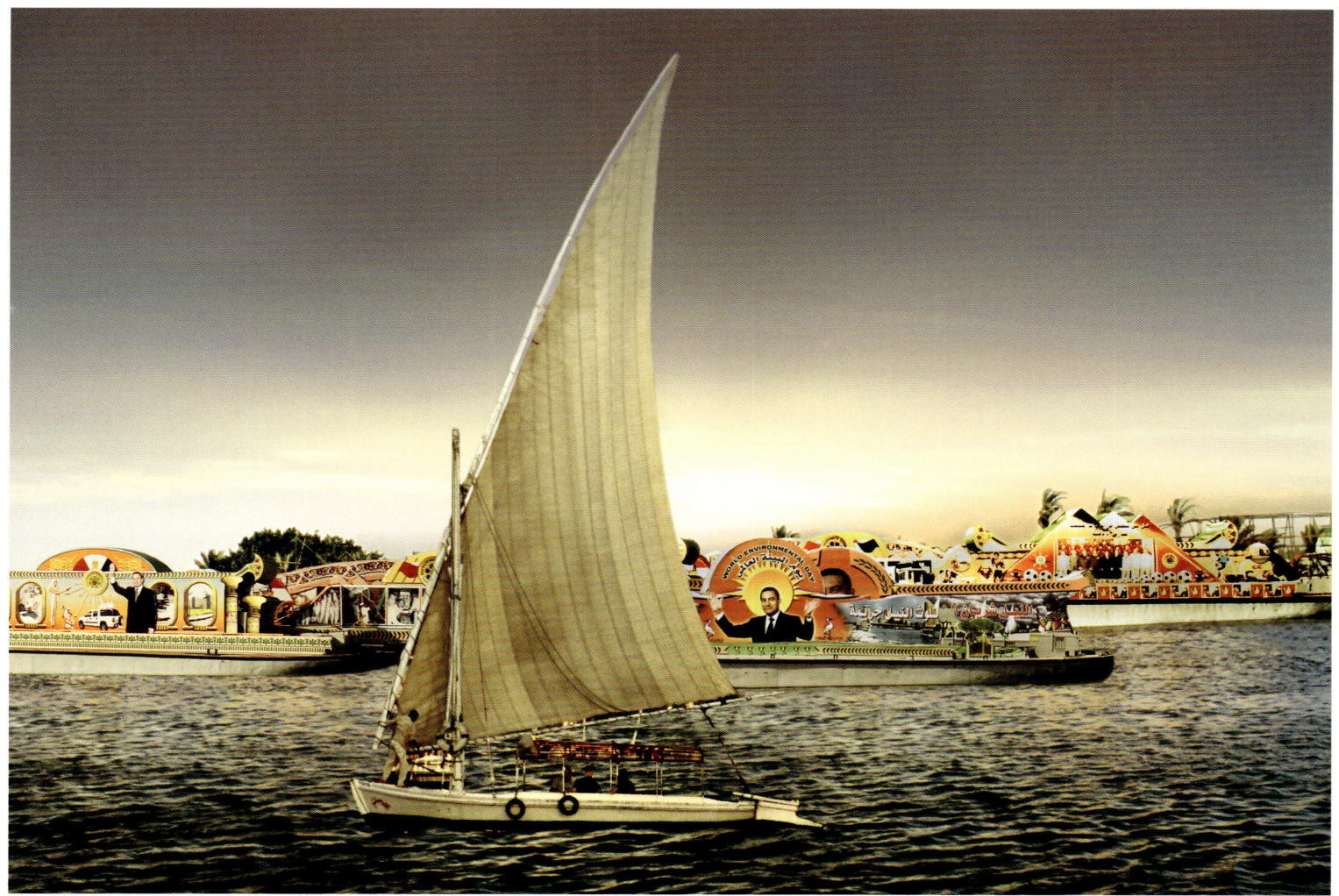

This page:
Felucca, from the series
Domestic Tourism I, 2005

Opposite:
Cairo at Night, from
the series *Domestic
Tourism I*, 2005

Maha Maamoun
Domestic Tourism

Natalie Bell

Natalie Bell is an assistant
curator at the New Museum
in New York.

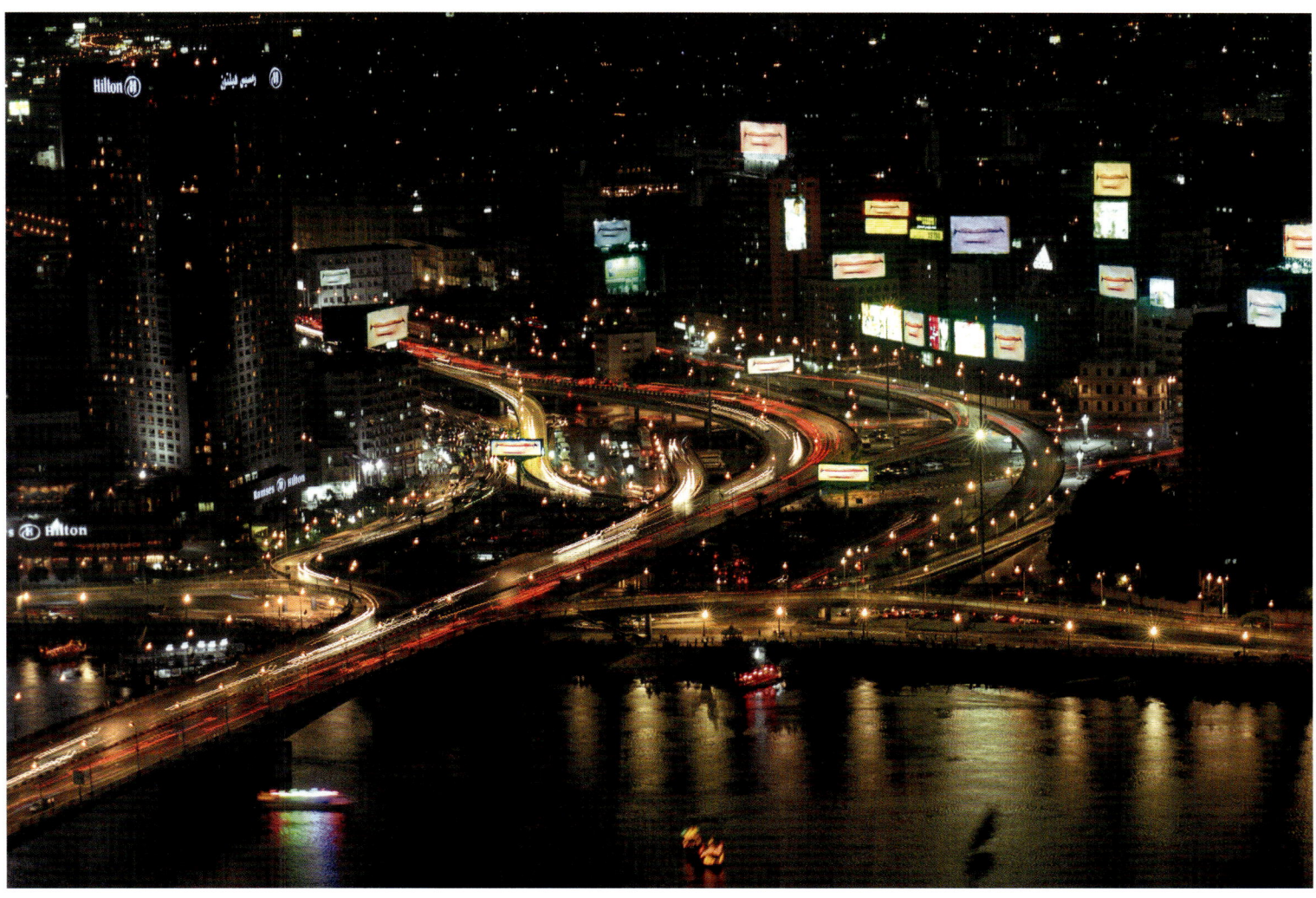

The Pyramids of Giza—vessels of history, myth, and mystery—have been a frequent point of reference in Maha Maamoun's work, which places a special focus on their persistent use as archetypes and clichés of travel photography. An Egyptian artist and photographer, as well as a founding board member of Cairo's Contemporary Image Collective, Maamoun is acutely aware of photography's critical role in representing ideas, forging narratives, and shaping media and society. Egypt's massive architectural icons, more often than not mediated by a foreigner's lens, have furnished countless imaginations with impossibly romantic and exotic representations that persevere to this day.

Maamoun, who regularly challenges systems of representation and ways of looking, lives in Cairo, the labyrinthine, ten-centuries-old city of nearly seven million people whose sprawl now inches upon the ancient pyramids. Her sustained reflection on the pyramids in *Domestic Tourism II* (2008), a sixty-two-minute video, emerged not from a fascination with the pyramids or conventional archival images —the picture postcard, for instance—but from the way these monuments of antiquity have been portrayed in popular Egyptian cinema footage from the 1950s to the

present, which, in keeping with the constantly encountered idealism of travel photography, often deceptively suggests that the pyramids are in the middle of the desert, fictionally segregated from Cairo. For this work, Maamoun also reproduced a selection of film stills as postcards, positioning them, ironically, as appropriated souvenirs.

Maamoun's survey describes the pyramids' role in a range of genres she defines, such as "Past Glory vs. Present Corruption" and "Espionage/Nationalism." Sequenced in a pyramidal structure, *Domestic Tourism II* begins with scenes from the 2000s, rises to the 1950s, and returns to the present. In films from the 1960s—the height of pan-Arab nationalism—characters' contrasting ideologies cast the pyramids as either emblems of an earlier socialist ethos or icons of an historical abuse of power. By the 1970s and '80s, however, the pyramids serve as a backdrop for "lamentation scenes" and are made to evoke nostalgia for the communal sacrifice associated with an idealized period of pan-Arab nationalism.

In her earlier series *Domestic Tourism I* (2005), Maamoun takes on the tradition of postcard photography more explicitly,

training her camera on urban scenes within Egypt that subvert the allure of tourist photography through bold opposition and subtle, digitally rendered alterations. In *Beach*, Maamoun frames a montage of bathers below a traffic bridge at a public beach in Alexandria—a cynical twist on idyllic Mediterranean beach scenes. In another, *Cairo at Night*, a bird's-eye view of downtown Cairo's knotted traffic belts initially resembles a typical nighttime cityscape. Upon closer examination, though, all the illuminated billboards can be seen to share the same motif of a closed mouth with a simpering smile. Throughout this series, an inviting scene is distorted to hyperbolic effect: the places depicted become subtly dystopian, oddly banal, or even eerily totalitarian. In one sense, Maamoun's photographs reveal a public typically invisible in picture post-cards, taking us deep into the psychological recesses of the quotidian lives of the Egyptian middle class in images that might not otherwise travel outside of Egypt. By identifying acts of leisure for this segment of Egyptian society, however, Maamoun not only presents a perspective that counters luxury tourism, but gestures toward a more unsettling idea—that these prosaic middle-class pleasures are symptomatic of a dangerous political complacency.

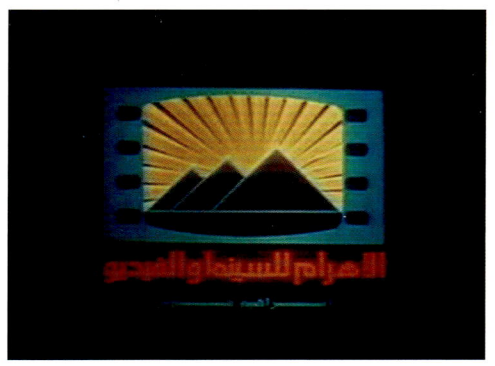 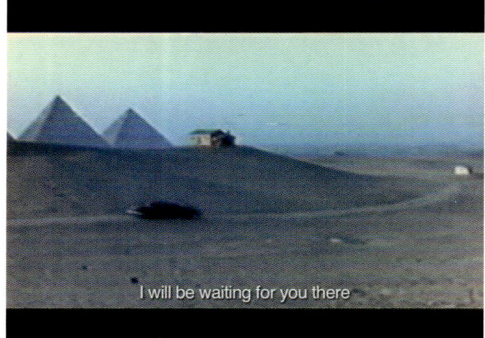 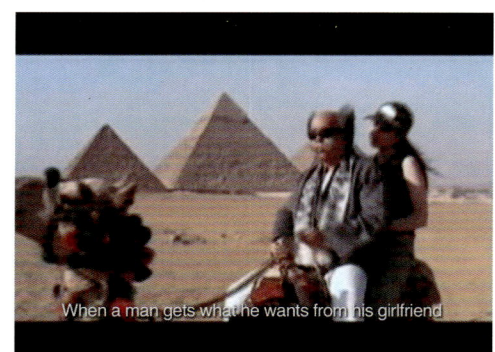

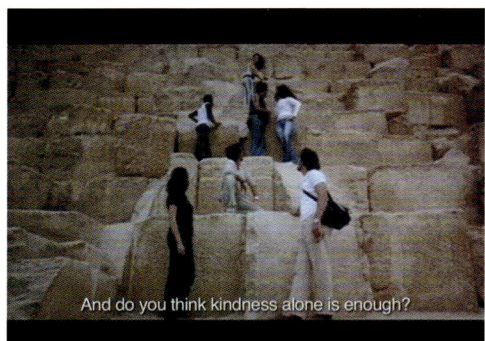 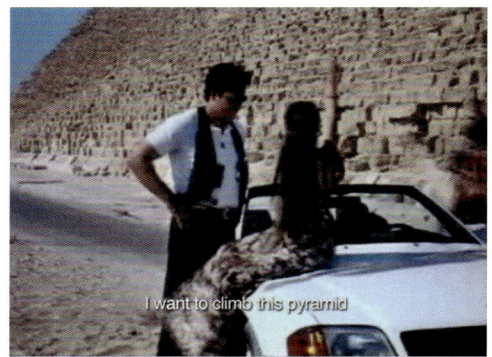 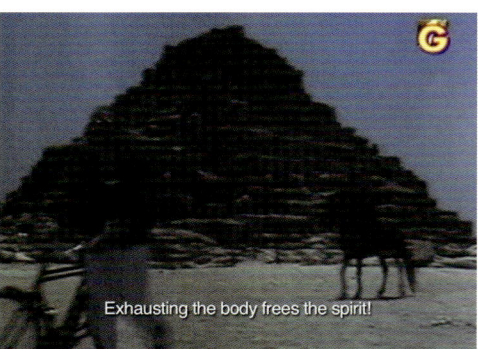

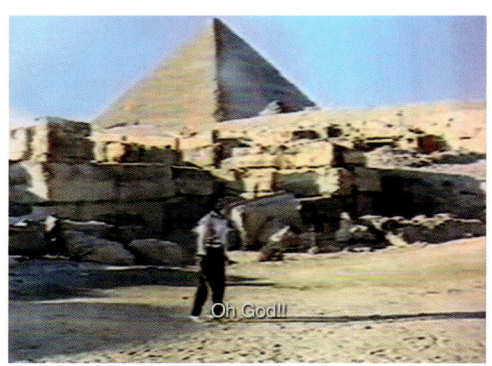 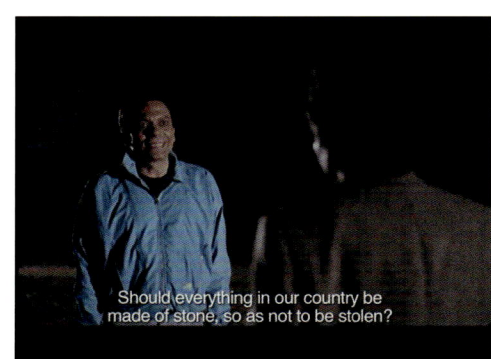 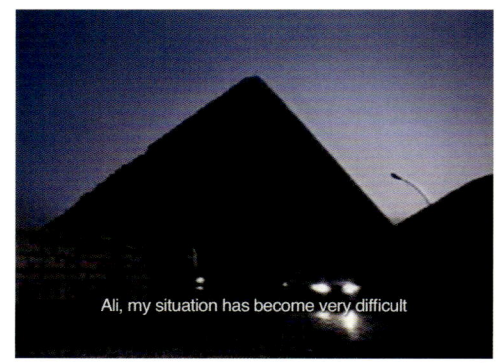

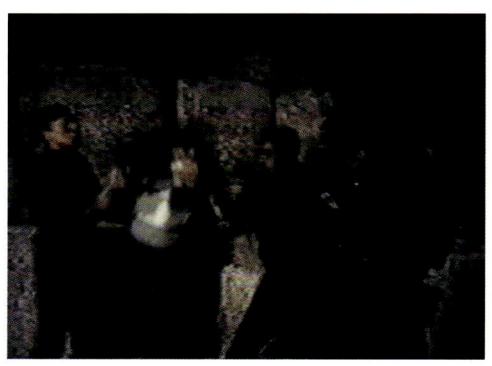 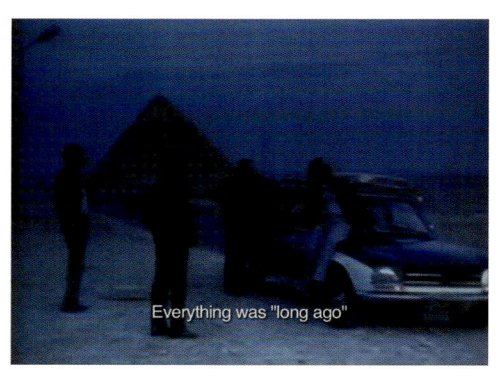 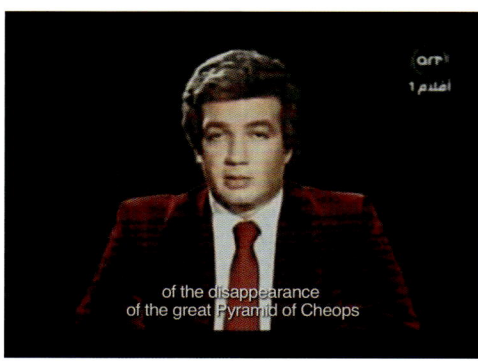

 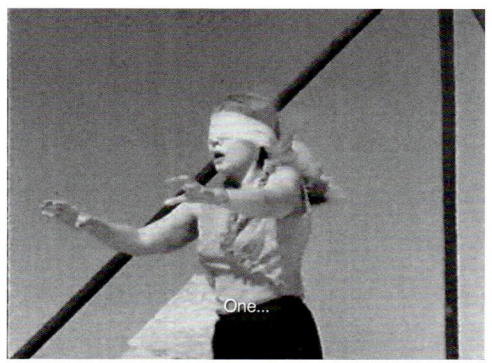 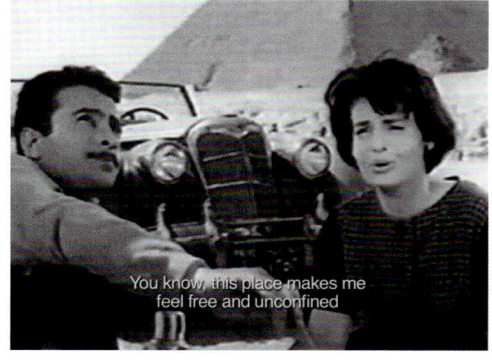

Video stills from _Domestic Tourism II_, 2008
All works courtesy the artist;
Gypsum Gallery, Cairo; and
Rosa Santos Gallery, Valencia

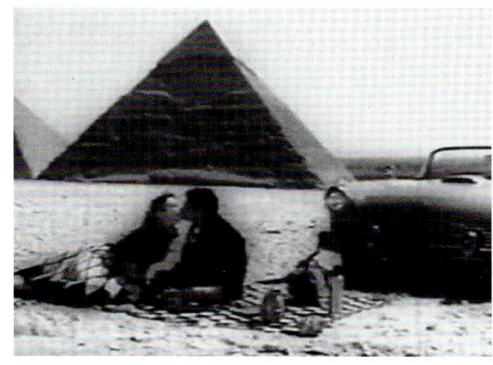

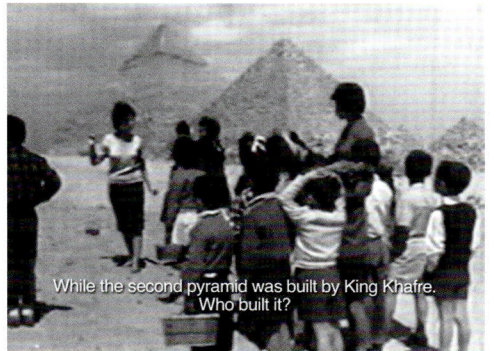

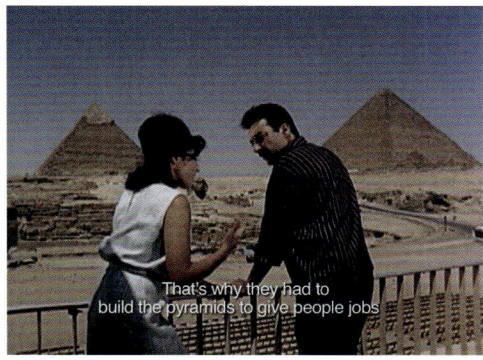

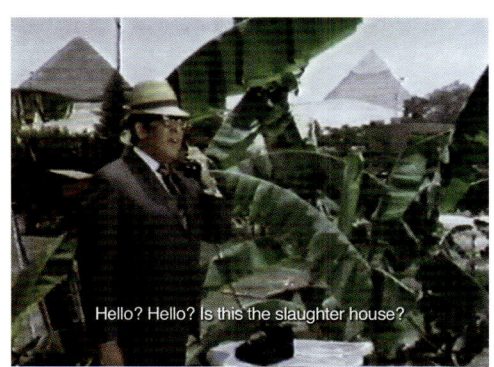

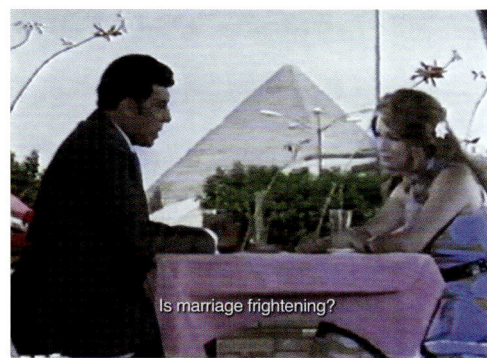

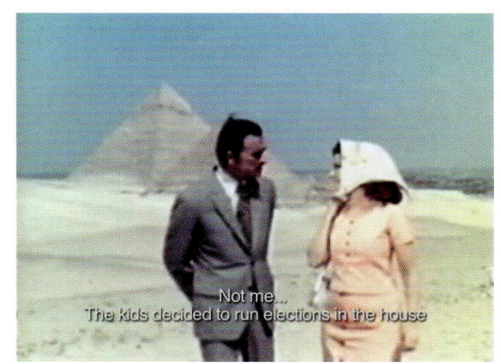

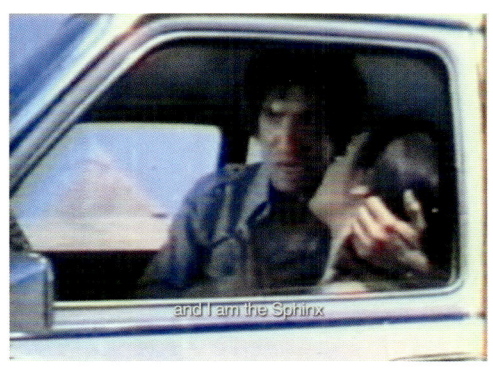

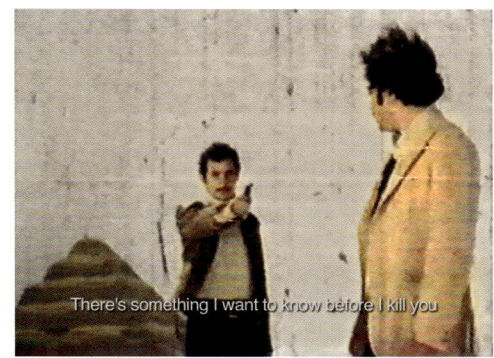

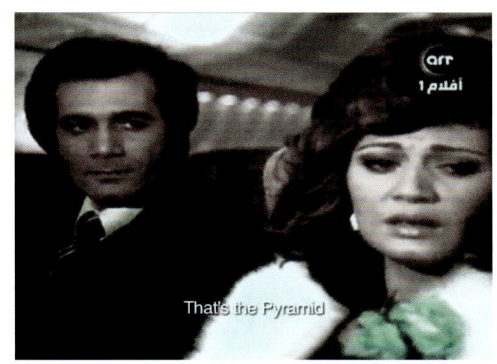

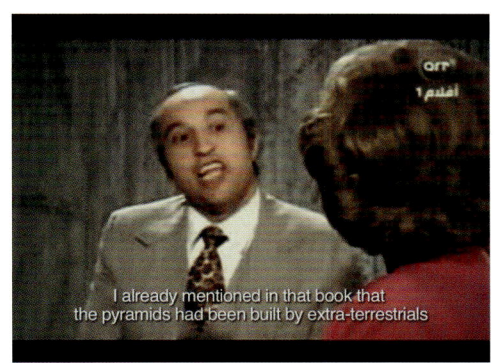

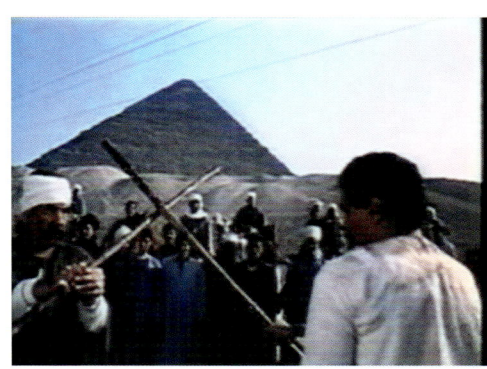

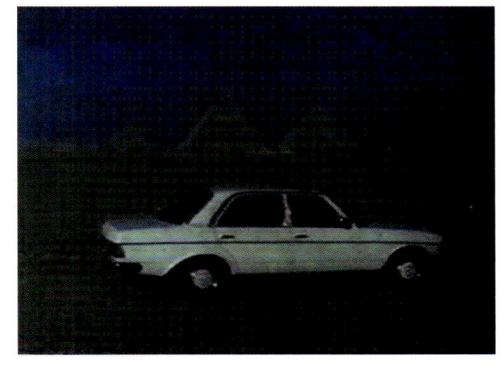

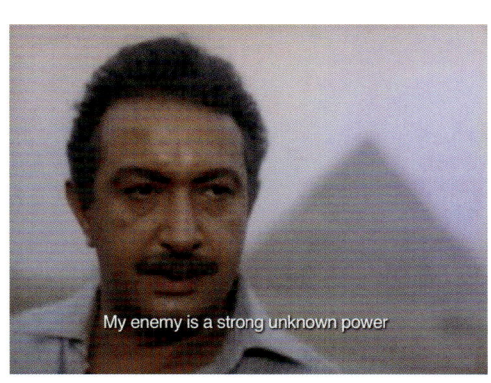

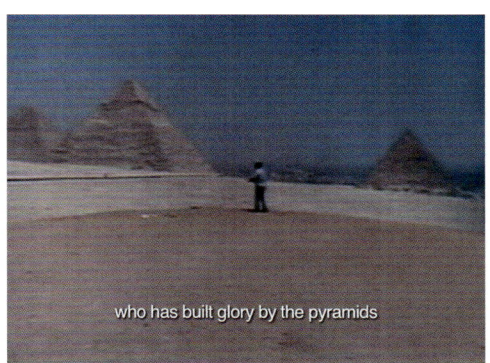

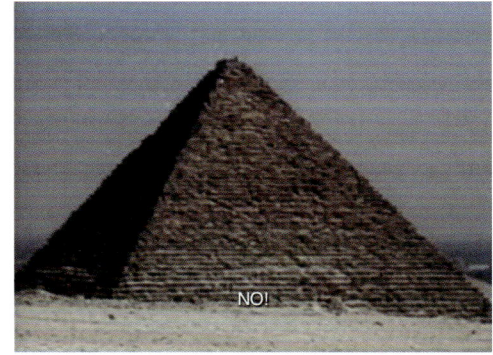

Search the words "Sahara desert tour" or "Morocco fossil holiday" on the Internet and find hundreds of results. Companies like Sahara Tours 4×4, Atlas Geo Tours, and GeoWorld Travel, most based in and around Casablanca and Fez, promise the near-unlimited collection of goniatites, graptolites, trilobites, and other materials from Cretaceous sites. By all accounts, Morocco is open country for mineral and fossil seekers. While laws exist to protect aspects of the nation's geological and cultural heritage, they are spottily enforced. Fossil tourism, much like the safaris of Eastern Africa, is big business: a ten-day trip can run as much as $3,500 per person, with the promise of collecting and exporting at least sixty pounds of fossils including, but not limited to, Middle Jurassic Period dinosaur bones that are 160 million years old.

Yto Barrada's series of photographs from *Dinosaur Road*, part of her larger body of work *Faux Guide* (2015), tracks a road through the High Atlas mountains— a range in central Morocco—plied by government agents, local geologists, paleontologists, and mineral- and fossil-hunting tourists alike. Barrada, who splits her time between Tangier and New York and has long investigated geographical territory as a site of power and material exchange, pictures the road as it curves over and between arid, red hills. Inactive mineral mines and related industrial factories can be seen in the near background, reminding the traveler that the history of paleontology in North Africa and elsewhere is entangled with the history of European colonialism and land exploitation. In Niger, the first dinosaur bones were incidentally discovered in 1963, when French mineral companies were digging for uranium; it's a story that came to be repeated throughout North and Central Africa in the decades to come. On one geo-safari website's testimonial page, an "adventurer" points out how interesting it was to remove precious objects so close to the mines where another kind of extraction was done by his recent, imperialist forbearers: "I felt history was coming full circle." One of Barrada's collages assembled for this portfolio— a photograph of the "dinosaur road" landscape and a thrown-away, vernacular geological painting in the style of Mohammed Melehi—could be understood as a reference to a history of territorial overlay.

Dinosaur Road ultimately leads across the Atlantic to the Arizona Mineral & Fossil Show in Tucson, which has been active since the 1950s and is considered one of the most impressive fairs of its kind in the world. Yet instead of picturing the bustle, Barrada looks toward an empty hotel pool, a fluorescent-lit closet, the handwritten label "Dino Bones" on a storage box. These photographs, like the landscapes and archaeological museums Barrada shot six thousand miles away in a different desert, are devoid of the animal remains themselves. Except for a single worker vacuuming the carpet of a convention center ballroom, human beings too are absent.

Barrada's subtle imagery suggests that without the objects or the people who seek them out, we are left looking for narrative in the land itself, which is continually shaped by human and planetary intervention. After all, the High Atlas mountain range, through which "dinosaur road" runs, was formed by the tectonic merger of Africa and America millions of years ago—and Tucson had far fewer hotels and gem fairs before being colonized by Spanish missionaries in the sixteenth century. Maneuvered by occupying governments, local politics, scientists, farmers, tourists, and looters alike, *Dinosaur Road* offers cultural history as a cycle of discovery and myth, erosion and ruin. Some kind of full circle.

Yto Barrada
Dinosaur Road

Carmen Winant

Carmen Winant is an artist, writer, and Professor of Visual Studies and Contemporary Art History at Columbus College of Art and Design.

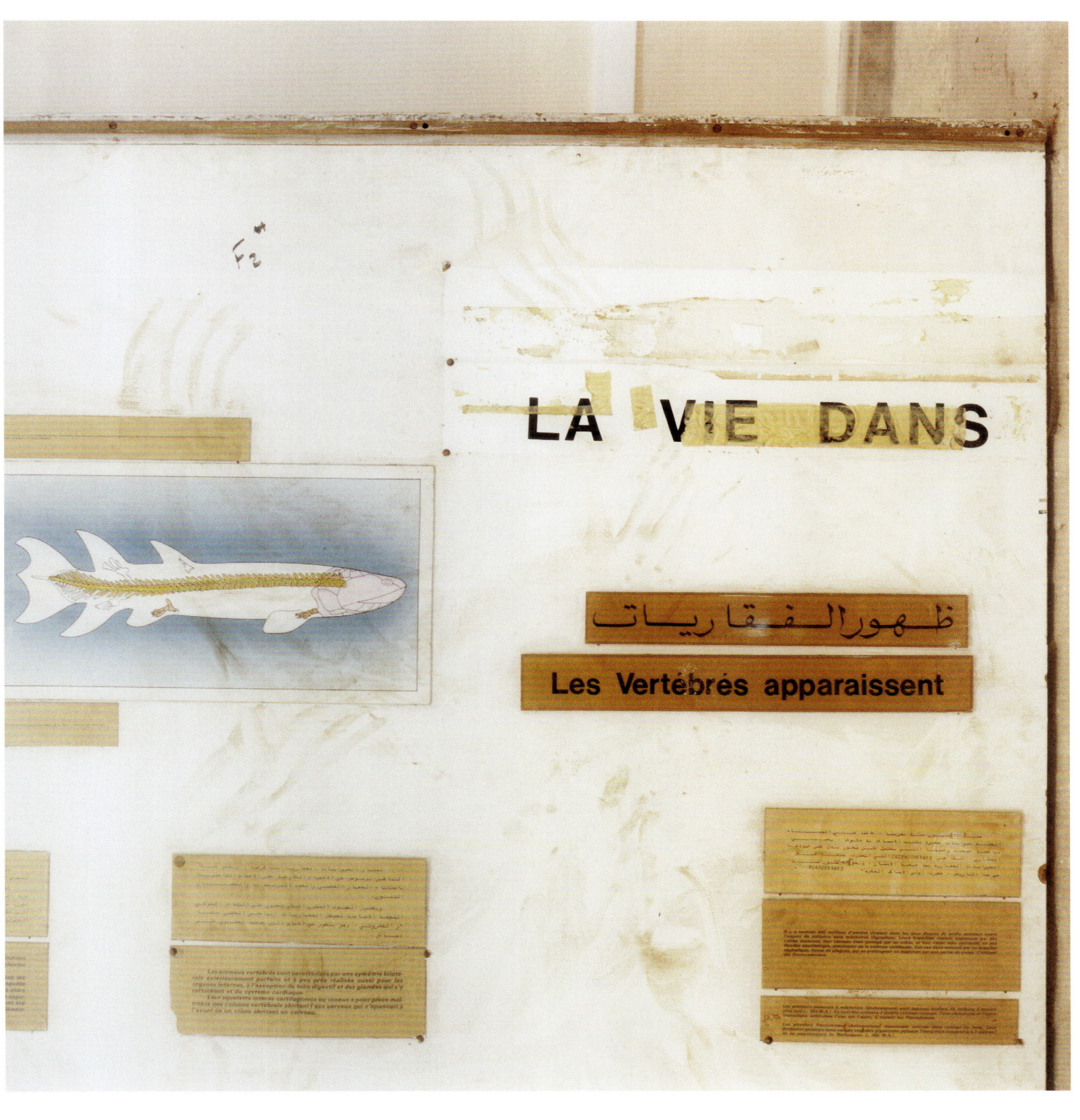

Fe^+_2

LA VIE DANS

ظهور الفقاريات

Les Vertébrés apparaissent

Page 112:
Untitled (*Dinosaur Road*
series, High Atlas, Middle
Atlas, Morocco; painted
educational board found
on site of Azilal Museum
Project, Morocco), 2013–15

Page 113:
Untitled (*Dinosaur Road*
series, Bin el Ouidane Dam,
Middle Atlas, Morocco;
Dinosaur Road series,
Graffiti, Imi-n-Ifri, High
Atlas, Morocco), 2013–15

This page:
Untitled (painted
educational board found
on site of Azilal Museum
Project, Morocco),
2013–15

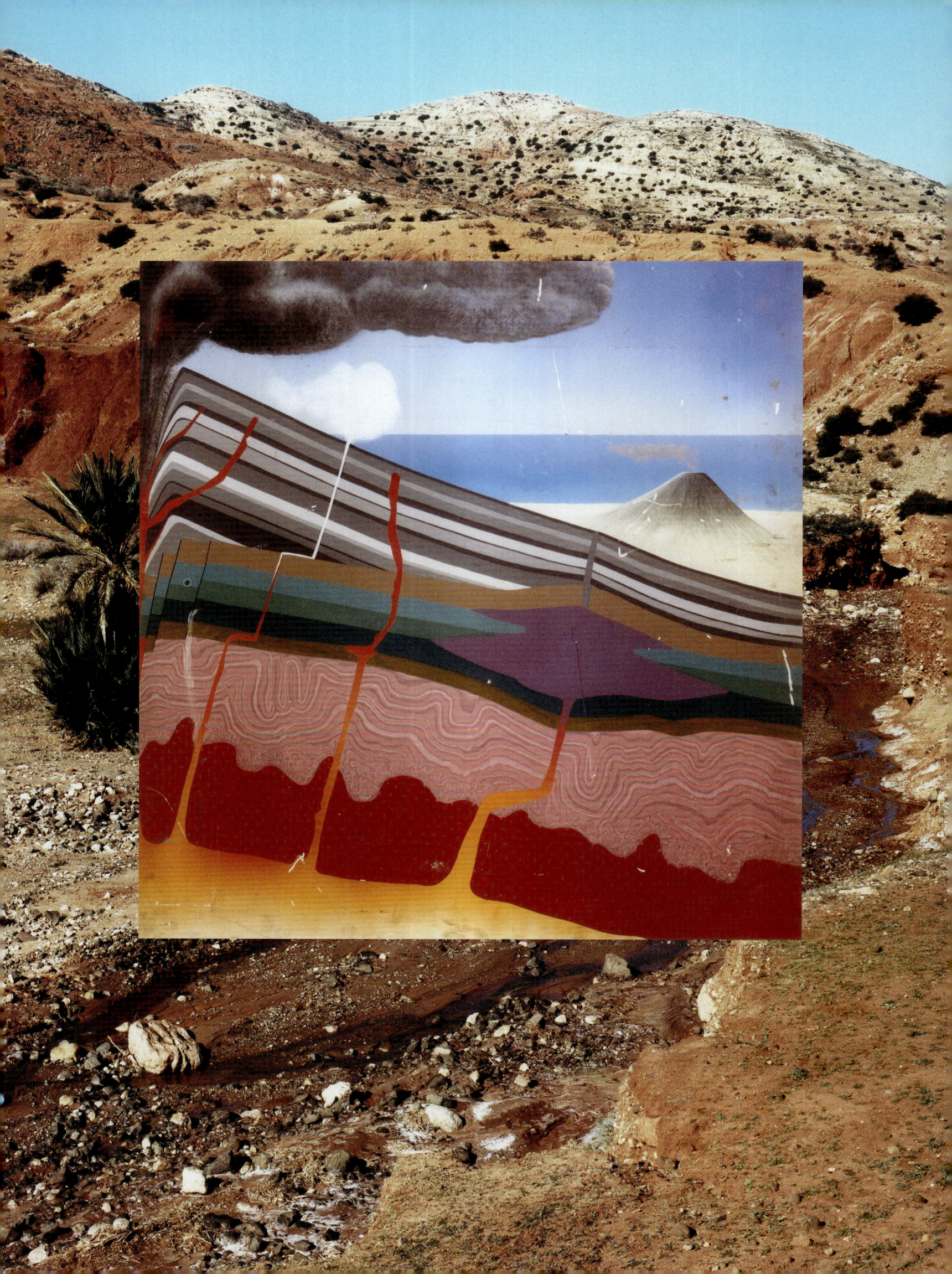

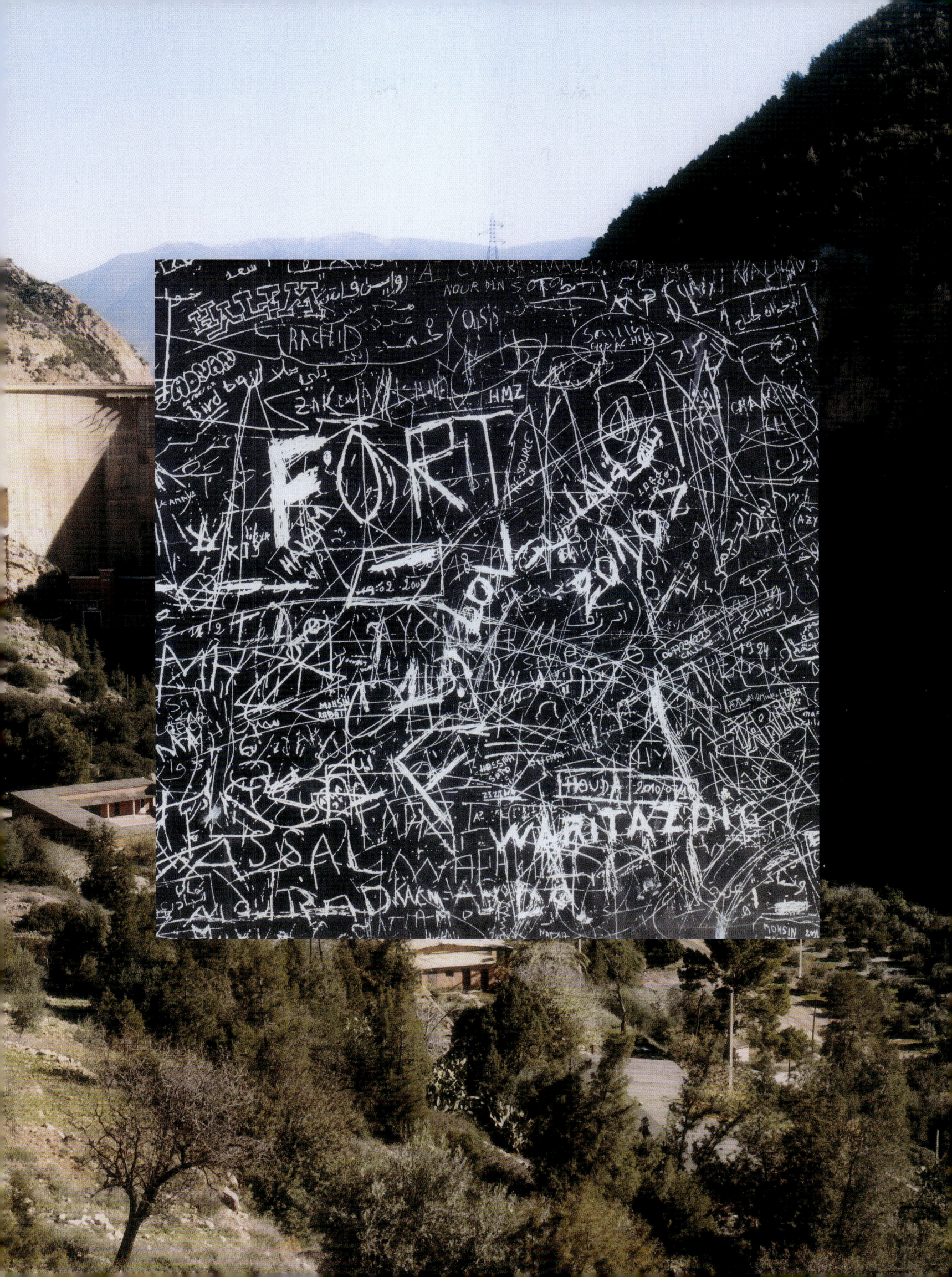

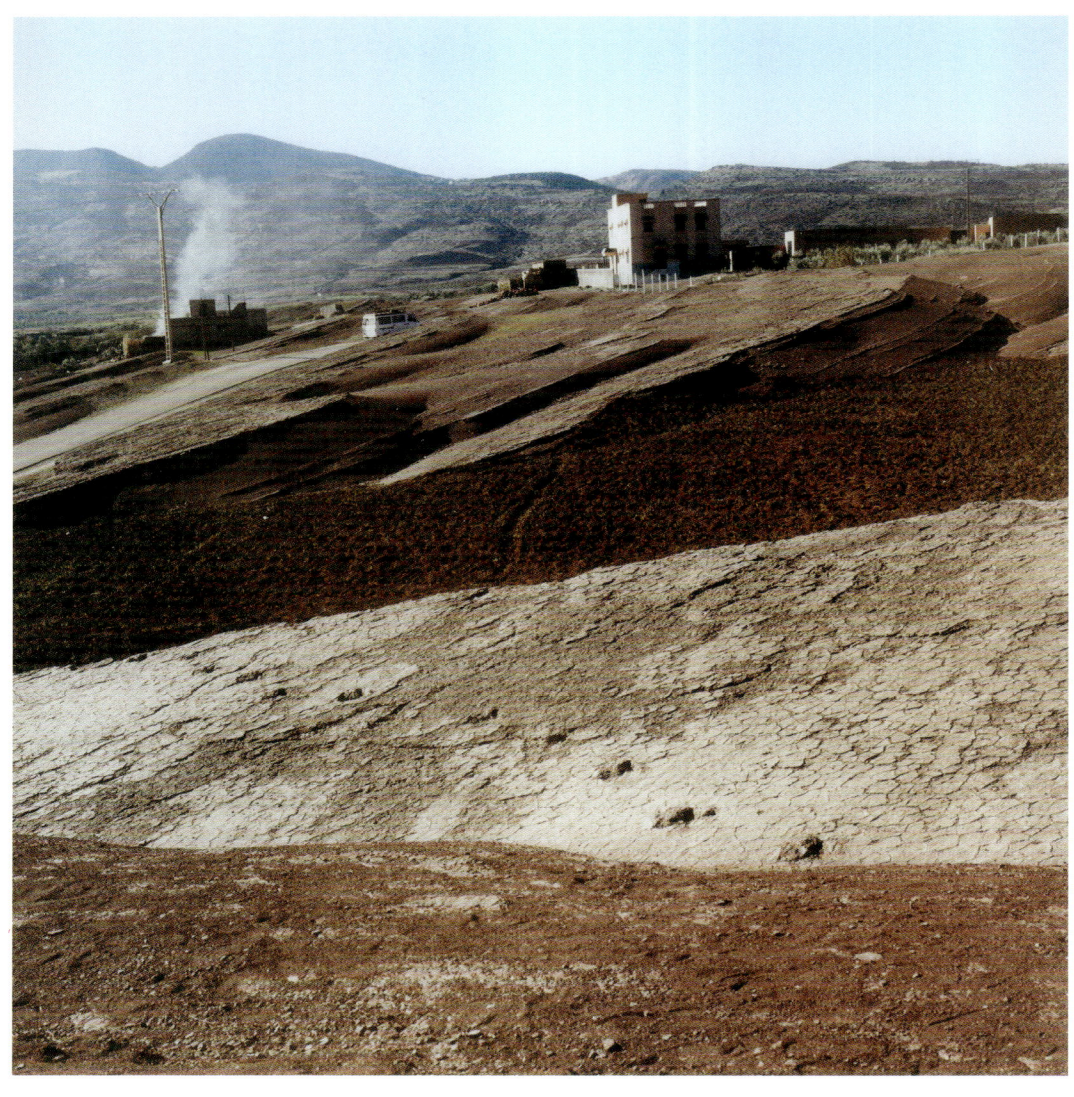

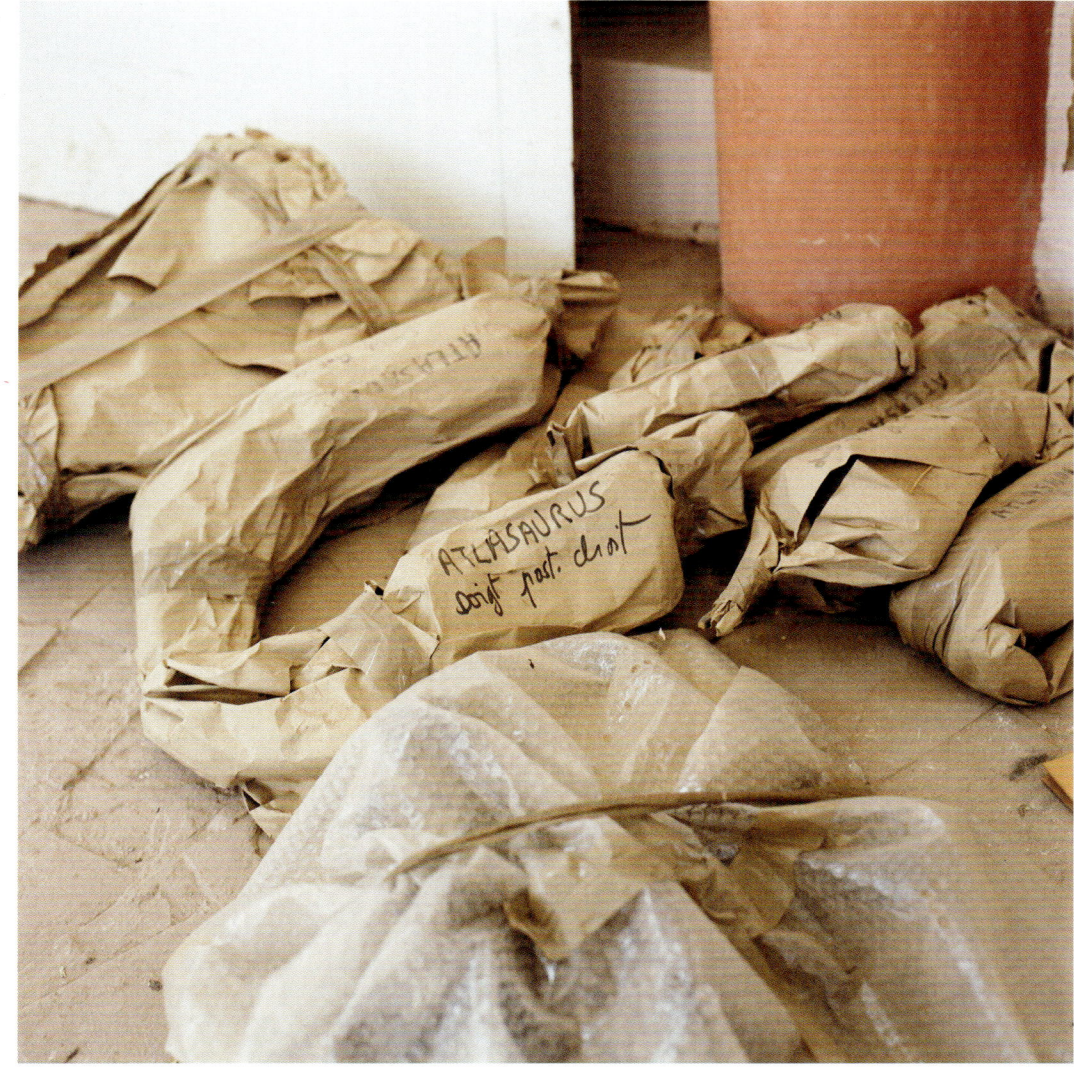

Top:
Untitled (*Dinosaur Road*
series, Dinosaur Footprints,
Iouaridene, High Atlas,
Morocco), 2013–15

Bottom:
Untitled (Azilal Museum
Project, Morocco), 2013–15

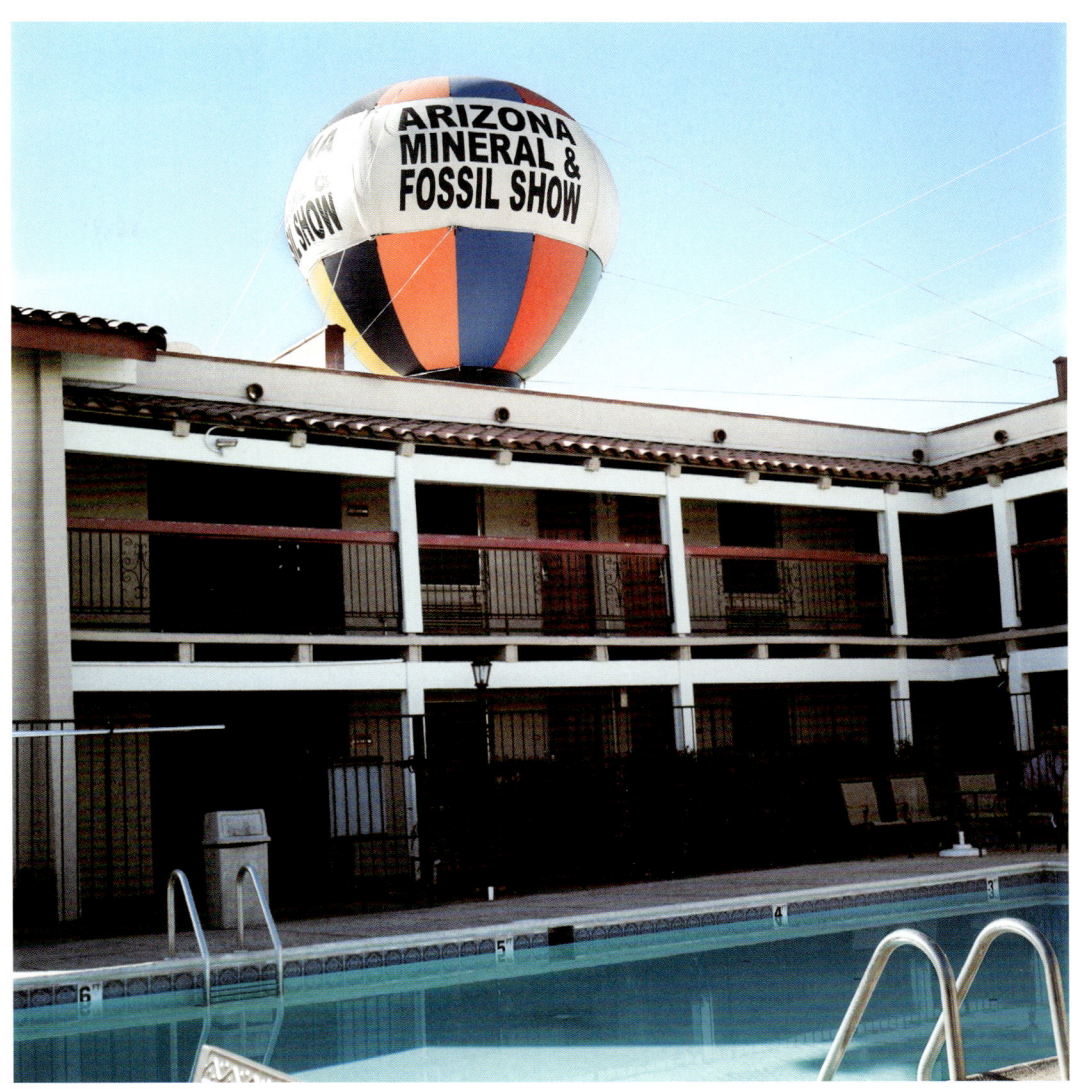

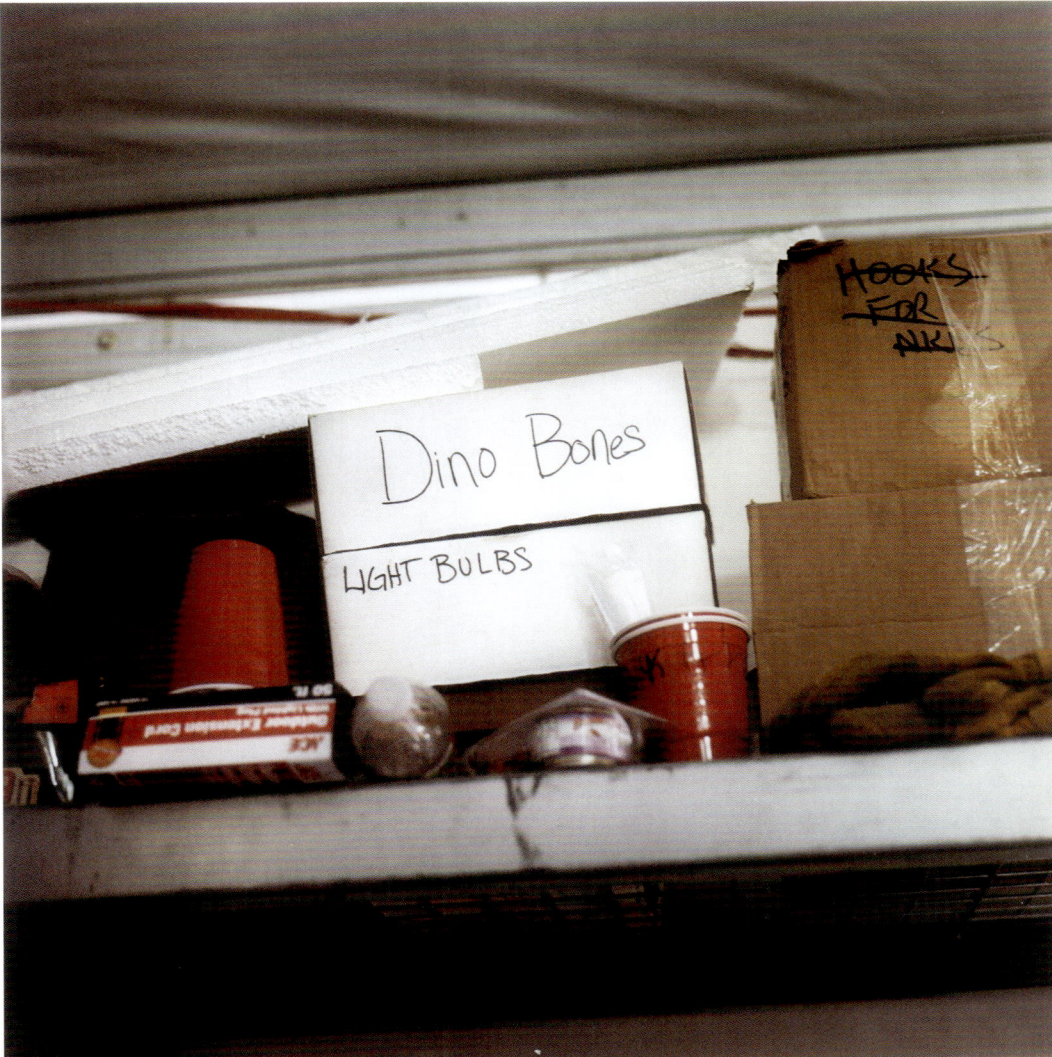

Top:
Untitled (*Arizona Mineral
& Fossil Show* series,
Balloon, Arizona),
2014–15

Bottom:
Untitled (*Arizona Mineral
& Fossil Show* series,
Dino Bones, Arizona),
2014–15

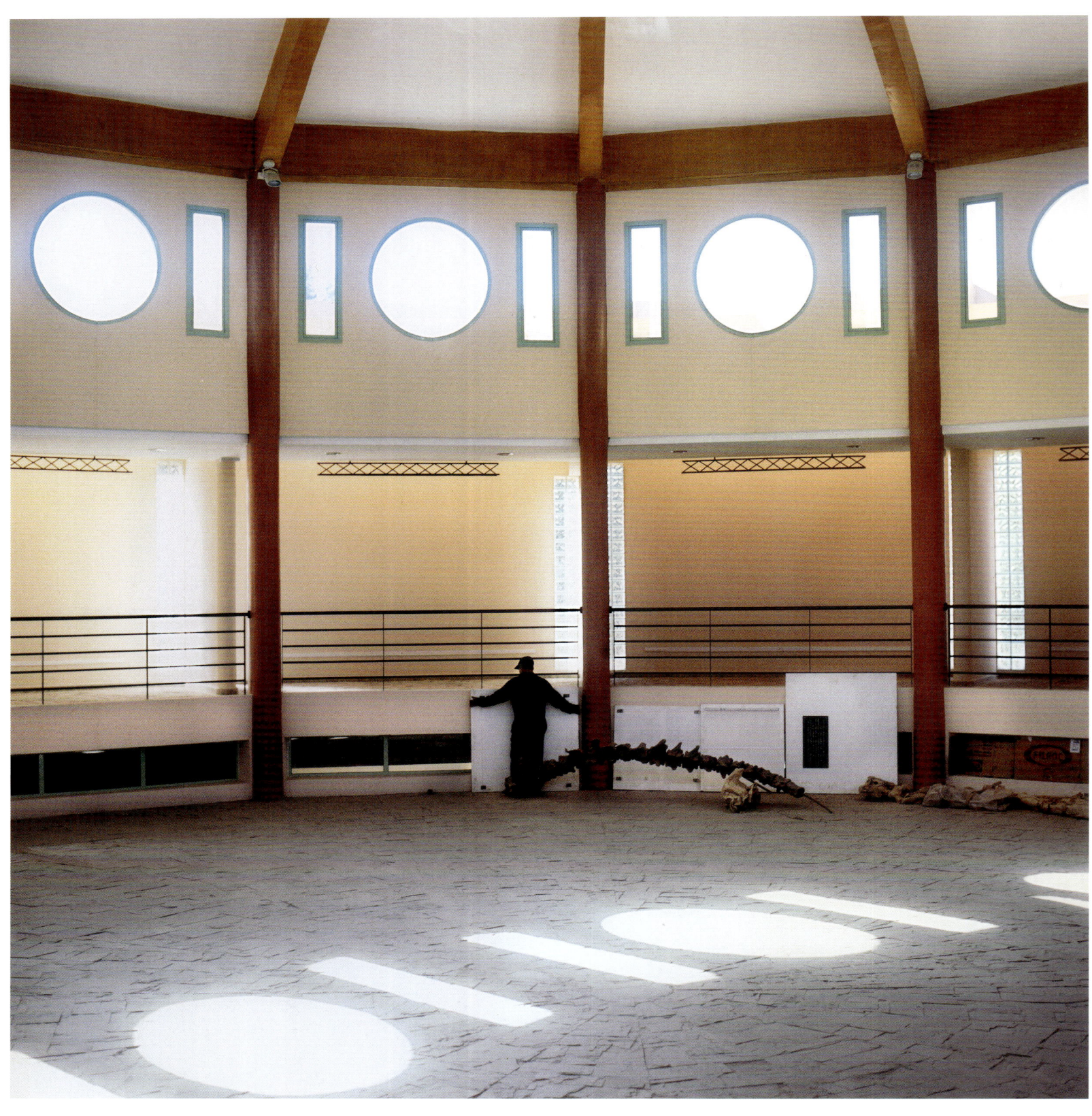

Untitled (Future Azilal
Museum, Morocco),
2013–15

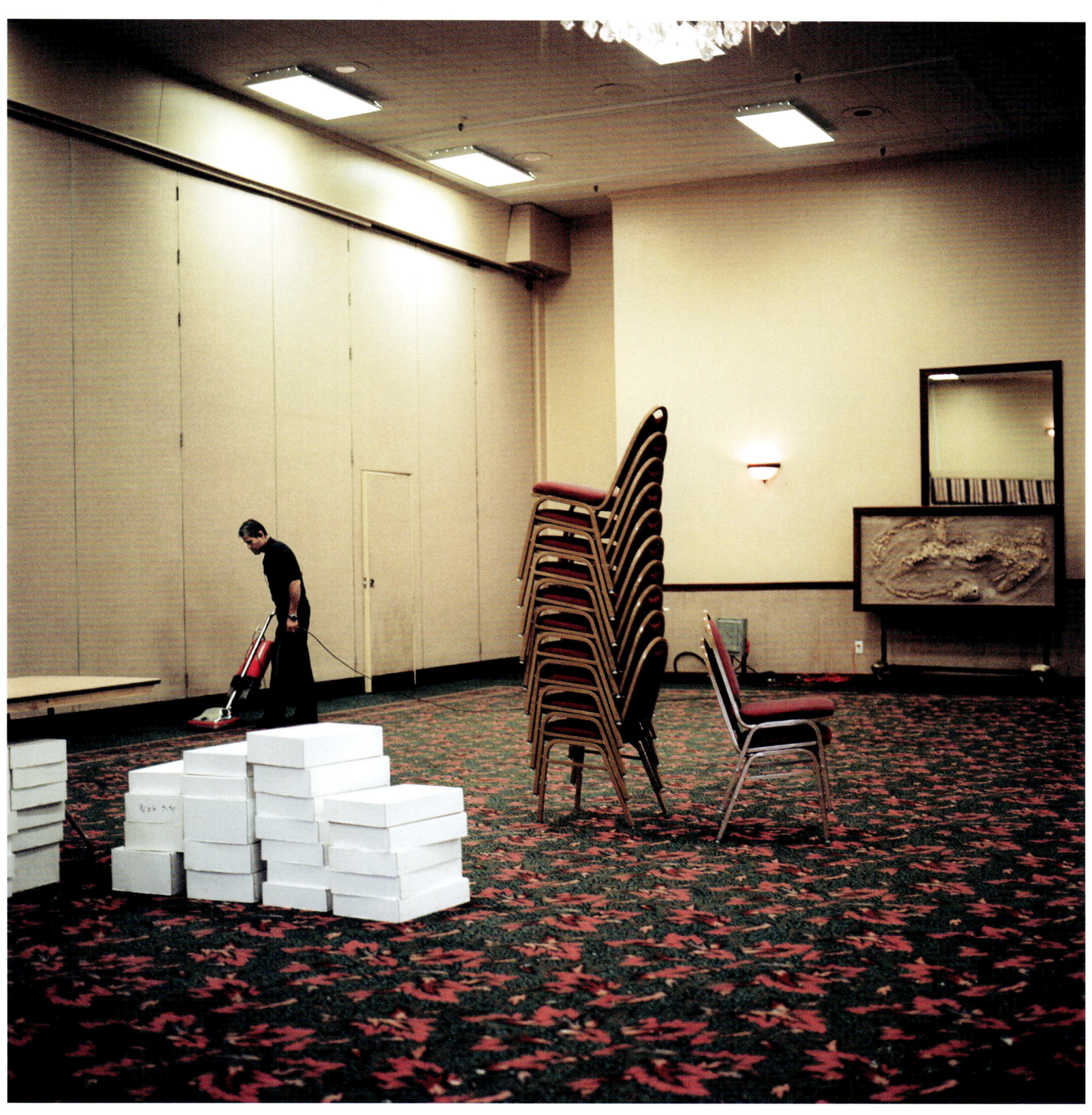

Untitled (*Arizona Mineral & Fossil Show* series, Ballroom, Arizona), 2014–15
All photographs courtesy the artist; Pace Gallery, London; Sfeir-Semler Gallery, Beirut and Hamburg; and Galerie Polaris, Paris

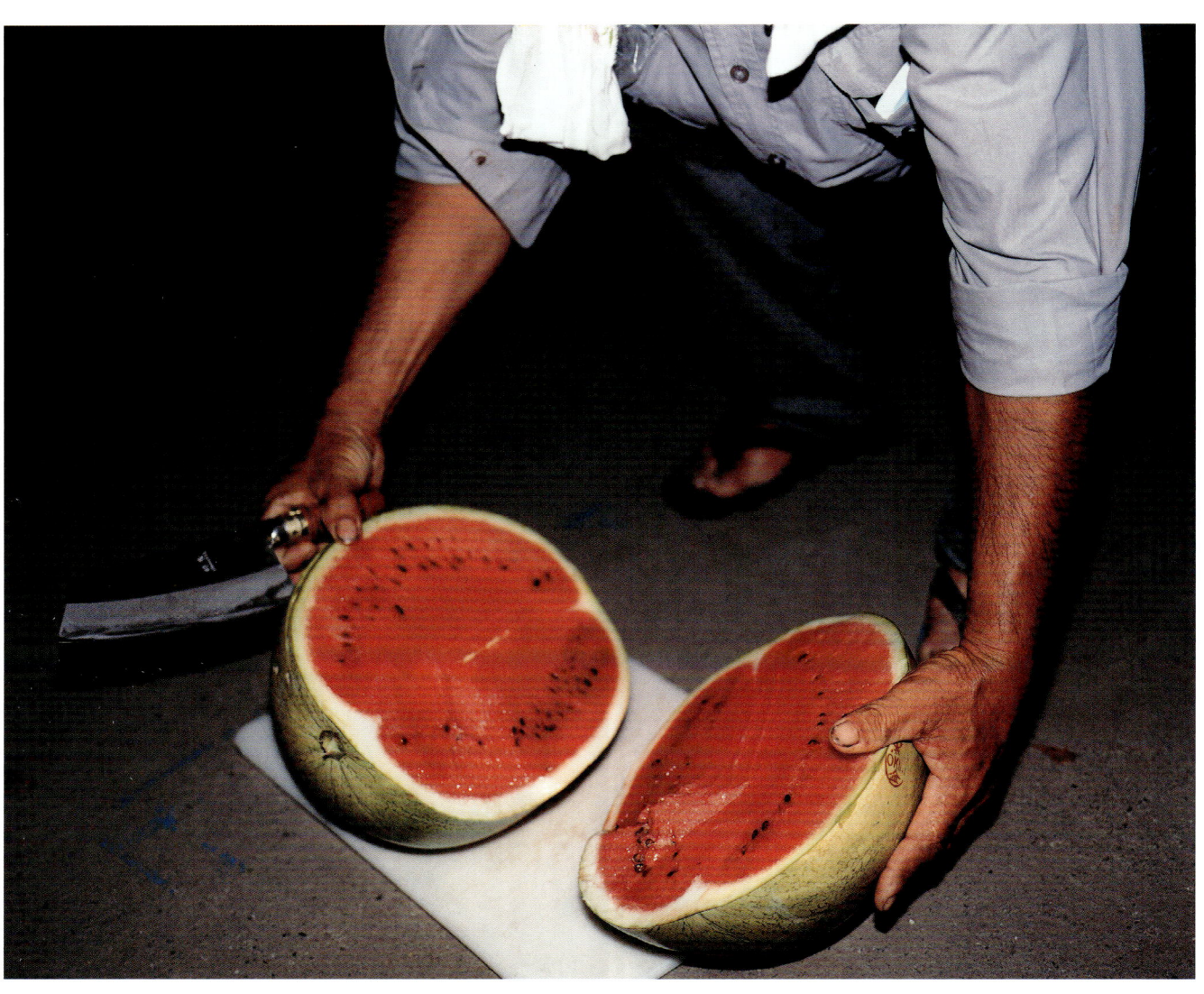

An adventurer turned photographer, Ishikawa Naoki has journeyed from the North Pole to the South Pole using only human-powered vehicles. He is the youngest person ever to have scaled the highest peaks on all seven continents, as well as K2, one of the world's most hazardous mountains. But Ishikawa, who was born in Tokyo in 1977, doesn't travel out of a desire to conquer nature—but rather, as he says, in order to relativize his own perspective.

For his series *Archipelago* (2009), made over ten years, Ishikawa traveled around the numerous island chains in the seas to the north and south of Japan. The artist's twenty-first-century project to reposition Japan—once seen as being on the far edge of the world ("the land where the sun rises"), as one cluster in a long chain of islands in Asia—and to reconsider its history and culture in that context is an act redolent with implications. From the southernmost tip of Kyushu he traveled to Okinawa, the Yaeyama Islands, the Ryukyu Islands, Taiwan, and Kinmen, a tiny group of islands situated within a hair's breadth of the Chinese mainland that has several times become the site of fierce territorial battles between Taiwan and China. For his travels in the north, he went to Sakhalin, the Sea of Okhotsk, the Bering Sea—and even as far as Haida Gwaii in the Gulf of Alaska.

Throughout the islands, Ishikawa devoted himself to documenting local festivals and practices, as well as people's daily lives. "There are certain realities that disappear when you package them up in language," he says. "My idea is to break through all that, and simply present the things in the world." His work attempts to view afresh customs and ceremonies, teasing out histories and cultures on the margins that have been overlooked in favor of cities like Tokyo and Osaka.

Festivals in the Tokara Islands, to the south, and also in further islands, are quite different from those you might find on Japan's main island of Honshu, having more in common with traditions in Southeast Asia, the Philippines, or Taiwan. In a world we are continually being told has shrunk with the power of the Internet and the effects of globalization, fascinating customs and practices abound that are unique to particular cultural and spiritual topographies. "Before we had political boundaries, it was each local area, each locality—that was all that mattered," Ishikawa explains. "The world was made up simply of individual places." As we gaze at such places through Ishikawa's eyes we experience this topographical uniqueness in a direct, unmediated way.

The photographs in this series are often compared to Shomei Tomatsu's prizewinning 1975 book on Okinawa, *Taiyo no empitsu* (The pencil of the sun). But the impulse behind Tomatsu's images is different in character—his are real-time documents shot through with experiences of the political realities of the postwar years. Ishikawa's work, set in present-day Japan, well past the postwar period, is impelled by a more epistemological project, an attempt to express the idea of what it is to know. Facing both north and south, he fits together the various pieces of an archipelago of his own design. Today, in 2015, pivotal changes are occurring in Asia that could never have been foreseen when this collection first came out seven years ago—the China–U.S. summit meeting, the historic meeting between President Xi Jinping of China and President Ma Ying-jeou of Taiwan. The archipelago that Ishikawa envisioned now seems situated like the long arc of a bow taut with the tension of what was yet to come in the relations between Asia and the rest of the world.

Ishikawa Naoki
Archipelago

Niwa Harumi

Niwa Harumi is a curator at the Tokyo Metropolitan Museum of Photography.

Translated from the Japanese by Lucy North.

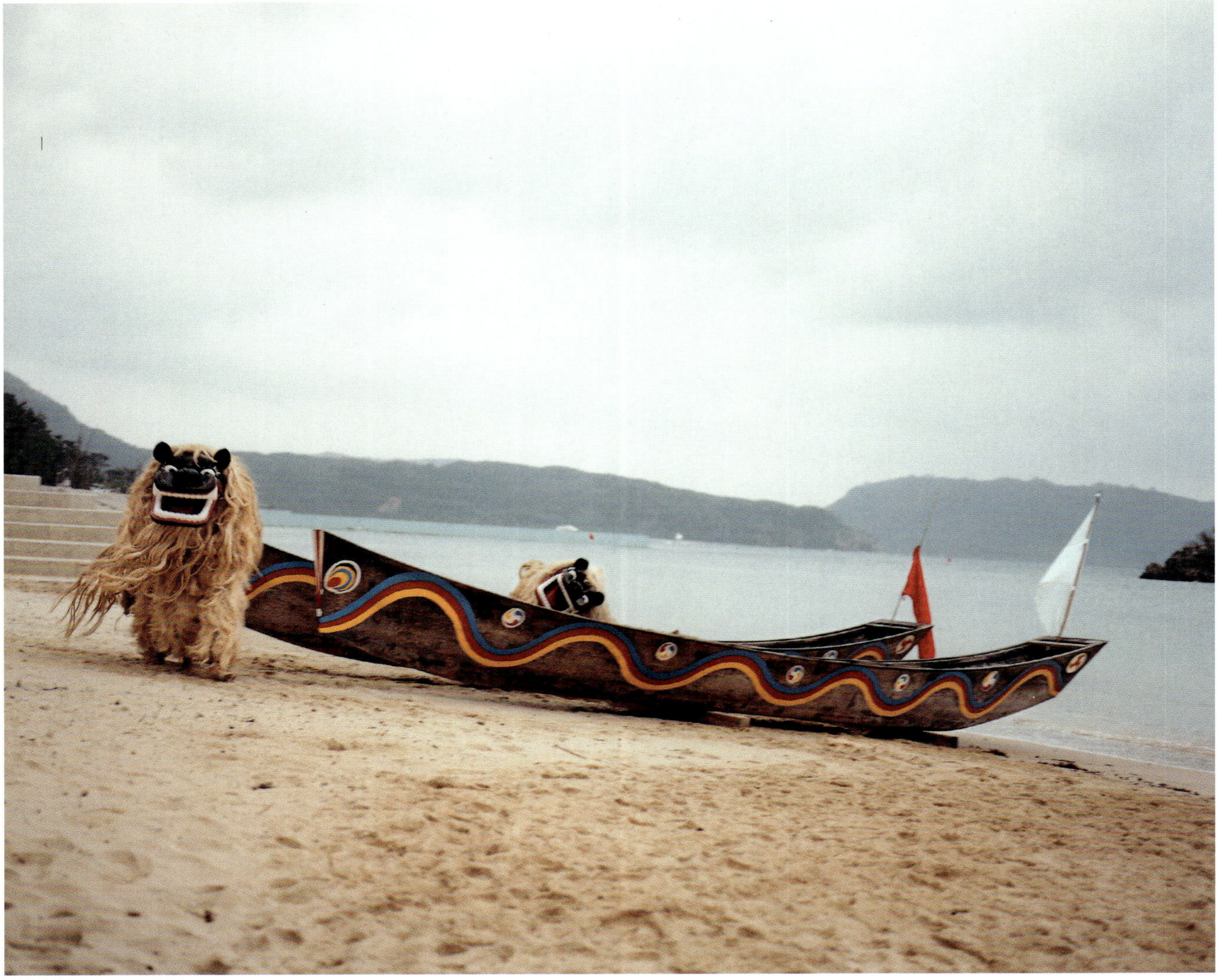

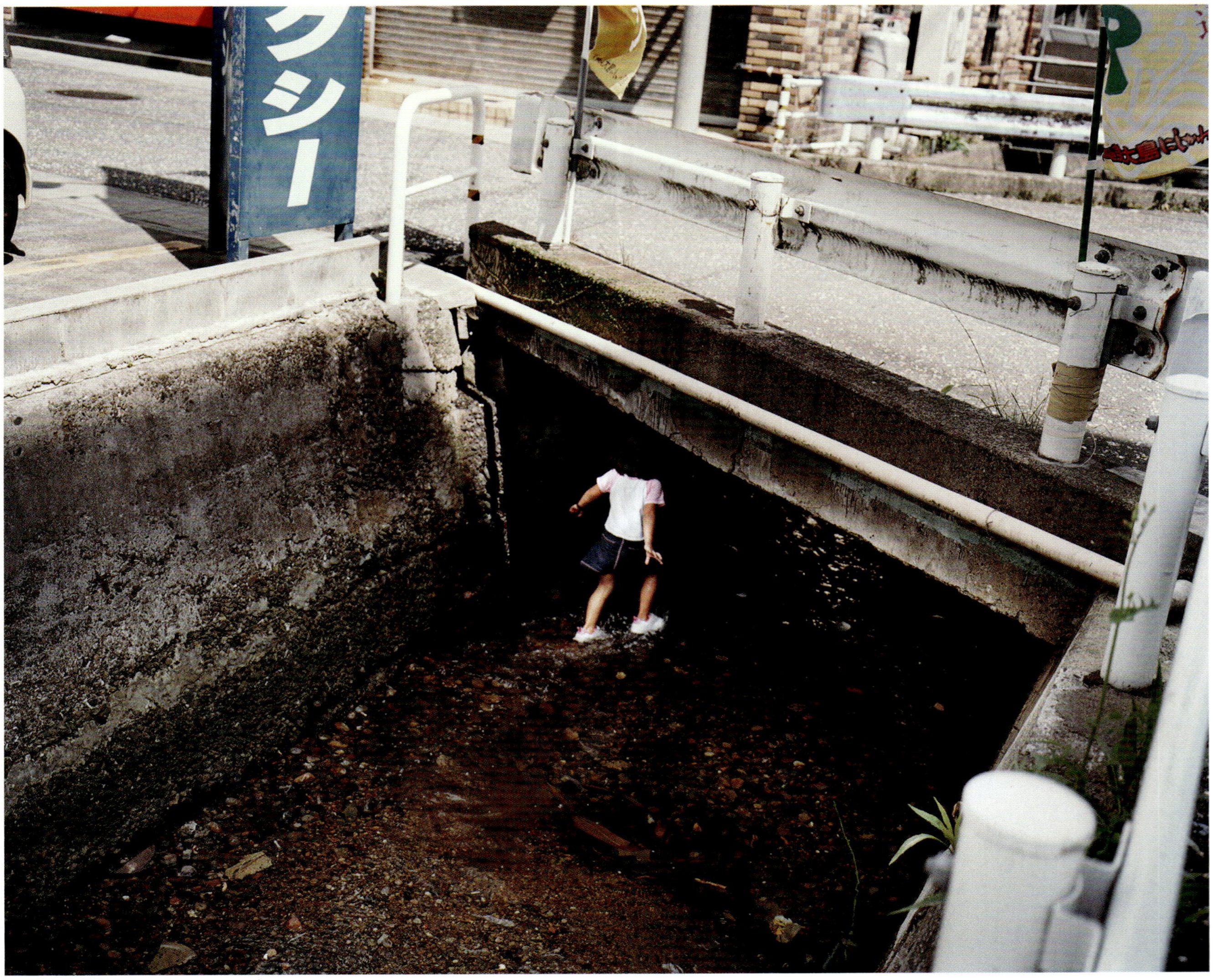

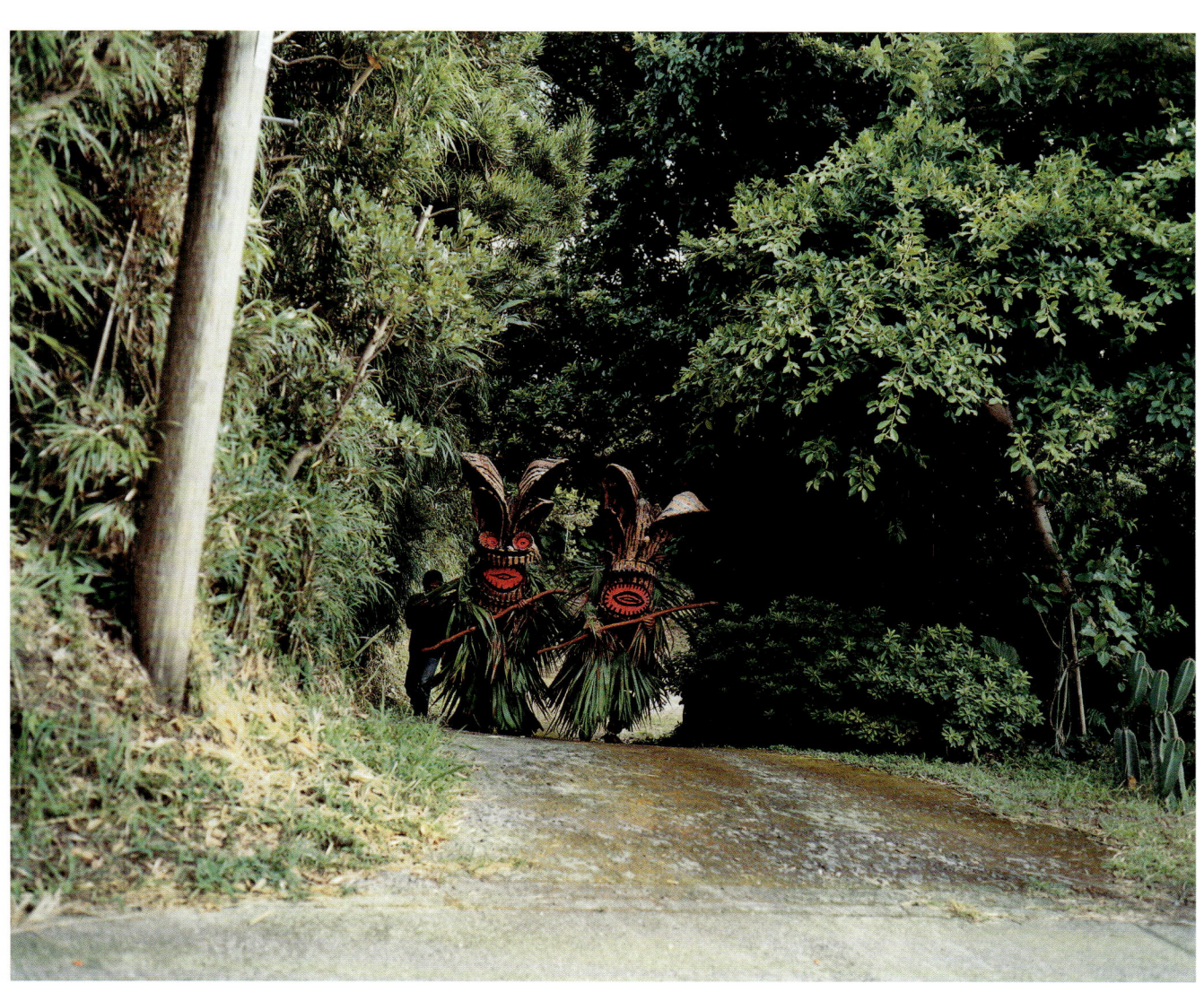

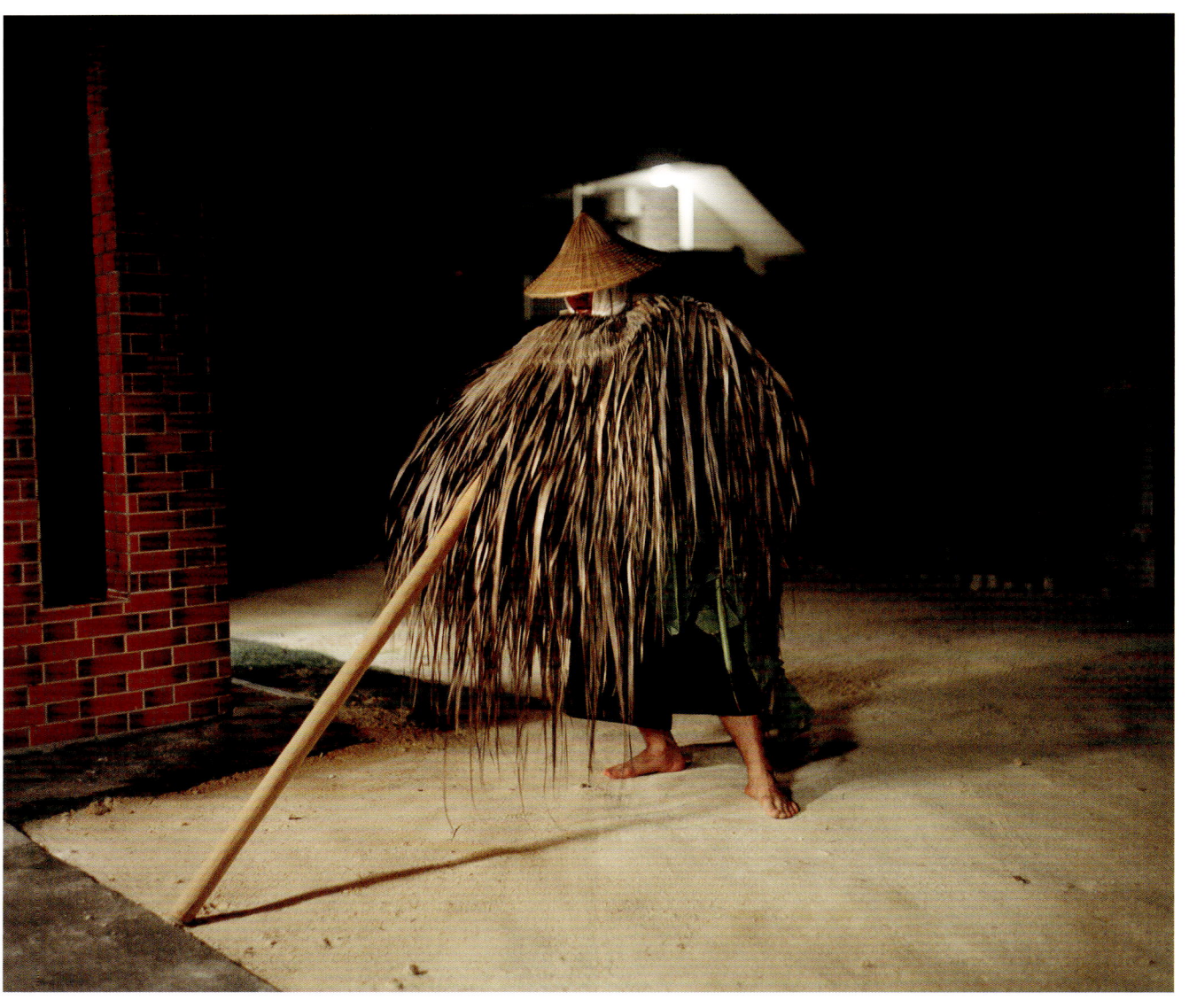

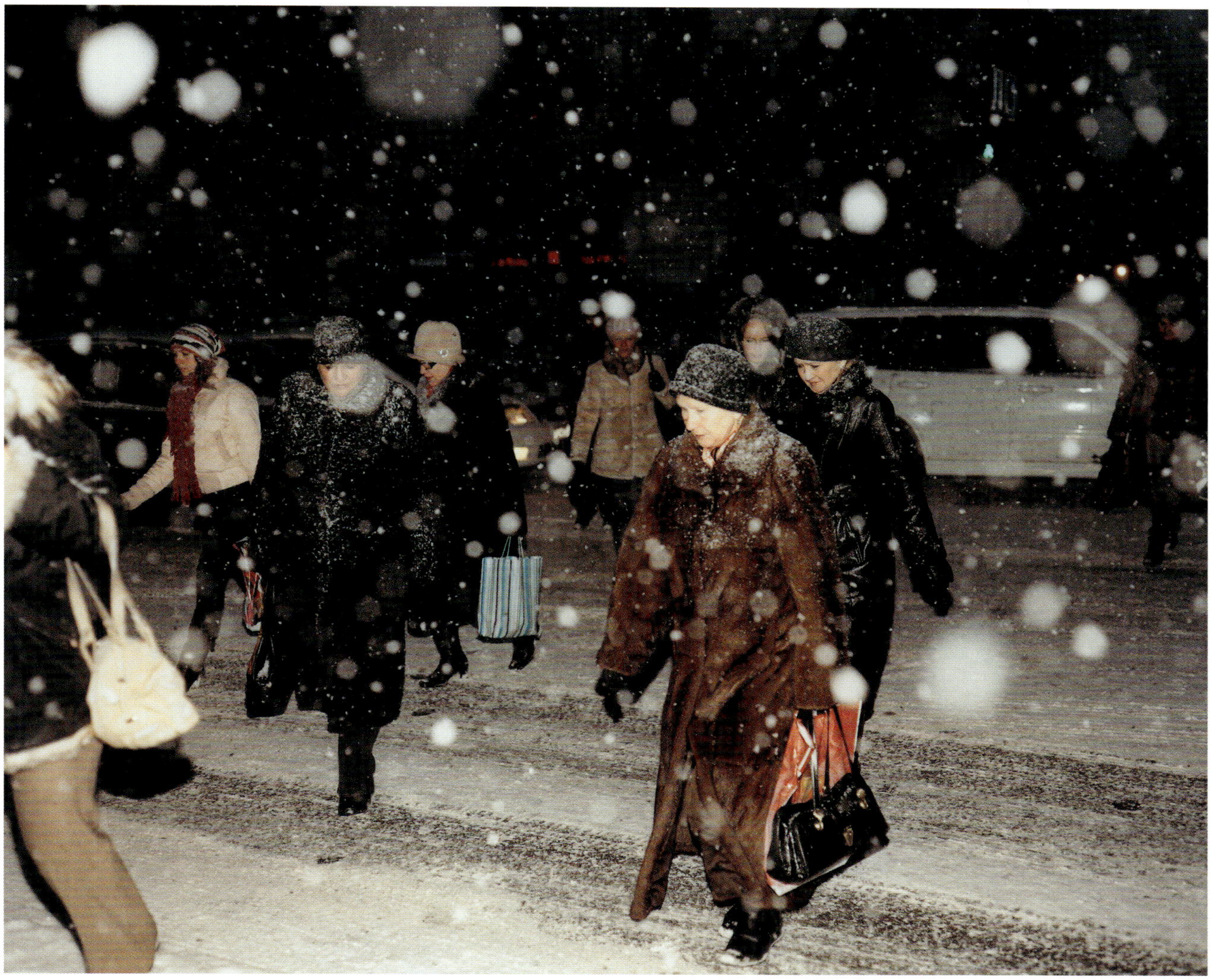

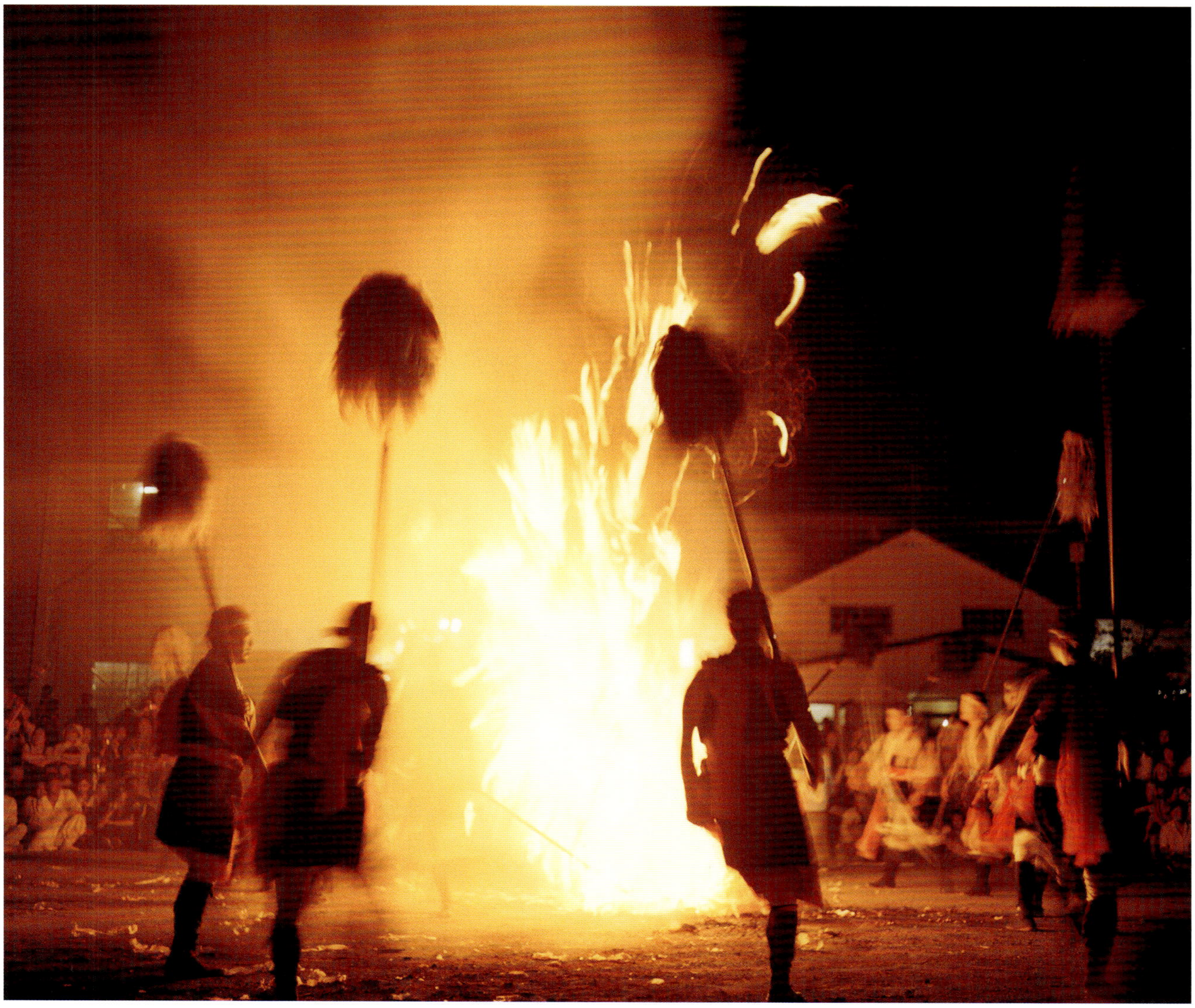

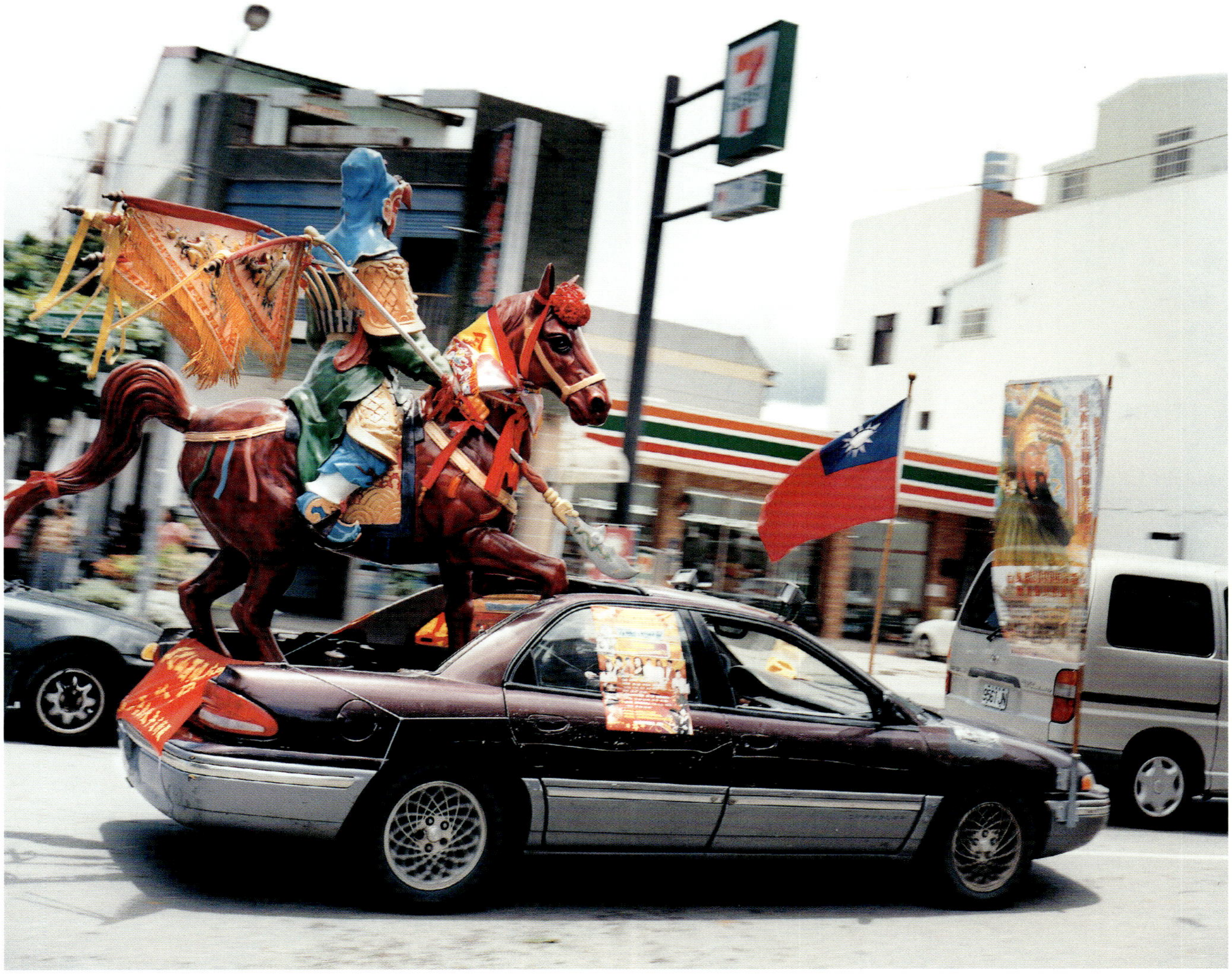

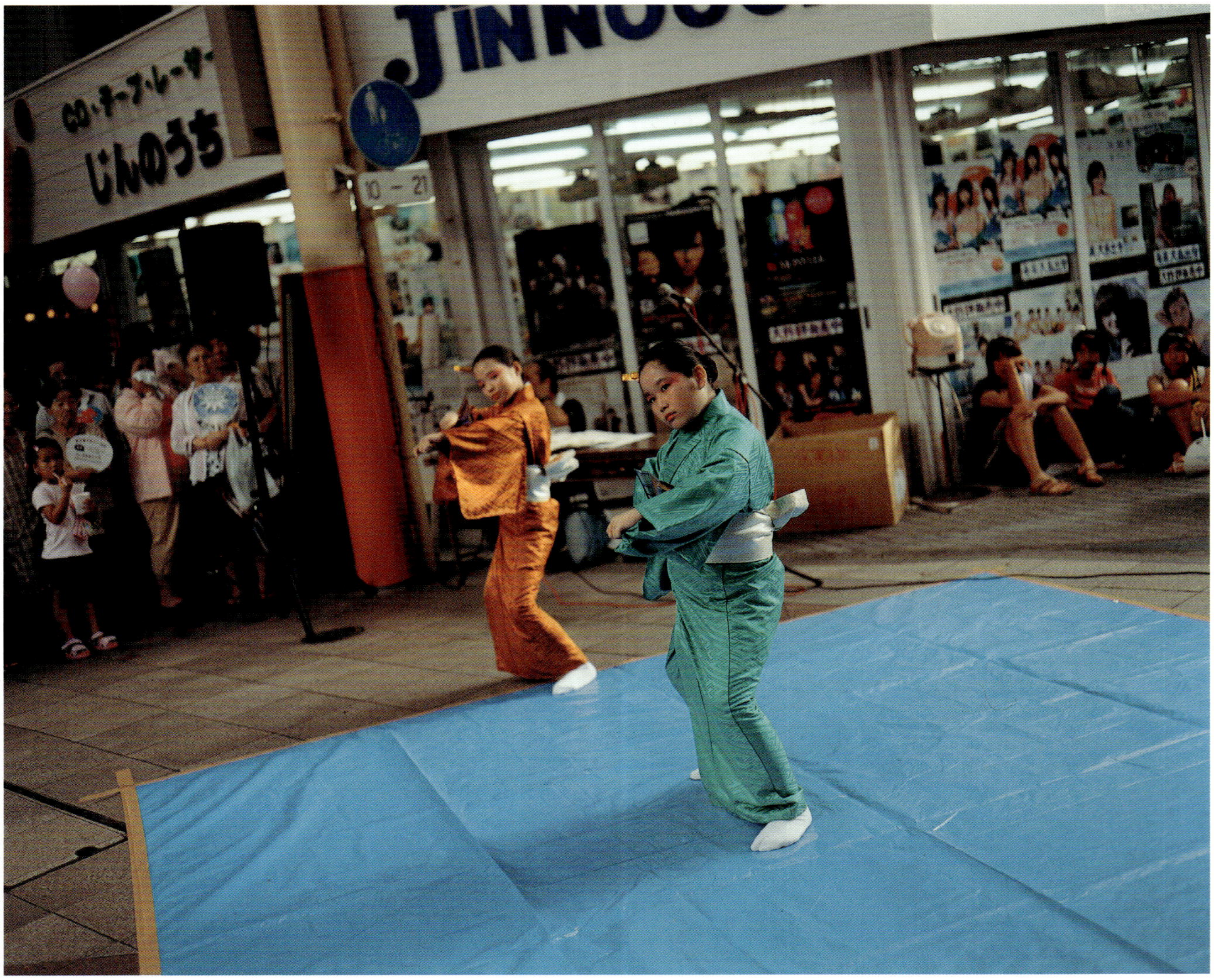
CD・テープ・レーザー
じんのうち
10 − 21

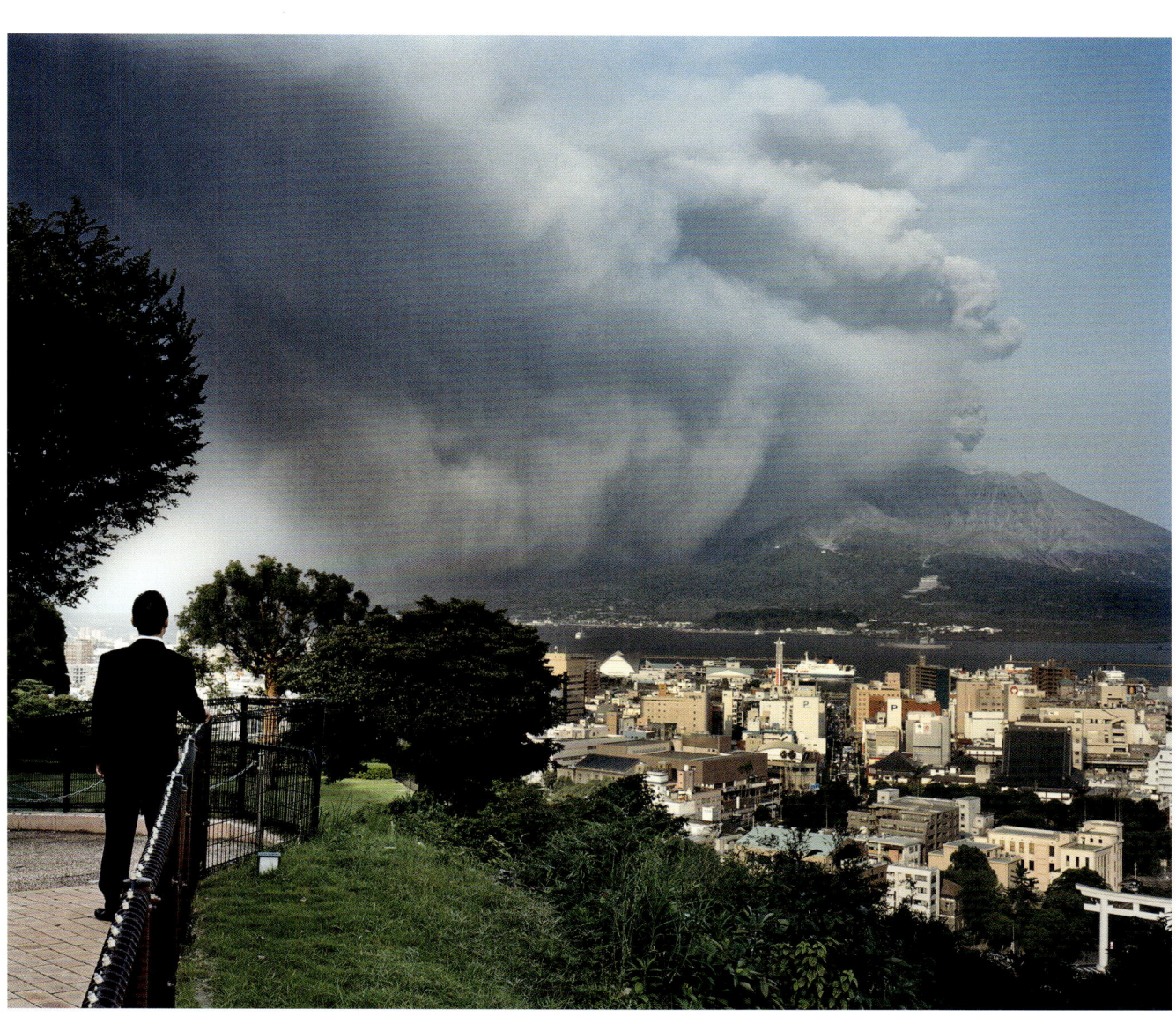

The actualities and the myths, the facts and the metaphors. Justine Kurland photographs America's tangled sense of itself. How do we see when seeing has been so anticipated by images? Through the filter of all that has gone before, can a photographer describe lives and places anew? In the last few years Kurland's pictures have emerged in groupings, with names like *This Train Is Bound for Glory* and *Sincere Auto Care*. Gathered here in eloquent sequence is a small sample from her forthcoming book with Aperture.

A train snakes like a toy across the desert between Nevada and Utah. The view looks unchanged for decades but those are boxcars of cheap consumables from China, bound for Walmart. The photographer's son, Casper, a regular companion on these trips, throws back his head and refreshes himself. He looks like a feral creature, a pioneer, and a twenty-first-century boy, chugging juice from a plastic bottle. The excess trickles down his belly to his diaper. When Casper was six, Kurland took a teaching job. It reconnected her with the work of Eugène Atget, Walker Evans, and the long tradition of intelligent documentary photography. For now, this is her idiom—wide, generous, and testing.

Her road trips are long and her van is eleven years old. With 250,000 miles on the clock, it gets patched up often. Since nobody feels entirely positive about cars these days, breakdowns and crashes feel like larger symbolic deaths. But as Evans wrote in "The Auto Junkyard," a 1962 photo-essay published in *Fortune*, "There is a secret imp in almost every civilized man that bids him delight in the surprises and in the mockery in the *forms* of destruction. At times, nothing could be gayer than the complete collapse of our fanciest contrivances. Scenes like these are rich in tragicomic suggestions of the fall of man from his high ride."

The auto yard is a place of pragmatic resurrection. Indeed, the fall of man, or more exactly *fallen men*, have their own erotic pathos. Kurland's pictures of mechanics and car culture are touching and affectionate. They leave the ambivalence to us. Casper had his own little fall from Mom's parked van, catching his mouth on the bumper. That's his tooth in his hand.

One day she met a man who looked uncannily like Casper, all grown up and coming down from a junkie's high. With a head full of worries about keeping her boy safe and the knowledge that he won't be hers forever, she photographed this man. She accepted him, watching him almost pray with his hands around a Coke. Her camera is respectful but it wards off the fears.

And here is Cuervo, on horseback, no car in sight. Kurland got to know him and photographed him over three years. He can hunt, prepare food, and light fires without matches. His past includes drug running and incarceration in Mexico. He has just crossed the Sierra Nevada with his animals. Kurland recalls his words: "I'm a man with a man's needs, and if you want to get some photography done you are going to have to satisfy my needs." She walked away. "When I came back he was completely naked. Somehow that was the final straw. I haven't talked to him since."

We all know the easy failings of men. The pride, arrogance, narcissism, and fragile vanity. Yet, nobody is quite sure what a man is supposed to be. Myth and history were once on his side but no longer. In these photographs, made with young Casper at her side, Kurland offers her own brave contemplation of it all.

Justine Kurland
Highway Kind

David Campany

David Campany's most recent book is *A Handful of Dust* (2015).

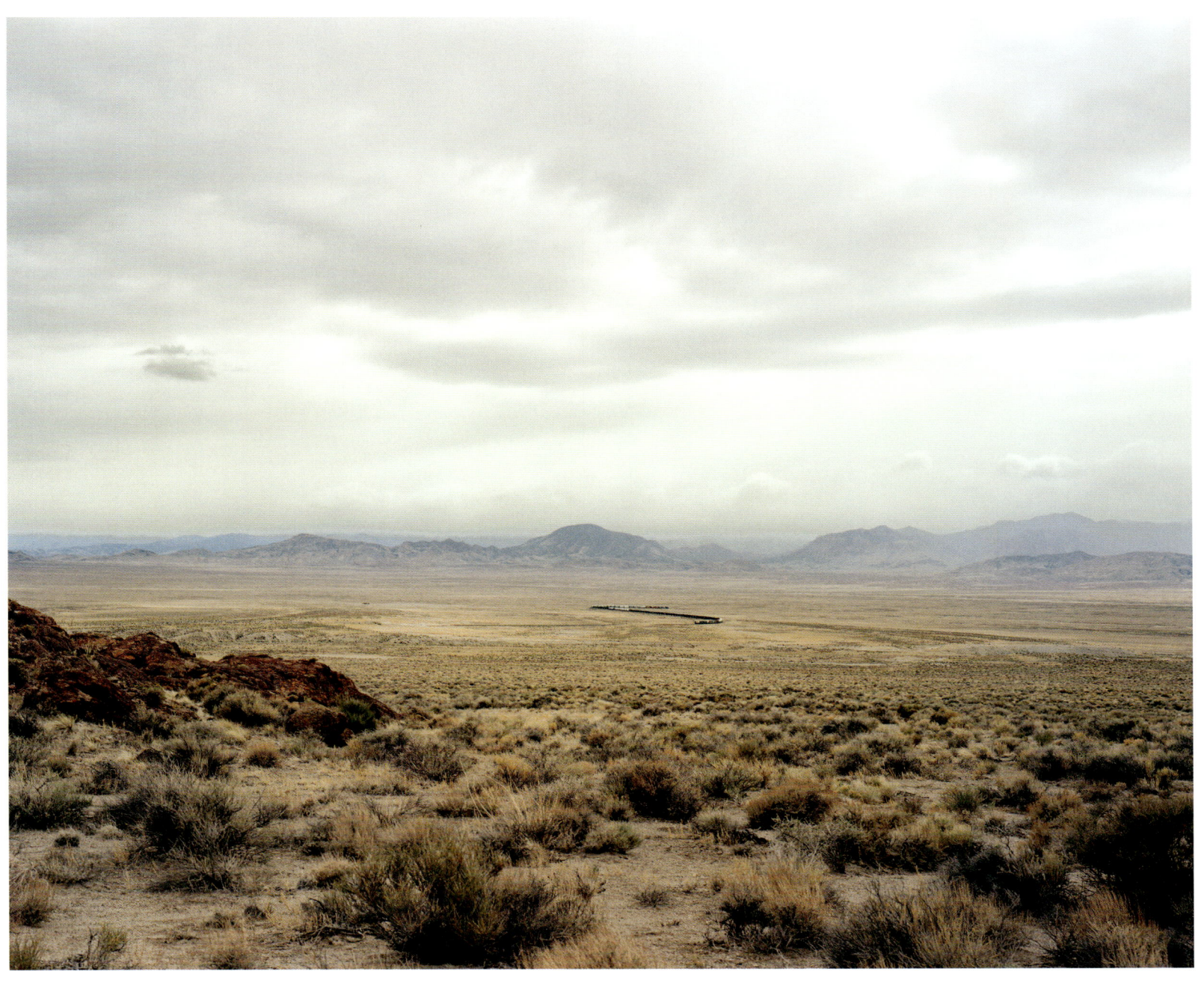

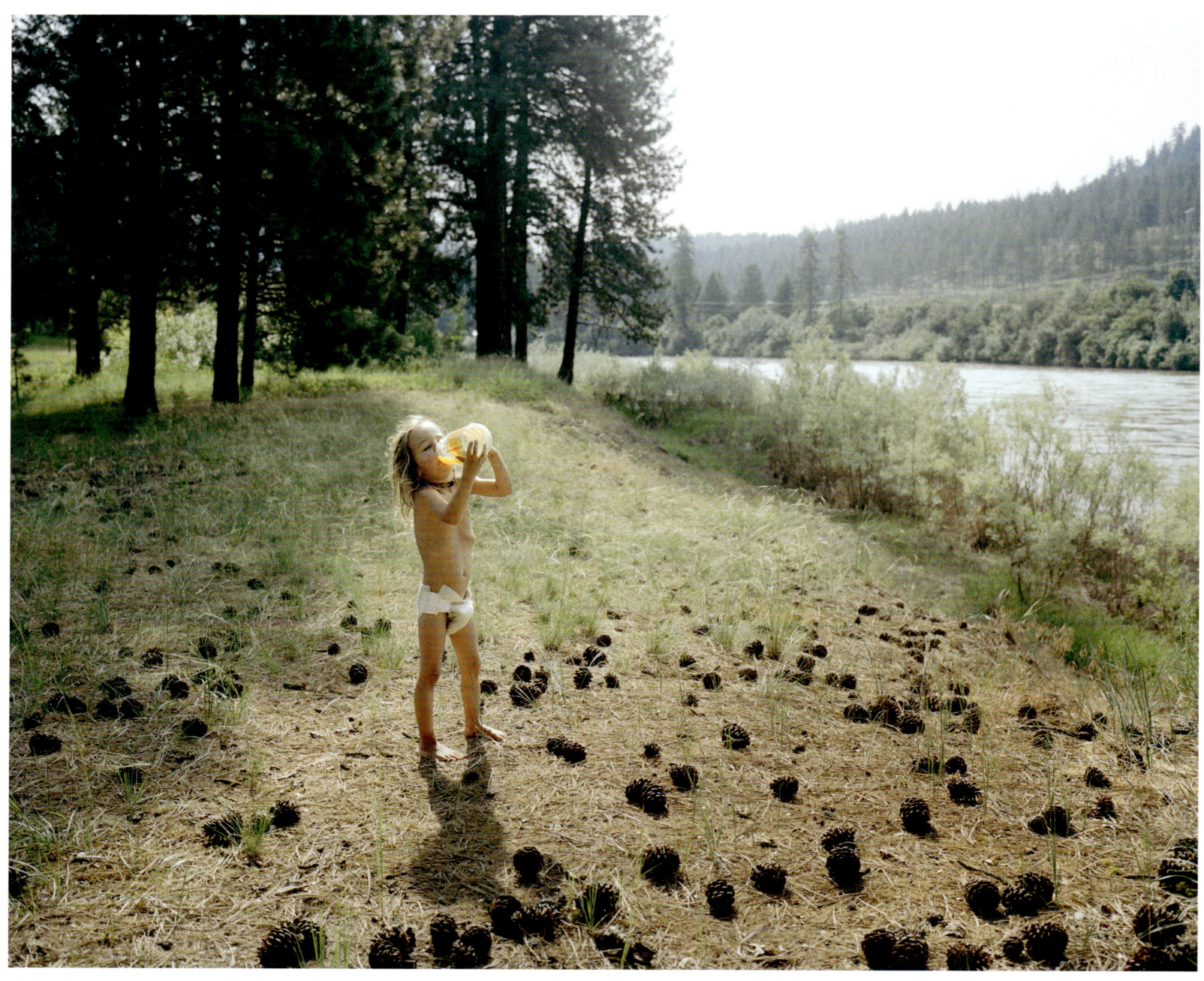

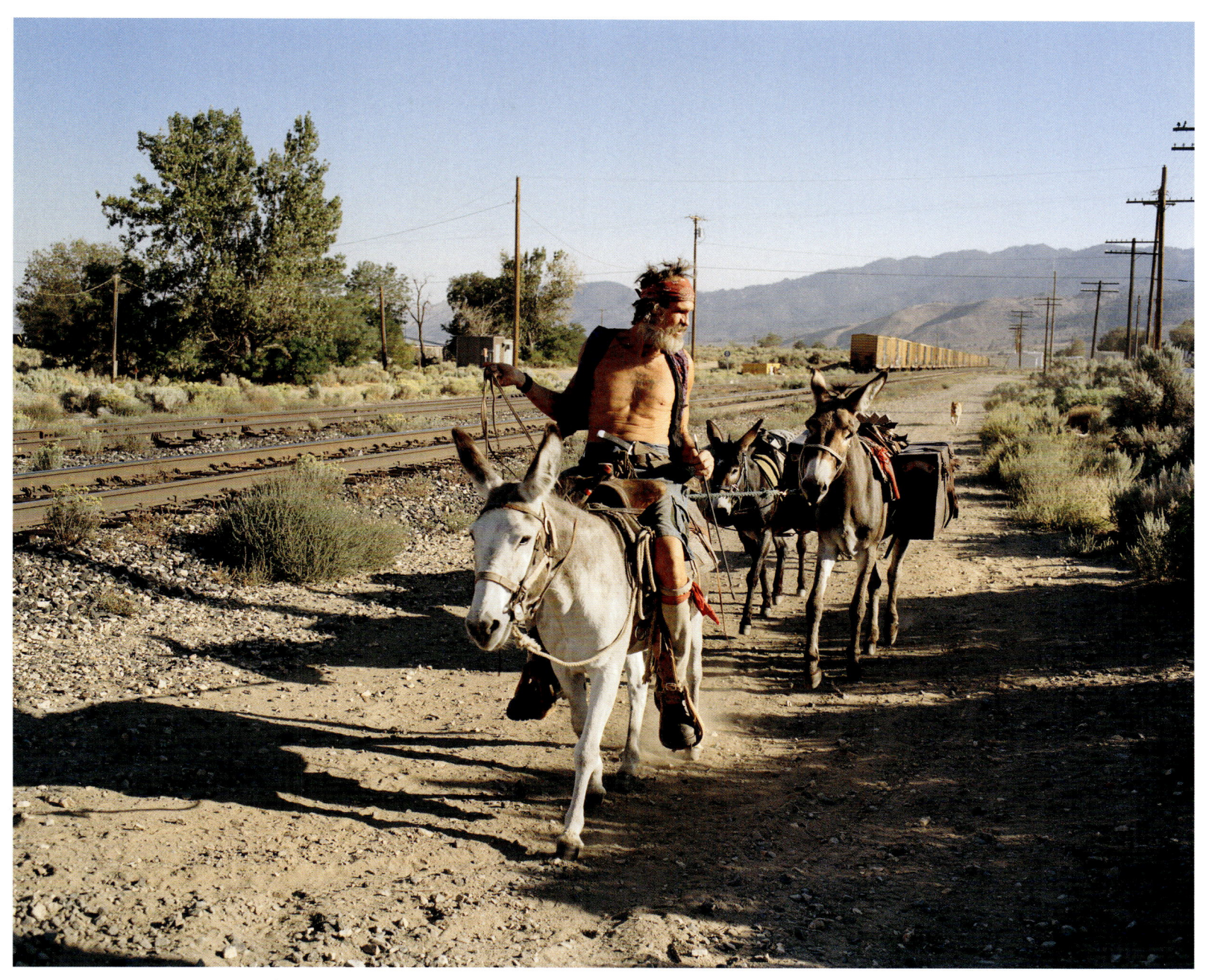

Framed Headlight, 2012

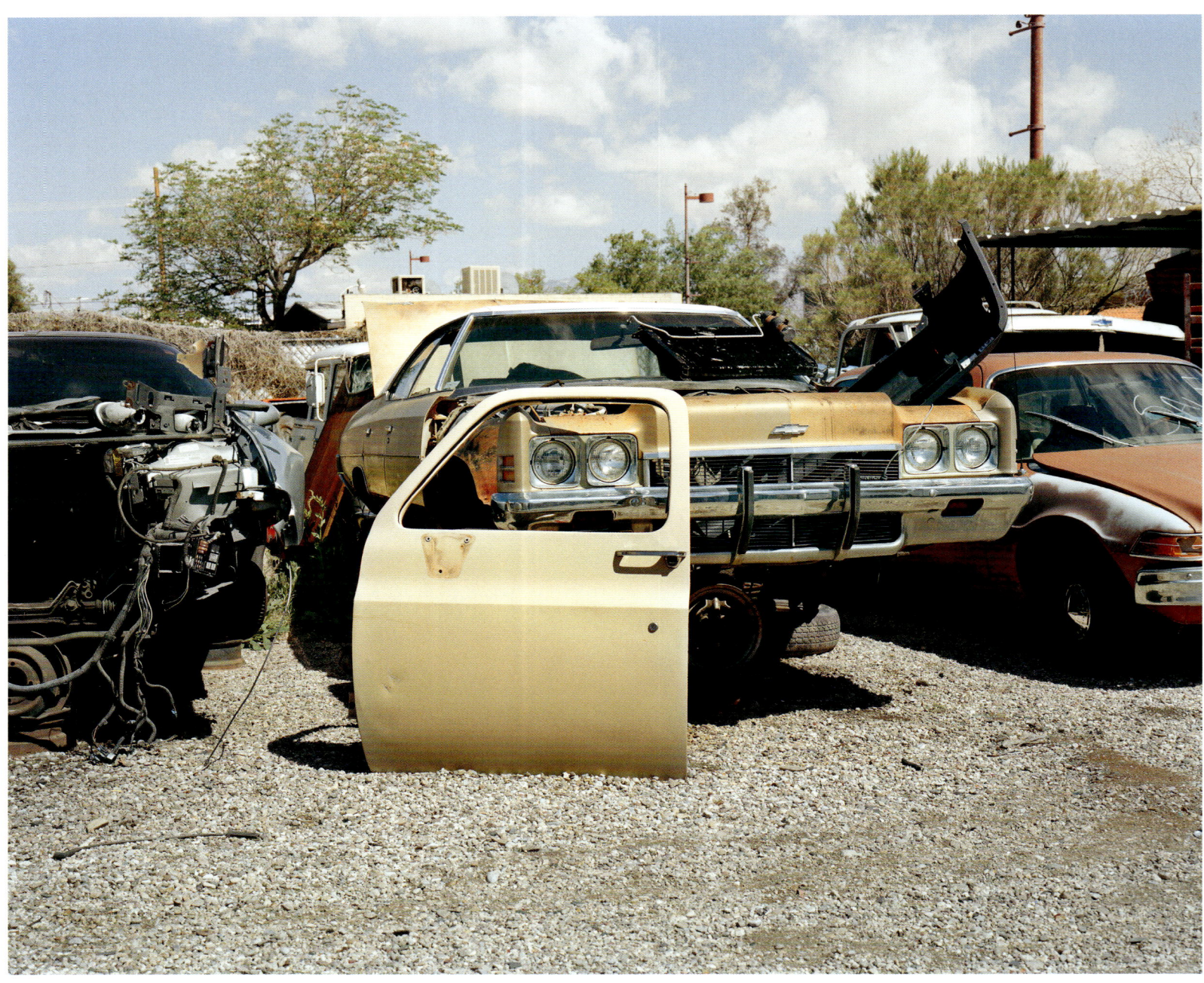

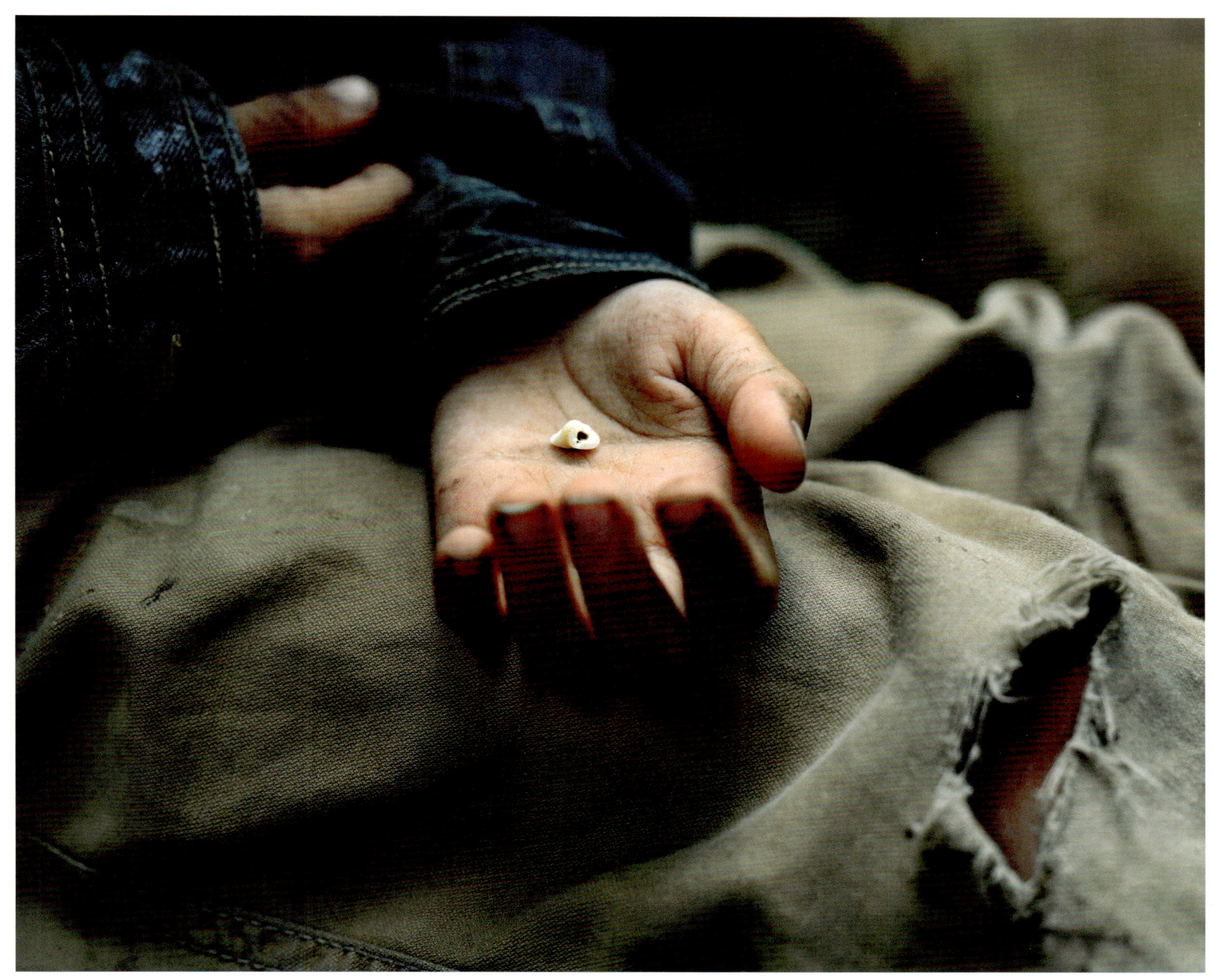

*What Casper Might
Look Like if He Grew Up
to Be a Junkie in Tacoma,*
2013

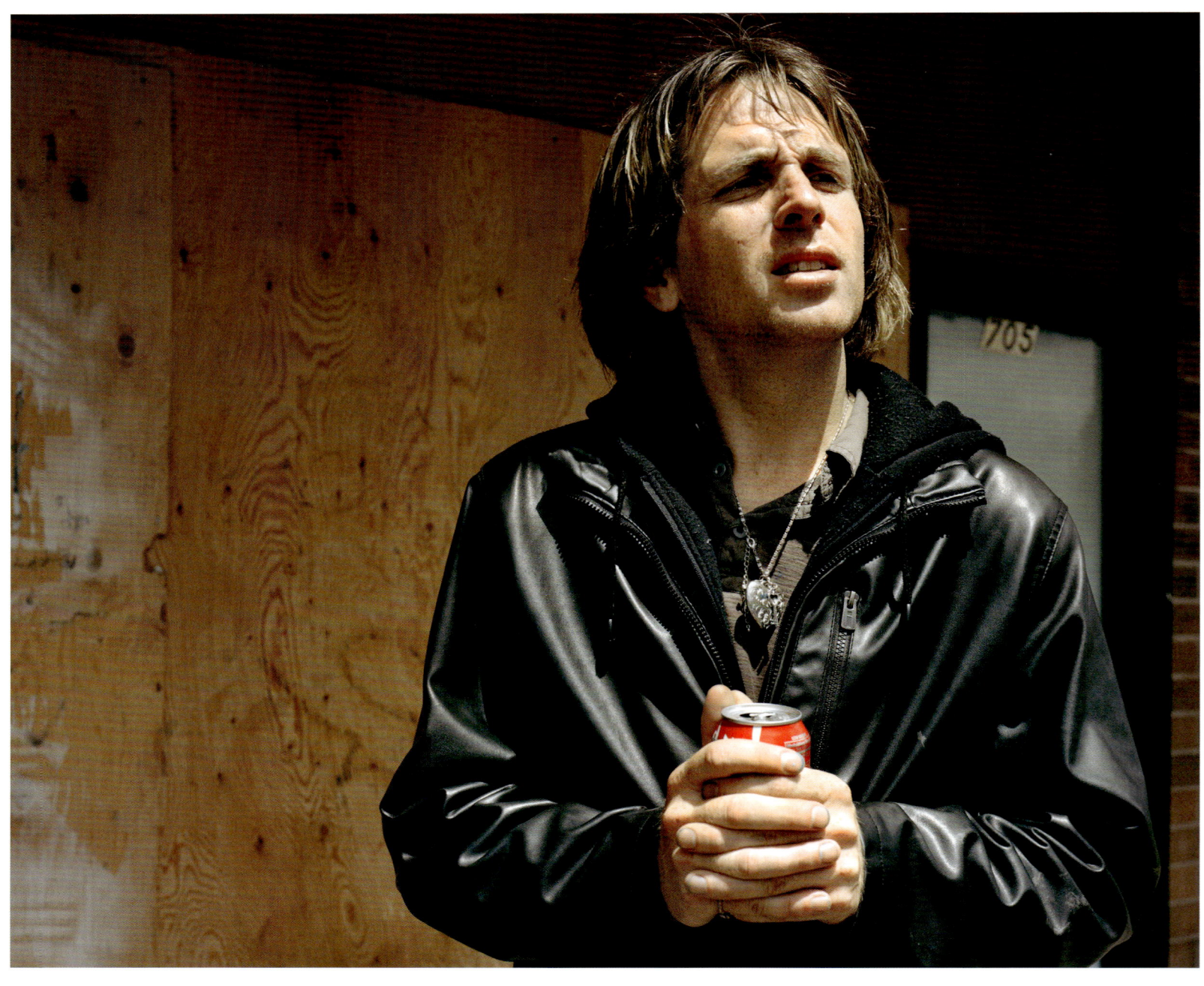

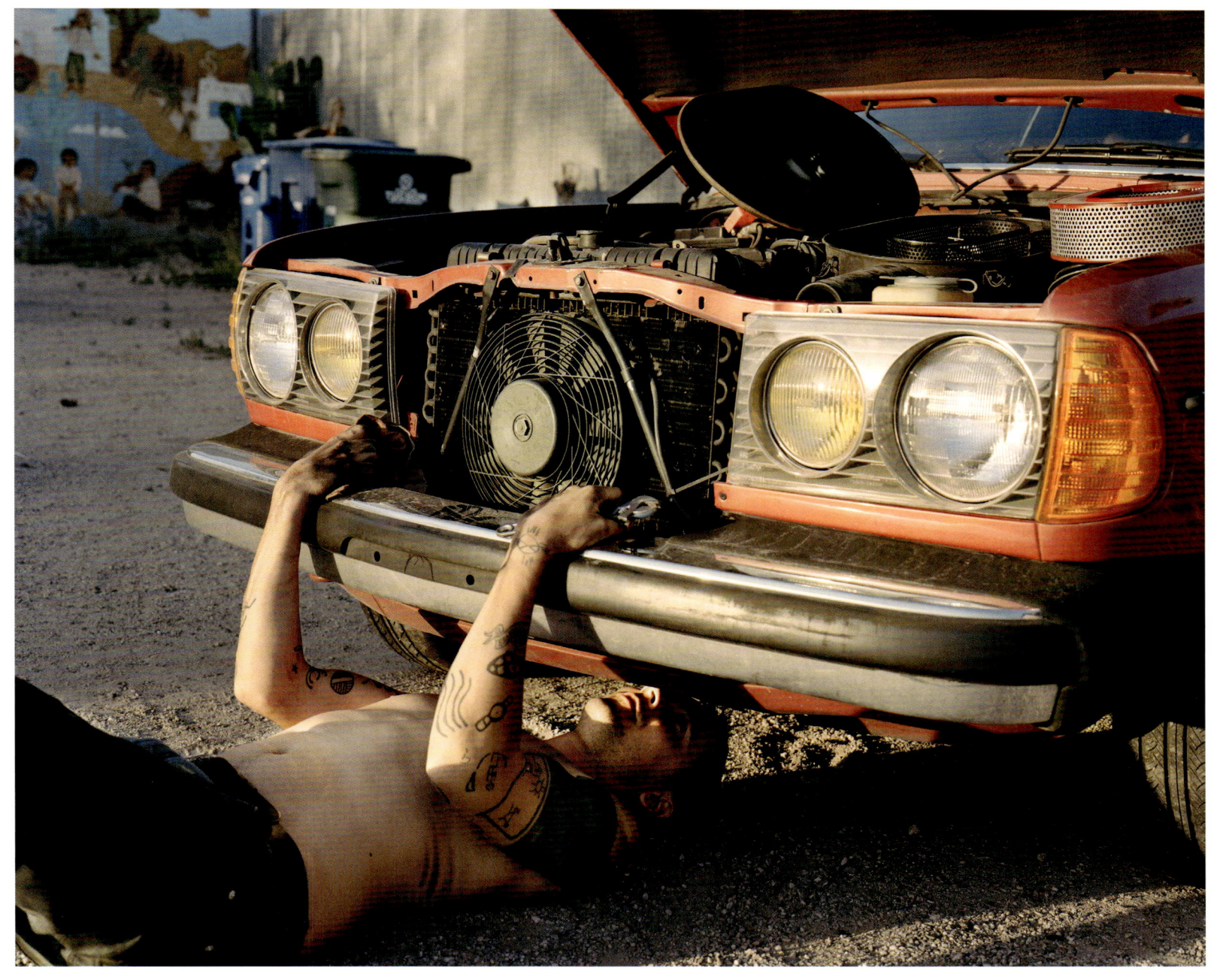

280 Coup, 2012
All photographs courtesy
the artist and Mitchell-Innes
& Nash, New York

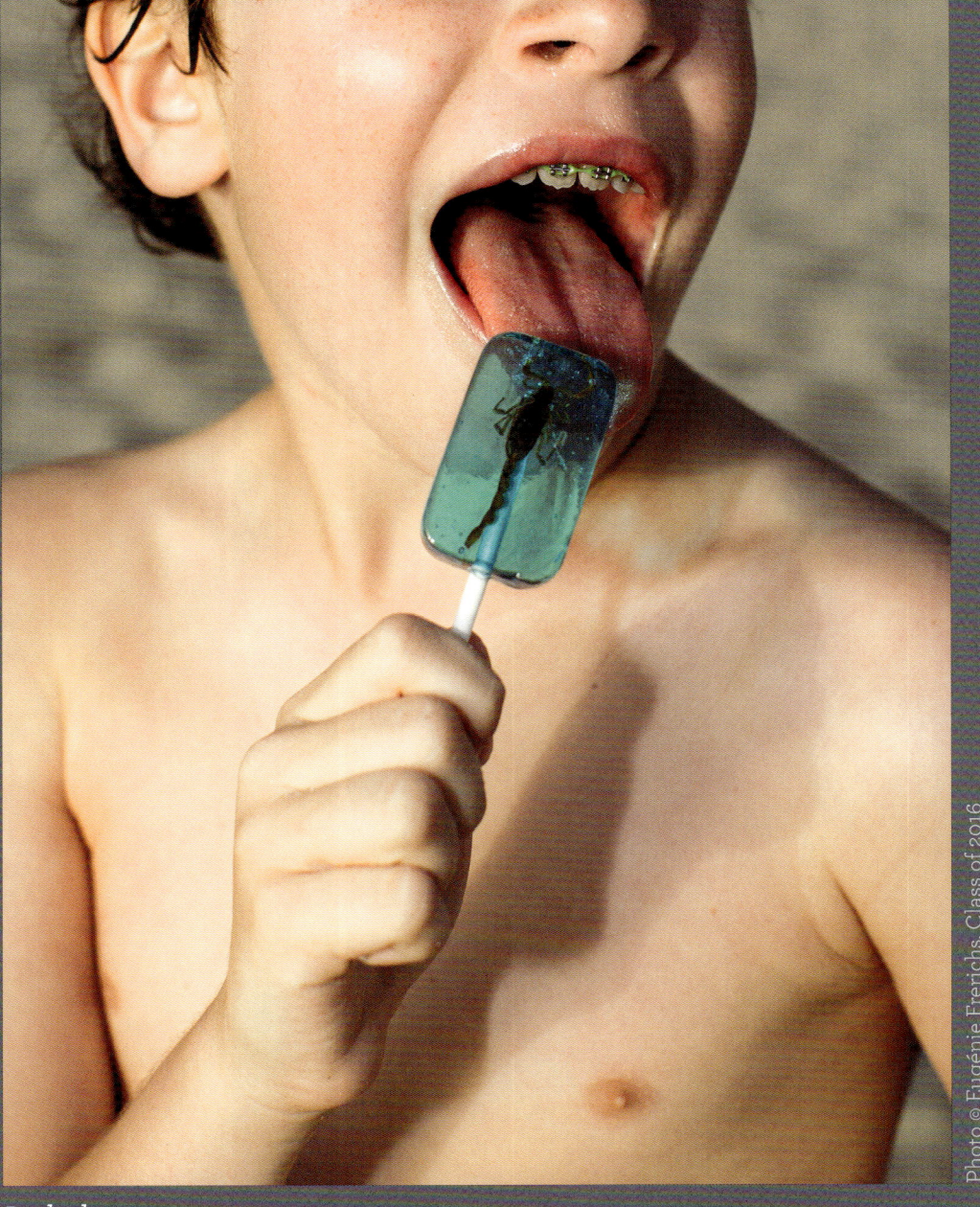

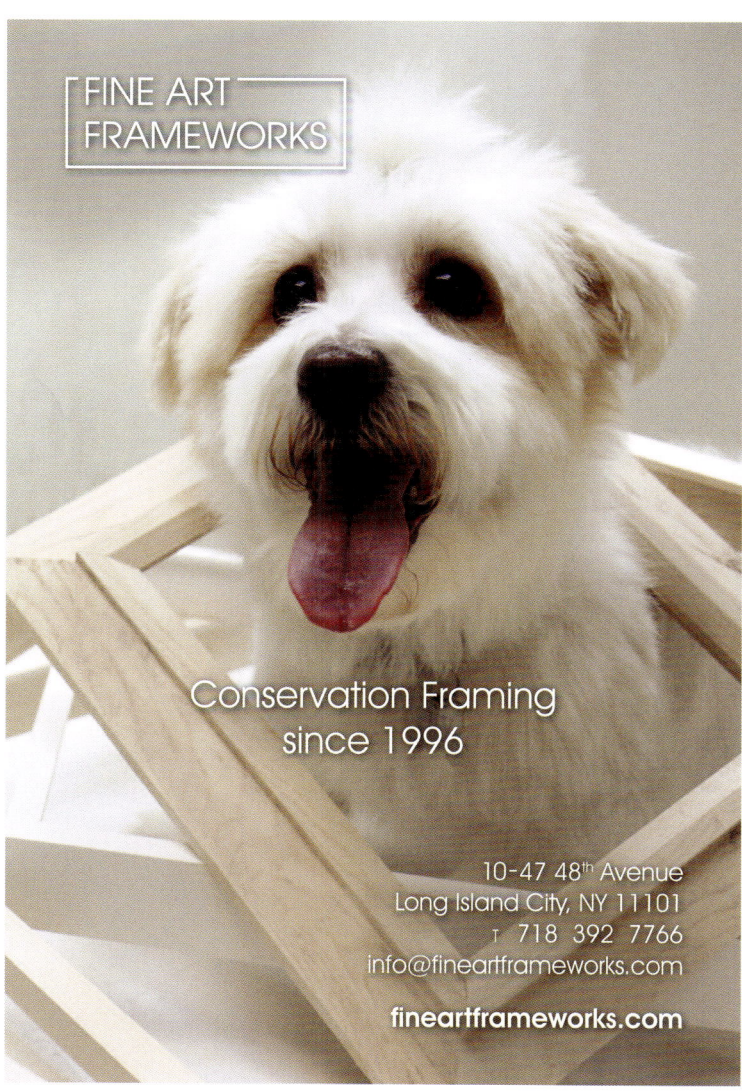
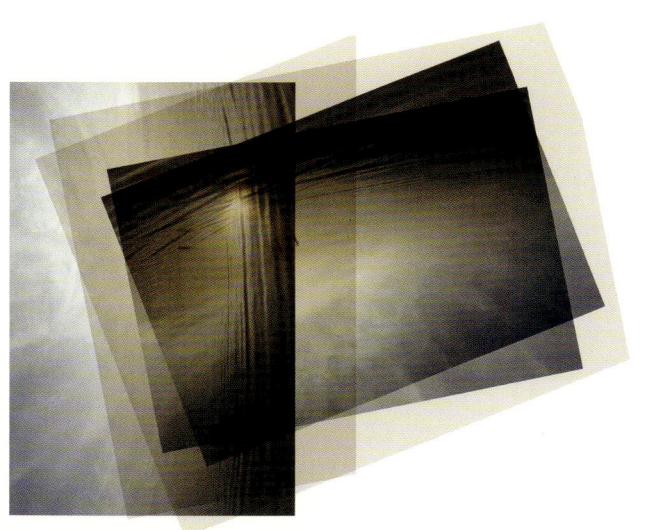
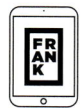

Object Lessons
Annie Smith Peck's Postcards, 1908

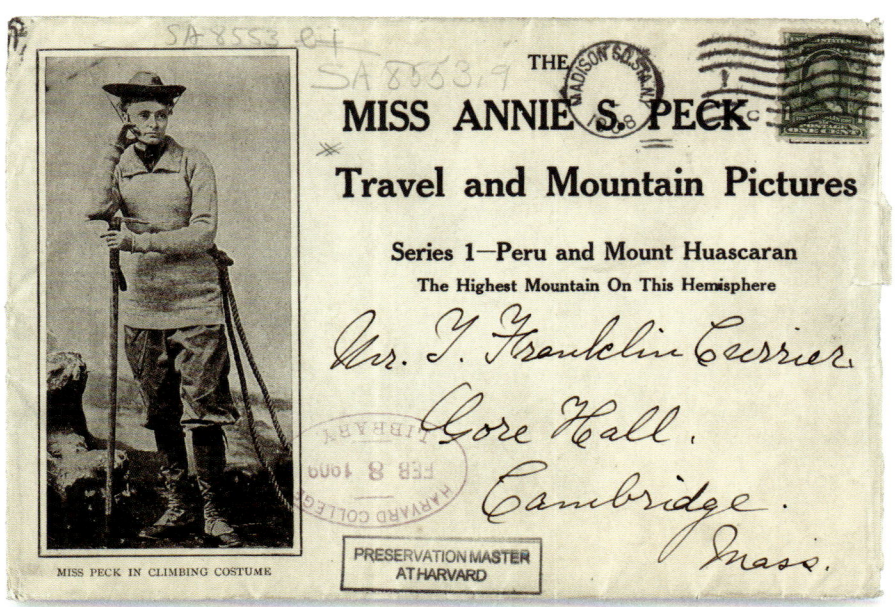

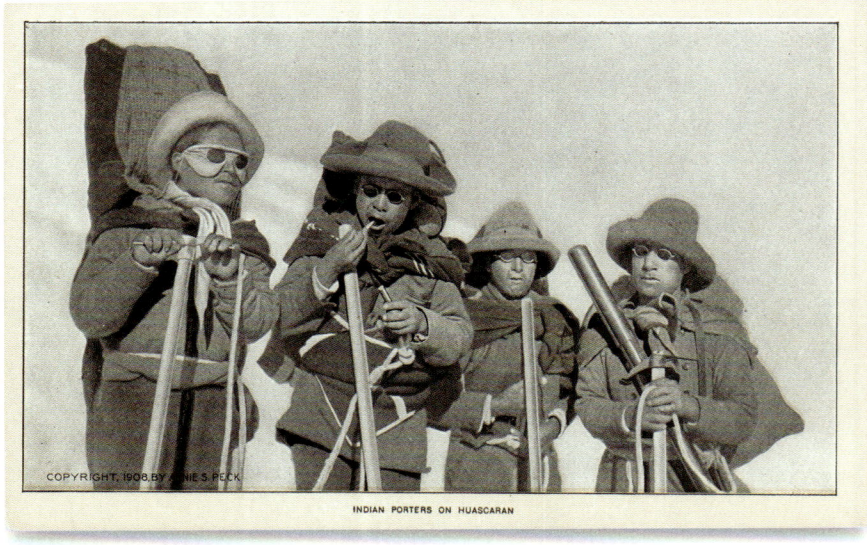

The Miss Annie Peck Travel and Mountain Pictures, 1908 Courtesy the Latin American Pamphlet Digital Collection, Harvard University

"President Roosevelt has expressed his lively interest in the enterprise," Annie Smith Peck wrote in 1908, soliciting a small donation. Ten cents—"a mite toward the large sum needed for the important expedition to set out June 29"— could buy a set of pictures taken by Peck, then fifty-eight years old, printed in support of her quest to ascend Mount Huascarán in the Peruvian Andes. A suffragist and a distinguished, multilingual American scholar of classics and archaeology, Peck was renowned for her mountain climbing, even as fame invited skeptical criticism. (Upon her descent from the Matterhorn in 1895, Peck attracted a flurry of press coverage for conquering the mountain—in pants, instead of a skirt.) Peck's picture postcards for the Huascarán fund-raiser, some featuring photographs taken in 1906 on previous climbs, show street scenes and bullfights in the town of Yungay, Peru, and visions of the peak from base camps.

On the reverse sides are lively descriptions of the sites Peck photographed, together with advertisements for Singer Sewing Machines stating "Singer Talks to Thinking Women." Pictures of Peck herself range from formal portraits showing the estimable mountaineer in her rugged sportswear, accessorized with ropes and tools, to a pastiche in which she dons a "rather superfluous painted moustache." Unlike other notable women explorers of the era, Peck remained unmarried—a feat that forced her, for the sake of propriety, to bring along at least one man on every expedition. Peck, who lectured frequently and published articles on her South American tours, was admitted into the Royal Geographical Society in 1917; ten years later, the north peak of Huascarán was named in her honor. At eighty-two, she embarked on her last climb, to the summit of Mount Madison, New Hampshire. "My home," Peck once said, "is where my trunk is." —The Editors